The Great Urban Transformation

The Great Urban Transformation

Politics of Land and Property in China

You-tien Hsing

OXFORD
UNIVERSITY PRESS

OXFORD
UNIVERSITY PRESS

Great Clarendon Street, Oxford ox2 6DP

Oxford University Press is a department of the University of Oxford.
It furthers the University's objective of excellence in research, scholarship,
and education by publishing worldwide in

Oxford New York

Auckland Cape Town Dar es Salaam Hong Kong Karachi
Kuala Lumpur Madrid Melbourne Mexico City Nairobi
New Delhi Shanghai Taipei Toronto

With offices in

Argentina Austria Brazil Chile Czech Republic France Greece
Guatemala Hungary Italy Japan Poland Portugal Singapore
South Korea Switzerland Thailand Turkey Ukraine Vietnam

Oxford is a registered trade mark of Oxford University Press
in the UK and in certain other countries

Published in the United States
by Oxford University Press Inc., New York

© You-tien Hsing 2010

British Library Cataloguing in Publication Data

Data available

Library of Congress Cataloging in Publication Data

Data available

Typeset by SPI Publisher Services, Pondicherry, India
Printed in Great Britain
on acid-free paper by the
MPG Books Group, Bodmin and King's Lynn

ISBN 978–0–19–956804–8

To my father, for his 90th birthday; and my daughter, for her 10th birthday.

Contents

Acknowledgments

In the long process of completing this book, I have accumulated enormous *renqing zhai*, or "debts of human feelings." I could never pay these back in full. I do wish, however, to acknowledge the following people to whom I am forever indebted.

My first expression of thanks goes to Manuel Castells, who has unfailingly provided intellectual stimulation and regular nagging for the past twenty-two years. My community of colleagues in different parts of the world also helped shape this project (but are not responsible for its shortcomings) and commented on all or parts of the manuscript. Among them, special thanks go to Fred Block, Richard Walker, Ching Kwan Lee, Yuan Shen, Trevor Barnes, Lixun Li, Lei Guang, Larry Ma, George Lin, Michael Burawoy, Michael Johns, Kevin O'Brien, John K.C. Liu, Linda Li, Michael Watts, Gillian Hart, Wen-hsin Yeh, Aihwa Ong, Li Zhang, Mark Selden, Thomas Gold, Neil Smith, Mayfair Yang, Kam Wing Chan, Maureen Sioh, Miriam Chion, Boy Luethje, Stanley Lubman, Anthony Zaloom, Dan Abramson, and Dan Buck.

Several institutions have been fundamental for this project. Foremost among these is my intellectual home of Berkeley Geography. I am deeply indebted to my departmental colleagues for their generous support and am proud to share their vision of deepening the understanding of the inter-connection between space, society, and environment. I also thank my graduate students at Berkeley, especially Max Woodworth, Xiaohui Lin, and Youjeong Oh for their indispensable help with this project and critical reading of my manuscript. Staff members at Berkeley Geography are true Godsends: Natalia Vonnegut has administered my research projects with amazing efficiency and Darin Jensen demonstrated, once again, his superb mapmaking skills. Also, the librarians at the Berkeley Chinese and East Asian Libraries, especially Susan Xue and Jianye He, worked magic, finding crucial materials from only they know where. To them I owe deep gratitude.

I have also benefited tremendously from my affiliation with the Department of Sociology at Tsinghua University in Beijing. I thank in particular

Professors Qiang Li, Yuan Shen, Liping Sun, and Yuhua Guo, as well as their energetic graduate students Yunqing Shi, Xiangyang Bi, and Xiang Wen, for sharing with me insights on China's social transformation. The Graduate Institute of Building and Planning at National Taiwan University, where I received my first introduction to grassroots environmental planning more than twenty years ago, has served as a resource-rich academic base in Taipei and has kept me connected with the place I grew up. My very special thanks go to Professors Chu-Joe Hsia, John K C Liu, Hungkai Wang, and Hernda Bi, and their graduate students for their inspiration and warmth.

I also wish to sincerely thank my editor at Oxford University Press, David Musson, for his encouragement and insightful suggestions. I also wish to acknowledge the fine editorial work of Matthew Derbyshire, for his patience and professionalism during the production of this book at Oxford University Press.

My gratitude also goes to my friends whose camaraderie has sustained me as a single mother and academic. This village includes Jerlian Tsao, Yifen Li, Szeyun Liu, Miriam Chion, Chaoyin Liu, Keiko Ono, Kimmy Chen, and more. I am extremely lucky to have a family that is very good at spoiling me: my father and my late mother, my brothers I-tien and Chih-tien, my sister Mei-tien, and their families are the source of love. Finally, I thank my daughter, Tina, for the privilege of being a part of her growth, and for her incredible patience while waiting for mom to finish the book.

List of Figures

Tables

List of Chinese Terms

Bading 拔釘 ("pulling out the nails," or getting rid of the trouble maker)

biaozhunzu 標準租 (standard-rent housing)

cehua 策劃 (strategic planning)

chengshi yunying 城市運營 (urban operation and management)

chaiqianhu 拆遷戶 (evicted household whose house is demolished)

chaoda chengshi 超大城市 (super-large city)

cunji 村籍 (village membership)

dashilan 大柵欄 (an old neighborhood in Beijing)

daxuecheng 大學城 (University Town)

chaiqian jingji 拆遷經濟 (economy of demolition and relocation)

dayoufei 打游飛 (flying pests)

da-za-qiang 打砸搶 (beating, smashing, and looting)

dingzihu 釘子戶 ("nail households," or holdouts)

erbashou 二把手 (the second man in charge)

fabu zezhong 法不責眾 (law should not, and could not penalize the majority)

fenjiadi 分家底 (dividing the family assets)

gaizao 改造 (reconstruction)

guihau 規劃 (urban planning)

Hexi xincheng 河西新城 (Hexi New Town)

hongguan tiaokong 宏觀調控 (macroeconomic adjustment and control)

jihua 計劃 (economic planning)

jiao 交 (Submitted)

jingzufang 經租房 (state-managed rental housing)

jianfu 減賦 (reducing peasant burdens)

kaifaqu 開發區 (development zones)

kouzi 口子 (exceptions to rules)

lanluhu 攔路虎 ("tigers blocking the road," or barrier of progress)

lingdijia 零地價 ("zero-cost" land)

liuyongdi 留用地 (reserved construction land)

nongmin jizi jianzhen 農民集資建鎮 (peasants raising funds for town construction)

nongzhuanju 農轉居 (conversion from agricultural to urban residency)

peiben zhuan yaohe 賠本賺喲喝 (running red to win cheers)

qiangqianhu 強遷戶 (households of forced eviction)

ruanying jianshi 軟硬兼施 (mixing gentle and tough approaches; using both carrots and sticks)

shangfang 上訪 (visiting government offices to lodge complaints)

sannong wenti 三農問題 (Three Agricultural Problems)

shiguan xian 市管縣 (city governing counties)

shidai xian 市帶縣 (city leading counties)

shidi nongmin 失地農民 (displaced peasants who also lost the land)

tai gong tian 太公田 (lineages' land holding)

tiao 條 (vertical chain of command)

wushiliu jian shishi 五十六件實事 (Fifty-Six Concrete Tasks)

wanren dasusong 萬人大訴訟 (Grand Litigation of Ten Thousand Plaintiffs)

wanren dajubao 萬人大舉報 (Grand Petition and Revelation of Ten Thousand petitioners)

weifang gaijian 危房改建 (reconstruction of unsafe housing)

xiangchanquan 鄉產權 (housing with township-granted ownership certificates)

xiao jinku 小金庫 (internal coffers of government units)

xinfang 信訪 (writing petition letters)

xitong 系統 (vertical chain of command)

xin cheng 新城 (New city)

xin quandi yundong 新圈地運動 (new land enclosure movement)

xiuxian shangwuqu 休閒商務區 (Recreational Business District [RBD])

yangiu jingji 眼球經濟 (economy of spectacle)

yibashou 一把手 (the number-one boss)

yidi shengcai 以地生財 (get rich through land)

yizhibi shenpi 一枝筆審批 (one-pen approval)

Yeman chaiqian 野蠻拆遷 (employing violence in eviction and demolition)

yi-xian-tian 一線天 (thread-like sky, the sky between buildings is as thin as a piece of thread)

List of Chinese Terms

Zhujiang xincheng 珠江新城 *(Zhujian New Town)*

zading 砸釘 ("crushing the nails," or using violence against trouble makers)

zejuquan 擇居權 (rights to choose the location of residency)

zhen-ya-cun 鎮壓村 (the township dominates the village)

zhanbu pingheng 占補平衡 (balancing between land converted for non-farm uses and expansion of farmland)

Zhongyang juzhuqu 中央居住區 (Central Living Districts [CLD])

Zhongyang wenhuaqu 中央文化區 (Central Cultural District [CCD])

Prologue

This book was born out of frustration. Until the mid-1990s, I had been preoccupied by questions of industrialization and capitalist expansion in my study of contemporary China. By then, however, I found myself increasingly annoyed by the fact that contacts and friends in China were changing home addresses and phone numbers too often for me to maintain contact. I noticed too that during repeated visits, my hopes of discussing technology transfers and private entrepreneurs were stymied by the drift in the conversation toward their recent purchases of apartments and cars, and of their moves to new housing complexes in the urban outskirts.

My interviews with local government officials were often disappointing as well. Officials' eyes would light up only when I dropped my own pet topic of technology upgrade programs and switched the discussion to their industrial park or new town center. Factories, they thought, were dull. They much preferred to take me on a tour of the new town plaza, the new industrial park, and the new wholesale market. Hoping to take advantage of my background in planning and architecture, local officials would ask my opinion about their urban expansion plans. Meanwhile, I saw large sections of "industrial parks" and "high-tech zones" being devoted to commercial housing, restaurants, resorts, and amusement parks. I was also told that revenues from land lease sales exceeded the income derived from industrial taxes. I often left local government offices knowing little about industrial policy, but a lot about local construction projects. My camera was loaded with pictures of me standing in front of new structures next to proud local officials. China had clearly come a long way from the rural collective industries that marked the success of reforms in the 1980s.

By the late 1990s, I began to think that if my questions failed to excite, I would need to figure out what, after all, did command people's attention in China. I would need to seriously consider why so much energy and expectation were focused on something that I deemed a distraction from the "main event" in China's capitalist development. Perhaps, I began to wonder, the industrial parks are the core of industrial policy, and the condos and office towers are central to the new political economy? Perhaps the theater of accumulation has shifted from industrial production to urban construction, and construction had become the motor of productivity? If urbanization has triumphed over industrialization as a policy priority, and urbanism has superseded industrialism in development discourse, how did the transition occur?

These questions proved to be a Pandora's box. First, the figures were hard to ignore. Between 1980 and 2002, the urban portion of China's total population grew from about 20 percent to about 40 percent. In other words, 250 million people were added to the urban population.[1] While a 40-percent urban population is lower than the world average of 50 percent, the scale and pace of urban growth make the Chinese case exceptional. Between 1978 and 2003, the number of cities with a population larger than a million increased from 13 to 49; the number of cities with a population between half a million and one million increased from 27 to 78; the number of middle-sized and small cities grew from 174 to 533.[2] By way of basic comparison, China's 250 million new urbanites in the last quarter century are four times the total population of the United Kingdom and about 84 percent of the total population of the United States in 2007. China's urban population, as of 2006, stands at an astonishing 577 million. And the increase in China's urban population from 20 percent to 40 percent occurred in the span of just 22 years, while the same increase took 120 years in Britain (1720–1840), 40 years in the United States (1860–1900), and 30 years in Japan (1925–55).[3]

The eye-popping scale and pace of urban expansion came at the expense of farmland. A frenzy of land conversion from agricultural to nonagricultural uses between 1987 and 2003 reduced China's already limited cropland by 10 to 12 million hectares, about one-tenth of the country's total.[4] While much of the debate over China's farmland loss has focused on its implications for national food security, it is the process of land rights transfer that exerted the most immediate and violent impacts on people's livelihoods. Together, between 1990 and 2007, farmland conversion and inner-city redevelopment have displaced between 60 and 75 million people in both urban and rural areas.[5] The new logic of urban expansion seemed to be based on dispossession, which triggered increasingly explosive and widespread social unrest.

With these facts in mind, it became clear to me that the significance of China's urban expansion demands more attention. Stated plainly, cities have taken center stage in the politics of accumulation and distribution in China today. The physical reality and the political economy of urban expansion, as well as the ideology of urbanism combine to dominate the logic of China's transformation.

What makes the story of China's great urban transformation even more intriguing is that the contradictions inherent to industrialization and urbanization are compounded by China's simultaneous transformation from state socialism to a market-oriented economy. Urban expansion therefore served as the platform of capitalist accumulation, the restructuring of socialist state power, and the changing relationship between the state and society.

On the state/market front, socialist state land tenure continues to dictate the politics of commodification of land. As local governments act as landlords, developers, city planners, and urban boosters, the interconnection between the state and market consequently shapes the logic of market regulation and competition in the new economy. On the state/societal front, massive displacement and dispossession go hand in hand with the abrupt retreat of the state from social welfare provision. The destruction both of homes and social protection leads to intensified social contestation, thus challenging the legitimacy of the state.

China's triple movement of industrialization, urbanization, and marketization over the past three decades hardly provides a case of gradualism, a word often used to compare China's reforms with Russia's "Big Bang" reforms in the early 1990s. With this book on Chinese cities, I hope to contribute to the understanding of the radical and profound transformation in China today.

Notes

1. See Lin, George C. S., 'The growth and structural change of Chinese cities' 2002 and Zhou, Yixing, and Laurence J. C. Ma, 'China's urbanization levels', 2003.
2. Song, Yan and Chengri Ding, Smart Urban Growth for China, (2009), p.1.
3. Lu, Dadao et al., *Zhongguo quyu fazhan baogao—chengshihua jincheng ji kongjian kuozhang* (Report on China's regional development: Progress in urbanization and spatial expansion 2006). For US data, see also http://www.census.gov/population/censusdata/table-4.pdf. The exact figure is 19.8 percent in 1860, and 39.6 percent in 1900. For Japan, see http://www.e-stat.go.jp/SG1/estat/ListE.do?bid=000000030587&cycode=0. This set of data shows that the Japanese urban population grew from 21.5 percent of the total population in 1925 to 37.3 percent in 1950, and 56.1 percent in 1955. Therefore, it took Japan more than 25 years, but less than 30 years, to reach the 20 percent growth in urban population.
4. The figures of land loss vary greatly, depending on the sources and methods of data collection. This figure is from the following: Ho, Sammuel, and George C. S. Lin, 'Emerging Land Markets in Rural and Urban China,' 2003; Lichtenberg, Erik and Chengri Ding, 'Assessing farmland protection policy in China,' 2008.

5. Yu Jianrong suggests that the total number of displaced peasants caused by land grabs and development projects was about 66 million as of 2002. Wang Guolin's figure was 50 million between 1996 and 2003—the figure of 50 million was also used in official reports. As for inner-city displacement, based on extremely scattered and vague sources of information and my own conservative estimation, the figure is between 8 and 10 million nationwide. Between 1996 and 2008, at least 1 million people (both peasants and urban residents) were displaced in Beijing; in Shanghai, between 1991 and 2006, about 4 million were displaced. For information of peasant displacement see Yu, Jianrong, 'Protection of peasants' land rights and urbanization in China,' 2006, Wang, Guolin, *Shidi Nongmin diaocha* (*Investigation of Peasants Who Lost Their Land 2007. For data on displacement in Beijing, see* 'Aoyun jingji' (*Olympic Economy*) <*http://big5.bjoe.gov.cn/hayjj/ wz/200705/t176957_2.htm*>, *and He*, Qinglian, 'Cunchaiqian xingwei kan zhongguo zhengfu xingweide heishehuihua' (*Mafia behavior of Chinese government from the perspective of demolition and relocation*), 2005. *See also,* 'Report at the national meeting on demolition and relocation' by Director of the Department of Housing and Real Estate, Ministry of Construction, Xie, Jiajin, October 16, 2001. Online. See <*http://law-lib.com/ fzdt/newshtml/22/20051028192134.htm*>, *accessed November 28, 2008. For numbers of displacement in Shanghai, see Shi, Mi (forthcoming),* 'The Evolving Law of Disputed Relocation: Constructing Inner City Renewal Practices in Shanghai, 1990–2005,' International Journal of Urban and Regional Research.

Chapter 1

Land and Urban Politics

Land has moved to the center of local politics in post-Mao China. It now shapes the restructuring of Chinese state power and radically impacts state–society relations.

The origin of this change came in 1988, when the country's land leasehold market was formally established, thereby separating land ownership from land-use rights. The change did not affect the bifurcation of land in China into urban and rural categories, nor did it overturn the state ownership of land enshrined in the PRC Constitution and the *Land Management Law*.[1] It did, however, allow urban land-use rights to be leased at a profit for a fixed period of time. Rural land, according to the same set of regulations, belongs to village collectives, but cannot be legally leased out for profit. Nevertheless, a significant black market for rural land has taken shape in highly industrialized areas like the Pearl River Delta and the Lower Yangtze River Delta.[2] Land has thus been commodified in the cities and the countryside, though its ownership is not privatized under either category. These market-oriented changes set the stage for massive urban expansion and fueled skyrocketing land values in the 1990s. As a consequence, land quickly came to dominate China's politics of accumulation and distribution.[3]

The politics of accumulation under state-land tenure unfolds as intra-state competition for land control and land rents intensifies. This competition has reconfigured the power dynamics between the central and local governments, between rural and urban governments, and also between the state bureaucracy and the peasantry. The resultant power dynamics subsequently shape the land-centered accumulation project in which various state actors are dominant. Further, the emergent power dynamics condition the manner in which the land market is regulated, deregulated, and reregulated.

Land-centered accumulation has also become the main aspiration, the tacit and explicit mandate, and the key strategy behind local state building.

Local state leaders seek to legitimize themselves as urban promoters and builders, and urban agendas dominate local development policy, while local politics predominantly revolves around farmland conversion and industrial or commercial development projects. Urban construction has therefore expanded from an accumulation project to a territorial project of local state building. Urban modernity, more than industrial modernity, now captures the political imagination of local state leaders. I call this dynamic the "urbanization of the local state."

The urbanization of the local state defines the relationship among the local state, the market, and society. It also triggers three types of distributional politics that challenge the legitimacy of the local state's urban identity and its projects. The first is a politics of resistance, calling for property and social rights. Forced eviction and inadequate compensation in urban redevelopment projects has been the primary trigger of widespread contention and social activism in the urban core. The second is a nonconfrontational politics for economic rights in which land-owning village collectives at the rapidly developing urban fringe bargain with the urban government, profit from urban property markets, and define and defend their territorial autonomy under metropolitan governance. I call such nonconfrontational dynamics "village corporatism." The third type of distributional politics concerns more than 50 million displaced peasants in rural areas. Displaced peasants share with their urban counterparts grievances over forced and violent eviction and inadequate housing compensation, as well as demands for property and social rights. However, while the number of peasants pushed off their land in the last twenty years has been growing, and land-related rural protests are increasingly frequent and violent, peasants' mobilization remains largely fragmented and localized. I attribute the gap between the peasants' destitution and their lack of successful mobilization to the politics of deterritorialization.

Responding to the current politics of distribution, various social groups in different places adopt different strategies for self-protection. Through their actions, territoriality takes different forms, and achieves different results. I use the term "civic territoriality" to highlight my bottom-up approach to understanding territory and to capture the spatial dynamics in the distributional politics of land.

In the politics of land-centered accumulation and legitimation, local states are built and transformed by urban agendas. In the politics of distribution, social groups act upon and react to urban transformation. Both the local state and society actively shape urban processes and are transformed by them. Here, I place these two key concepts—the "urbanization of the local state" and "civic territoriality"—in the broader context of relevant literature.

Urbanization of the local state

"State-led urbanization" revisited

Students of Chinese cities often label Chinese urban processes "state-led urbanization."[4] The thesis of state-led urbanization, framed by the state-market dichotomy, can be summarized as follows: the state's planning power, its persistent land tenure, and control over rural–urban mobility supercede the market and dictate the direction and pace of urban growth in Chinese cities. The "state-led urbanization" argument correctly points to the centrality of the state, especially the local state, in urban expansion. Yet, the argument assumes a passive role on the part of the city, whose dynamism is "led" by the state. I propose that the urban process is an integral part of the local state. It actively shapes the dynamics of the local state, which, in turn, shapes the territorial logic of the state at large. While the local state mobilizes its resources to try to expand the city, the struggle over urban expansion defines, legitimizes, and consolidates urban-based local state power. For sure, there are many cases of unsuccessful, scandalous, and even disastrous projects developed by the local state, some of which have de-legitimized and destabilized local governments and their overly ambitious and/or incompetent leaders. Nevertheless, successful or not, urban construction has become the key mechanism of local state building. Local accumulation is dependent on land sales and development, while the local state apparatus grows along with urban expansion. Further, local state leaders aspire to be landowners, planners, financiers, and builders, all at the same time. As a result, local politics centers on the politics of urban development projects, which define the dynamics of the local state and its relations with the market and society. It is the dialectical "urbanization of the local state"—more so than the linear concept of "state-led urbanization"—that characterizes the relationship between the local state and the urban process in China today.[5]

The state, land, and territoriality

In this book, the state is not assumed to be either a static or a coherent actor, as the term "state apparatus" might imply.[6] Instead, the state is treated as multitudinous power processes among segments that claim to be, and are claimed by others to be part of the state, and which have complementary, competitive, and/or contradictory mandates and constituencies. State power, therefore, should be treated as interrelated processes of "multiple centers of authority-building."[7]

Currently, the local state at various levels is among the most important authority-building centers in China. In the literature on the Chinese state in transition, Jean Oi's (1992) "local state corporatism"[8] captured the critical role of the local state in the phenomenal economic growth in post-Mao China. Michael Burawoy (1996) further suggested that local state corporatism sets China apart from other transition economies like Russia.[9] Here, I expand from Oi's treatment of the local state as an economic agent to see the local state as a territorial project with physical, political–economic, and ideological implications of state power restructuring.

Territoriality, defined as spatial strategies to consolidate power in a given place and time,[10] is the most important aspect of the local state's power strategy. Instead of identifying the local state as an agent to the principality of the central state or a crisis manager,[11] I view the local state as a territorialization of state power. Hinsley (1986) has framed territoriality as "local state sovereignty" and sees the local state as the site that brings together the "sovereignty abstraction" and the "territorial concrete."[12] In other words, the local state plays a more active role than merely being an agent of the central state. Its "territorial concrete" is a constituitive element of power, materialized through access and control over land, resources, and population. Instead of seeing the local state as a subsidiary to the central state, I treat the process of local state-building and territorial control as an integral and defining element of the dynamics of the state.

The processes that characterize the local state's territorialization, defined as the occupation and domination of a territory, are highly contested. They involve negotiating and strategizing to define and defend jurisdictional centers and boundaries and reduce gaps between nominal and actual authority over the jurisdiction. In the contentious processes of territorialization, the local state develops its agenda and finds its own agency. Territorial contestation is unusually intense when the status of the state is uncertain, as in post-reform China, where local state territorial jurisdictions change frequently and local state power is under-defined. This uncertainty leaves considerable room for local state actors to try to redraw, expand, and consolidate territorial control.

Land is among the most concrete of all the "territorial concretes" in that it provides the foundation of local state territoriality. The modern local state's regulatory authority is mainly exercised through land-use planning and zoning, as well as taxation on land development and land transactions. Land is among the most regulated of commodities.[13]

In China, under state-land tenure, the state not only regulates land use and transactions, but also owns land and profits directly from land rents. In post-Mao China, urban land-use planning has replaced economic planning as the main vehicle of state intervention in the local political economy. Land rents have become one of the most important sources of local state revenue since the 1990s. Development projects, especially high-profile ones like high-tech parks, Special Economic Zones, high-rise clusters in Central Business Districts, or gigantic New Cities, are all built by local states. The erection of massive physical structures and infrastructure projects intensifies the territorial presence of the local state, and provides a visual manifestation of its governing capacity. Organizationally, new urban projects justify and secure local state sprawl. To administer the flood of projects, existing agencies are expanded and new agencies established to take charge of land supplies, construction approval and certification, and demolition and relocation. Project-based agencies are also created to manage the construction of highways, airports, new industrial zones, and new towns. After these projects are completed, the agencies stay on to manage these territorial additions to the local state, thus helping to consolidate its expanded territorial authority.

As land rents become one of the most important sources of local revenue and capital accumulation, local state leaders identify themselves as city promoters and devote themselves to boosting the property value. Property prices are used to measure the success of urban development, and are openly referenced by local leaders as a primary political mandate. Mayors don suits and embark on road shows to promote real-estate projects in their cities, and compete with one another to hire advertising gurus for help in developing "urban strategic development plans" aimed at improving the image of their cities and boosting property values.

City marketing and property value boosting are performed at both the ideological and political levels. High-profile urban projects and property values are viewed as indicators of modernization, which in turn measure the political achievement of local state leaders. The local state builds its territorial authority, and finds its political identity in urban modernity. To the extent that the local state fails in urban accumulation and legitimation, as with the many development-related scandals and the abandonment of development projects due to financial problems, it also fails in state-building. In sum, the local state is built, and can be un-built by urban projects on physical, economic, political, and ideological fronts. Thus, the local state is urbanized in China's great urban transformation.

Space, power, and a typology of local state urbanization

The thesis of the urbanization of the local state is also my answer to the theoretical and methodological challenge of prioritizing the role of space in the study of society and space. I share Henri Lefebvre's (1991, 2003)[14] critique of the tendency to downplay space in social science. Too often, space serves as a passive container of sociopolitical processes that tends to reflect, but rarely initiates sociopolitical agendas or commands an independent logic. Also, as geographers like Neil Smith and Cindi Katz (1993)[15] have shown, space in many social-science literatures is treated as an all-encompassing element that transcends every field of inquiry, while the actual connection between physical and discursive space remains underdeveloped. To emphasize the active role of space, I use the urbanization of the local state to conceptualize urbanization as an active spatial force shaping the power process of the local state. In order to build a theoretical connection between the physical and the discursive dimensions of space, I stress that the urbanized local state is made and unmade by the interconnected physical, territorial, and ideological construction of urbanism.

A theoretical stance that treats space as an active force, and one that connects material space with discursive space leads me to operationalize this project through spatial concepts. These spatial concepts, in turn, emerged out of China's urban experience. China's current urban expansion follows three main trajectories:

- The first is an inward contraction of the inner-city areas that command the highest property values;
- The second is an outward expansion into villages at the urban fringe of the metropolitan region where the potential for increases in property value are the greatest;
- The third is the rural fringe of the metropolitan region, where townships and villages convert and lease out farmland for scattered industrial and commercial projects.

Before delving into the space-power relationship of these three types of places, a clarification of the term "metropolitan region" is in order.

The question of metropolitan regions has long been controversial in urban studies. Traditional Western urbanists held the view that a metropolitan region is composed of an urban core and its suburban ring or "commuting zone."[16] Others, such as Richard Walker (2008) and Bernadette Hanlon et al. (2006) have argued that the diversity within, and interconnection between the city and the suburb is much more complex than the dichotomous model of urban core and suburban periphery can convey; moreover, the model also underestimated the multilayered interaction between the city and the country.[17] Laurence Ma et al. (1987), Yixing Zhou et al. (2005), and George Lin (2006), among others, have tried to answer the question of what constitutes a city and a metropolitan region in the Chinese context. They point out the challenges of studying Chinese cities, which have multiple boundaries and definitions.[18] Kam Wing Chan (2007) helpfully drew a conceptual diagram to illustrate how administratively defined cities, especially large cities like Beijing, Shanghai, and Chongqing, are, in fact, regions that include a high-density urban core and an extensive rural area (Figure 1.1). Within this city-region, there are urban places of varied size and administrative rank, all of which are subordinated to the municipal government situated in the urban core. Some of

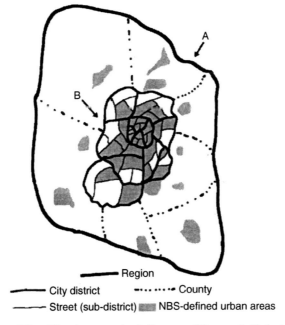

Figure 1.1 Kam Wing Chan's conceptual diagram of the spatial/administrative structure of a typical large city in China

Source: Chan (2007:5).

these city-regions are enormous, as with Chongqing at 82,300 sq km (nearly the size of Austria), Beijing at 16,578 sq km, and Shanghai at 6341 sq km.[19] While almost all large Chinese cities followed this model of city-region since the 1950s, Chan argues that they do not fit the definition of a metropolitan region, because their outer fringe remains predominantly agricultural and well beyond the "commuting zone." In other words, these large Chinese cities are administrative products that hardly qualify as genuine metropolises. For Chan, the bold line in Figure 1.1 showing the boundary of the municipal jurisdiction as a city-region is not the boundary of a metropolitan region.

In this book, I conceptualize the "metropolitan region" in a different manner. Instead of seeing the metropolitan region as a spatial unit defined by economic integration, I treat it as territorial dynamism, in which the administrative order sets the parameters for the restructuring of state power within the region. In a highly hierarchical state structure, the scale and scope of local state power corresponds directly to bureaucratic rank and jurisdictional boundaries. Local state leaders' territorial ambitions, which may exceed their jurisdictional rank and boundaries, must be affirmed and legitimized by adjusting ranks and redrawing boundaries through annexation, mergers, and detachment. Although jurisdiction does not determine the exercise of power, it shapes and is shaped by the politics of accumulation and legitimation in the place. A prominent Shanghai-based geographer, Junde Liu, has coined the term "jurisdictional economy" to emphasize the importance of jurisdictional boundaries in the organization of local economy and polity.[20] Because of the connection between the administrative order and territorial politics, I choose to follow the administrative boundary of large municipalities to define the "metropolitan region" in this book, notwithstanding the gap between its status as a "city" and the uneven level of urbanization within the jurisdiction. The "metropolitan" quality of the term, therefore, has a strong connotation of the central city's territorial dominance, particularly when it comes to a legitimate claim over land. Therefore, the line marking "region" in Chan's diagram (Figure 1.1), which is also the jurisdictional boundary of the municipality, coincides with the boundary of what I am calling the metropolitan region in this book. In other words, while Chan separated the administrative and economic definition of the metropolitan region, I treat them as interconnected forces in my analysis of territorial dynamism.

Within the metropolitan region, I use the urban core, the urban fringe, and the rural fringe to highlight the three areas of territorial dynamism and to build a typology of local state urbanization. Figure 1.2 shows the way

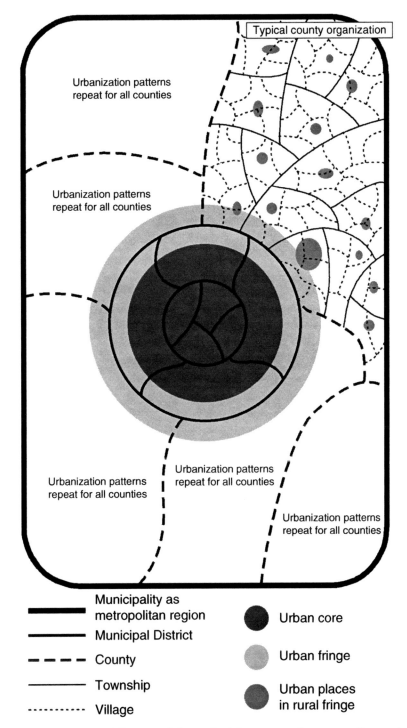

Figure 1.2 Conceptual diagram of the territorial structure of a metropolitan region (which coincides with a large municipality) and the typology of place in this study

I conceptualize the territorial structure of a metropolitan region, and the three types of place in this study. For each type of place, I identify the power vectors between the most active state agents. In inner-city areas in major cities like Beijing, the relevant power axis is between the municipal government, which seeks to consolidate control over land within its jurisdiction, and high-ranking state agencies that occupy and control premium land parcels in the urban core. At the urban fringe, the main state actors are urban and rural governments, which compete over land for conversion to industrial–commercial projects and commodity housing. At the rural fringe, the struggle is between the township government and villages. Though the townships are positioned at the bottom of the Chinese state hierarchy, they nonetheless represent state authority in villages. This intermediary position between the state bureaucracy and the peasantry enable townships to broker deals in the illicit land markets for construction of industrial and residential projects.

The sets of state actors in these three types of places are engaged in different territorial politics and development projects, which characterize the territorial restructuring of post-Mao China. But that is only half of the story of this book. The second half concerns the society, which is spatially conceptualized as "civic territoriality."

Civic territoriality

Territory is often associated with state sovereignty in geopolitical literature, and is aligned most closely with the nation-state. But territory is contested not only between the ruling elites of the state, but also between the state and society. Moreover, social actors develop territorial strategies that may contradict the state's own territorial logic. For example, local governments use urban redevelopment powers to destroy, displace, and rebuild, while inner-city protesters make legal, historical, and moral claims over their rights to property, housing, and livelihood in the city. Similarly, as an urban government initiates expansion in neighboring villages, villagers at the rapidly growing urban fringe strategize to avoid displacement, take advantage of urban real-estate markets, and even manage to secure a relative territorial autonomy. Meanwhile, in the remote rural fringe areas, large numbers of displaced villagers lose economic, social, and cultural resources and become deterritorialized.

In all three cases, territoriality is central to different social actors' cultivation of resources and collective identities, to the framing of grievances and demands, and to the choice of collective actions. Territoriality also shapes the results of their struggle, leading to territorialization or deterritorialization in varying degrees. I call social actors' conscious cultivation and struggles to form their own territoriality at both physical and discursive levels "civic territoriality." I emphasize that territoriality, when viewed from the ground-up, is as much a tool of resistance as it is of dominance. While the local state uses urban construction to consolidate and legitimize its territorial authority, societal actors use territorial strategies for self-protection. These territorial struggles have become a critical platform for emerging social activism. The notion of civic territoriality brings society to the center of territorial politics, and places it at the root of social actions.

Just as the state is not a homogeneous entity, neither is society. Social actors' territorial struggles and strategies vary in different places. Before going into the typology of civic territoriality. I will first review geographers' works on the relationship between location, place, and territory. Clarification of these concepts can help to elucidate the concept of civic territoriality.

Location, locale, place, and territoriality

John Agnew (1987) has defined "place" as composed of three elements: location, locale, and sense of place.[21] A place has a physical "location"; it is a "locale" if we include the material setting and its social relations; and there is a "sense of place" that represents people's emotional attachments. Geographers such as Tim Cresswell, David Harvey, Doreen Massey, Don Mitchell, and Geraldine Pratt have elaborated further on the politics of place, especially the exclusiveness and inclusiveness of place; and on the place-making capability of marginalized peoples. Place has social, political, cultural, and ideological meanings on top of the physicality of location and locale.[22]

Most analysts agree that location, locale, and place are not separate components, but are interconnected layers of meanings. At the core of a place is its location: where it is on the surface of the earth. The second layer is the material environment and its physical elements like rivers, roads, and buildings, which turn a location into a locale. The history and subjective perception of the locale makes a locale a place. I would add to this a fourth layer: "territory." The struggle over the control and occupation of a place turns the place into a territory. Territorialization is the politicization of place. The territoriality of society refers to the dynamics of society's struggle over place making in a locale; it also involves struggles over relocation and dislocation. Society's strategization to define and defend the occupation and control of a place is what I call "civic territoriality." Civic territoriality involves processes of territorialization, deterritorialization, and reterritorialization, as well as the possibilities of building society's own territorial logic and autonomy.[23] Here, autonomy refers to the degree of control over the social, political, and physical construction of place, which is gauged not by separation from the dominant force, but by the level of control over the connection with it, as proposed by Robert Lake (1994) and James Defilippis (1999).[24]

While the urbanization of the local state focuses on land-centered accumulation and legitimation politics among various state actors, civic territoriality conceptualizes land-centered distributional politics initiated by society. In what follows, I elaborate further the three types of land-centered distributional politics that contribute to turning places into territories.

Typologies of civic territoriality

The three types of place that define local state urbanization each produce their own distributional politics. In the inner city of metropolises like Beijing, for instance, protests are initiated by long-term residents evicted to make room for redevelopment projects. This group of urban residents writes letters and visits government offices (*xinfang* and *shangfang*) to lodge complaints, or launches administrative litigation against relevant branches of the local state government and their allied developers. They demand fair compensation and adequate relocation based on titled ownership of privately owned homes and on the right to a livelihood in the city.

Inner-city protesters frame their grievances and strategies in territorial terms. Their place identity is activated in the process of forced eviction, and in the face of a loss of livelihood. They use territorial strategies to assert their entitlement to their inner-city homes, neighborhoods, and urban services. Though uneven, the results of their actions have slowed down inner-city destruction and increased compensation rates. I do not foresee a more fundamental transformation of state–society relations directly provoked by inner-city residents' mobilization, and I am reluctant to leap to the conclusion that inner-city residents' protests mark the emergence of an "urban social movement" that promises to change the power structure of the city, as defined by Manuel Castells (1983).[25] Yet, it does indicate the beginning of a changing discourse in which accumulation through dispossession is no longer hidden behind the slogan of "development is the absolute principle"; nor is massive urban displacement considered unanimously a historical necessity on the road toward a higher modernity. Inner-city activists and their version of civic territoriality have put forth a territorial agenda toward redefining the state-dominant property rights regime in the inner city and toward recognizing urban residents' social rights to the city, regardless of their property ownership status.

A second type of distributional politics emerges at the urban fringe triggered by the expansion of the metropolitan urban center. Unlike the confrontational resistance in the inner city, the distributional politics at the urban fringe features nonconfrontational bargaining and negotiation between urban governments and villagers. In the rapidly expanding southern metropolises like Guangzhou and Shenzhen, for example, land-owning village collectives have skillfully bargained with urban governments. Taking advantage of the urban government's desperation for high-speed and low-cost urban expansion, villagers in the urban fringe have managed to stay in their village homes and share the fortunes of the growing urban real-estate market. In these villages, which are dubbed *"chengzhongcun"* or "villages in the city," villagers and village collectives intensify their use of village land by developing and renting out residential and commercial projects. Based on reinforced collective identity, consolidated collective assets, and restructured corporatist organization, these villages have generated what I call "village corporatism" in the expanding metropolitan region, and achieved a degree of territorial autonomy. It is a relatively successful case of territorialization.

Most peasants, especially those at the rural fringe of metropolitan areas, are not nearly as fortunate as corporatist villagers in the southern metropolis. Their struggle for livelihood marks a third type of distributional politics: the politics of deterritorialization. Between 1990 and 2002, an estimated 50–66 million peasants lost all or part of their farmland and homes to local government land grabs and development projects. Protests launched by aggrieved peasants have been on the rise since the late 1990s. In 2005, the Ministry of Land and Resources recorded 87,000 protests related to land grabs, a 6 percent increase from 2004.[26] Like their inner-city counterparts, peasants protest against forced eviction, demand fair compensation, and request adequate relocation by going through the "letters and visits" system, and by initiating litigation against government agencies, officials, and developers. Despite their grave plight and the large number of aggrieved peasants, these protests remain largely fragmented and localized. A territorial explanation posits that when peasants lose their land and are forced to relocate, their economic base deteriorates, collective organization disintegrates, and collective identities are ruptured. Physical relocation thus leads to economic, social, and cultural deterritorialization. Forced relocation makes it difficult to avoid deterritorialization; and deterritorialization makes sustainable mobilization a daunting task.

Many dispossessed and displaced peasants have resorted to individualized modes of protest, such as physically occupying homes and farms slated for demolition thus becoming so-called "nail households" (*dingzihu*). While the corporatist villagers' territorialization is built upon reinforced collectivity, displaced peasants' deterritorialization is exacerbated by individualized strategies of self-protection.

Finally, the varied politics of accumulation, legitimation, and distribution amid urban transformation also produce one another. Competition over land among various state actors affects and is affected by societal responses to land grabs. For instance, in the early 1990s, when inner-city resistance to rampant redevelopment and massive displacement began to take shape and to slow down redevelopment projects, and as state work unit, or *danwei*, land holders proved resilient in the face of moves against their land control, municipal governments shifted their focus for land development from the inner city to village land at the urban fringe. In doing so, they sought to expand the metropolitan region outward, and to capitalize on both the legitimacy of development zones and on the relatively low political and economic costs of appropriating village land. By the late 1990s, the "development zone fever" and industrialism was cooling down. Amid the failure of rural collective industries, and the dramatic surge in peasant protests against land grabs, policy discourse started to shift from Deng's "development is the absolute principle" to Hu and Wen's concerns over the "three agricultural problems" and building a "harmonious society." But this turn of political discourse did not produce a linear result of greater protection of farmers and farmland. Rather, it created a new platform for power struggles and opened a historical opportunity for higher-level local state entities such as municipal governments. Under the emergent discourse, rural townships and their illicit industrial parks became scapegoats in the new campaign for farmland protection in the 2000s. Municipal governments, with their greater political legitimacy and organizational resources, took the opportunity to move even more aggressively into the rural hinterland and build new towns of a greater scale on land previously controlled by rural township governments.

By the mid-2000s, urbanism largely took over industrialism as the basis for political legitimacy and policy discourse. The decline of rural collective industries, the expectation of fast returns from urban projects, and the glamour of urban modernity led local state leaders to pepper their policy reports with jargon like "city branding," "urban marketing," and "global cities." The basis for local state-building has conclusively shifted from industrial parks to urban spectacles. These urban projects took two general forms. One was the revival of inner-city redevelopment on a grander scale than during the previous decade, with brands like "Multinational Corporation Headquarters" and "Global CEO Clusters." These commercial–residential mixed-use projects were expected to boost property values for municipal and district governments. The second entailed farmland conversion at the rural fringe of the metropolitan region to create "New Cities." New Cities tended to be far larger than townships' industrial estates of the 1990s, ranging up to more than 100 sq km, and affecting much larger numbers of jurisdictions and residents in the rural hinterland.

As the project of urban accumulation and legitimation through massive destruction and dispossession got underway, the politics of distribution has grown even more contentious and widespread in the cities, the countryside, and areas in-between. The interwoven politics of the urbanization of the local state and civic territoriality tell the tale of the great transformation in post-Mao China.

Research design and data collection

This project has stretched out from 1996 to 2007. It did not flow from a singular research proposal that outlined each step from the beginning to end. Instead, this project was a process shaped by the great transformation of China itself from an agrarian to industrial, rural to urban, and socialist to capitalist like polity and society. Following the completion of my first book on overseas Chinese investment in China and its impact on rural industrialization,[27] I turned my attention to the process of breakneck urbanization, focusing especially on the relationship between the local state and land development. Also at this time, the development gap between the coastal and inland regions became increasingly pronounced, as a result of deepened market reforms. Thus, I extended my research sites from the three major coastal metropolitan regions (Beijing, Shanghai, and Guangzhou) to include three inland cities: Chengdu (capital of Sichuan Province), Changsha (capital of Hunan Province), and Zhengzhou (capital of Henan Province), and districts, cities, counties, and townships under their jurisdiction. In these inland cities, I found anxious local state leaders desperate to catch up with the prosperous coastal cities, and taking even more precipitous measures than their coastal counterparts to grab land and secure land rents. Between 2003 and 2007, I also visited Nanjing (capital of Jiangsu Province) and Jinan (capital of Shandong Province) and returned to Beijing, Shanghai,

Figure 1.3 Sites of interviews in China (Cartographer: Darin Jensen)

and Guangzhou once again to reassess the changes in these metropolises. Figure 1.3 shows the places I conducted interviews in China for this research.

It was during this period that widespread instances of contentious politics triggered by land grabs began to flare up across the country. As the scale and frequency of protests launched by displaced inner-city residents and peasants mounted, I expanded my inquiry from the local state's urban strategies to society's responses to, and active participation in urban transformation, and from the politics of accumulation to that of distribution. My analysis of society's self-protection is mainly based on fieldwork in the metropolitan regions of Beijing and Guangzhou.

The long gestation of this project has its advantages and disadvantages. On the plus side, I feel more confident making generalized statements about China's urban dynamics. I have visited some of my sites multiple times at different stages in their development process, and have witnessed changes on the ground. At the same time, the project's wide spatial spectrum means that it does not attempt in-depth study of a single city, or systematic comparison between two or three sites. Instead, I am able to build the analytical and comparative axis on a typology of urban places and territorial dynamics.

To cohere with my emphasis on the importance of cities in understanding China's transformation, I use place as the analytical anchor. I identify three types of places and their territorial dynamics that I consider salient to the analysis of China's urban transformation. These are: redevelopment in the urban core, expansion at the urban edge, and farmland expropriation at the rural fringe of the metropolitan region. To each of these three, I apply materials from different research sites collected at different times to outline the changing institutional and historical conditions and the power dynamics among the main players. Accordingly, I have structured this book in three parts, each part dealing with one type of place and territorial politics. For each type of place there is a chapter on the local state's strategies of accumulation and legitimation, and one on society's strategies for self-protection.

While the place-based typology of territorial politics between state and society has general applicability in China, the empirical information in each chapter is inevitably place-biased. To address this bias, I have integrated a large amount of secondary data from news sources, official reports, and Chinese academic and policy research papers that point to similar phenomena in different regions. While most of the secondary data does not provide sufficient information for systematic comparison with my own data, my long-term observation of China's urban transformation has helped to evaluate the secondary data factually, and thus to qualify my generalizations. I also read the data discursively, so as to reflect on China's changing social and political discourses on urban processes.

That this project extended over such a long period, and incorporated so many disparate sites is really the outcome of a set of compromises, one of which derived from the topic itself. There are many widely accessible sources of information concerning policies, plans, and institutions of urban development in China. Most large cities count among their tourist sites grandiose exhibition halls featuring sophisticated, three-dimensional models of the future city. In a similar vein, developers are eager to take visitors on tours through their projects and to explain their future plans. Urban planning officials are always ready to cite statistics on the pace and scale of urban construction in their cities, and are generous in offering glossy brochures intended for prospective investors depicting the city's economic zones and industrial parks. There are also published laws and regulations on land use, urban planning, land conversion and circulation, as well as demolition and relocation compensation to which researchers can refer. In other words, much of the data on urbanization is low-hanging fruit.

Yet, when it comes to the very real struggles among state actors over land or the operation of local state-sponsored development companies, information is not nearly as readily available. The exciting topic of the city's spectacular future can quickly turn into a prohibitively sensitive subject. The stream of land-related political scandals that have brought down thousands of local officials in recent years has made it even more difficult to gather specific information. Hurdles are thrown up almost as soon as one attempts to enter into this fraught territory. I have experienced a sudden freeze in cooperation from local officials in the middle of fieldwork because a high-ranking local leader was detained in a corruption investigation. Due to the fluidity of the political context in which research of this type is conducted, research sites and interviewees frequently chose me, rather than vice versa. I was compelled to conduct research where I had solid contacts, who then introduced me to others with whom I was able to build a mutually trustful relationship. I spent more time with these people talking about the parts of the story they were familiar with and willing to disclose. That connection may or may not have led to other interviews in the same place. Due to the sensitivity of the topic, carefully nurtured information networks and informant chains were far more brittle and tenuous when compared with my earlier study of Taiwanese manufacturing investment in southern China. As a result, the information gathered for this project was inevitably fragmented. My task then has been to reassemble disparate threads into a comprehensible tapestry. While all researchers wear tinted lenses and make compromises, I found ethnographic work on the politics of land development especially challenging. While born out of frustration, as noted in the Prologue, this book was executed with compromises. I only hope that my own frustration and compromises do not obscure my attempt to present the fascinating complexity of China's great urban transformation.

Organization of the book

The two main questions I raise in this book are: first, how does the state and society shape and become shaped by the unprecedented urban transformation of post-Mao China? And, second, how does space, in the form of territoriality, play a role in these contested processes? To explore these questions, I organize the book into three parts around the three types of place mentioned earlier. I consider these three types of place to be key sites in China's urban transformation. As urbanization is a dynamic process rather than a static condition, these three types of place—the inner city, the urban edge, and the rural fringe—are not three isolated containers of human activity and politics. Rather, they constitute a spatial continuum from the most concentrated, high-density urban core to the lower density, transitional zone between the urban and the rural, then on to the rural edge. The boundaries between them are constantly shifting, and the dynamics within one place often trigger changes in others. The place-based typology also has a strong temporal component. The inner city speaks most strongly for this, because it has the longest-established settlements and infrastructure, the most entangled land rights, and the highest stakes in land-rent competition. The land battle in the inner city is between the socialist past and the present market economy. The politics of land development in the urban edge, on the other hand, is a grab in the present for a bet on the future. Local government leaders bet on the future by grabbing land at the fringe as reserves for future urban expansion. Through massive infrastructure investment, they connect the existing urban core with projects on the urban edge for a profitable future. At the rural fringe, the temporal element is trickier. Rural township leaders' low status in the bureaucratic hierarchy is the root cause of anxiety over their future power positions. To cope with the uncertainty, township leaders try to squeeze as much as possible from the present, hence the large number of small-scale, scattered development projects aimed at immediate profits.

   In each of the three place-based parts of the book, I devote a chapter to the politics of accumulation and legitimation of local state actors, paired with a chapter on the politics of distribution initiated by a social group. While the place-based typology and the pairing of state and social actions is by no means exhaustive, this structure serves the dual purposes of anchoring the story line in spatial terms, and providing a theoretical frame for the political economy of urban transformation in China.

Part I, Redevelopment of the Urban Core focuses on the core area of metropolitan cities such as Beijing and Shanghai, and provincial capitals like Changsha and Nanjing. Chapter 2 focuses on land battles in the urban core between high-ranking state units (or socialist land masters) and municipal governments. It argues that while the socialist land masters occupy premium land parcels inherited from the planned economy, the municipal government's authority is reinforced by a modernist discourse, Western urban planning doctrines, and recent policies that grant authority over state-owned urban land to the territorial government. Rather than settling the matter of power in the city, however, municipal leaders' granted authority is tested and defined by their political, regulatory, organizational, and moral capacity in negotiations with those above, within, and below them. The municipal government's regulatory capacity is especially challenged by a fragmented real-estate industry that includes players from state, nonstate, and in-between sectors.

Chapter 3 examines two types of grassroot resistance in Beijing triggered by inner-city redevelopment. One concerns property rights protests launched by pre-Revolution private homeowners; the other focuses on residents' rights protests by long-term inner-city residents displaced by redevelopment projects. The homeowners succeeded in recovering their pre-Revolution homeownership, and their protests quickly escalated to challenge the more fundamental issue of the state's exclusive claim over land and land rents. The displaced residents, on the other hand, framed their grievances and demands not as property owners, but as residents whose livelihood is rooted in the inner city. While both groups used legalistic and territorial strategies to negotiate with the state, and to expand mobilization networks, the expansion of their demands from property rights to residents' rights is particularly meaningful in the pursuit of citizenship rights.

Part II, Expansion of the Metropolitan Region shifts the geographical focus from the urban center to the urban edge. The type of land at issue here is rural land owned by the village collective. Chapter 4 outlines the land battles between expansionist urban governments at the municipal and district levels, and rural governments at the county and township levels. The struggle between urban and rural governments is set in the historical shift in which industrialism has largely given way to urbanism since the late 1990s. Drawing on the changing political discourse, urban governments have moved to incorporate scattered industrial estates formerly controlled by rural governments. As a result, the urban fringe becomes a primary site of capital accumulation, territorial expansion, and consolidation vital to urban governments' local state-building projects. The urban government's logic of property-based accumulation and territorial expansion is materialized through massive-scale mega projects like "New Cities" and "University Cities" built on former village land in the outskirts of the city.

Chapter 5 turns to the villages located at the urban fringe that have actually benefited from urban expansion, and looks at the nonconfrontational form of social mobilization in those sites. Rapid urban expansion since the 1980s has turned many "villages by the city" into "villages in the city" and has transformed villagers from vegetable farmers to *rentiers*, taking advantage of immigrant-fuelled rental housing markets. These "corporatist villages," as I term them, are most successful in Guangzhou and Shenzhen. Corporatist villages are able to enjoy relative territorial autonomy under the expansionist regime of the metropolitan government because of their skills in bargaining with the local state, their strategic location, recollectivization of the village economy, and reinforcement of village identity. These southern corporatist villages thus represent a successful case of territorialization.

Finally, Part III, Urbanization of the Rural Fringe moves farther out to the rural edge of the metropolitan region, where the influence of the metropolitan government over its immediate hinterland gives way to low-ranking township governments exercising informal power over rural land. Chapter 6 focuses on land politics in rural towns. Acting as power and property brokers between the state bureaucracy and peasants, township leaders try to avoid scrutiny from above while intensifying downward control over village land to develop illicit industrial, commercial, and residential projects. Townships' power and property brokerage is exemplified by their issuing of home-ownership certificates that attract buyers of affordable homes, but are not recognized by the state. Townships' limited formal power is secured through construction projects and expanded through the operation of the black market for property.

Chapter 7 looks at peasants who lost their land to urban expansion in the last three decades. It seeks a territorial explanation for the gap between the magnitude of peasants' grievances and the frequency of protests on the one hand, and peasant's mobilizational capacity on the other. It argues that the mobilizational capacity of peasants is undermined by the snowball effect of forced relocation. Forced relocation often leads to the deterioration of villagers' household financial status, disintegration of village organization, and rupture of collective identity, all of which

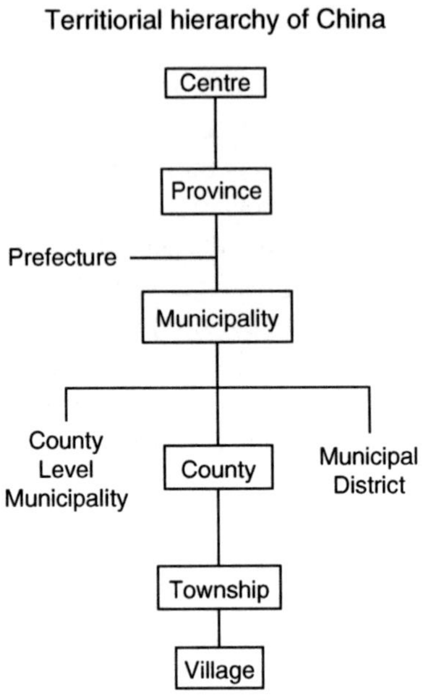

Territiorial hierarchy of China

Figure 1.4 Territorial hierarchy of China

contribute to village deterritorialization. More specifically, relocation produces deterritorialization through nebulous compensation negotiations that undermine mutual trust within villages, phased demolition and relocation that gradually destroys the physical environment as well as village solidarity, and switching peasants' status from members of village collectives to urban residents, thereby splitting the villagers' interests. These moves weaken the villagers' potential for successful collective action.

Chapter 8 broadens the scope of this book and makes programmatic connections both between the urbanized local state and China's emerging territorial order, and between civic territoriality and the prospects for grassroots mobilization in Chinese cities and the countryside. Both issues are at the center of the recent property crisis and rural reform. On the former, I propose that while state power is restructured through the double movement of power decentralization and reconcentration among competing local states, leading cities of metropolitan regions have come to dominate the new territorial order. On the latter, two theoretical connections can be made between civic territoriality and social activism. The first responds to debates on the relative importance of community and class in urban social movements; the second examines rural collectivism and suggests that while collective land ownership persists in China, peasants' collective organization and identity, which are integral to rural collectivism, have been paradoxically dismantled to a significant extent.

Notes

1. See PRC Constitution, Article 10. According to *PRC Land Management Law* (first adopted in 1986, amended in 1988, 1998, 2004), Article 2: "All urban land belongs to the state; land in the countryside and in suburban areas is under collective ownership."
2. Ho, Samuel and George Lin "The state, land system and land development processes in contemporary China," 2005.
3. Between 1980–2002 the urban population grew from 18–20 percent to 36–40 percent of the total population, or about 250 million in total were added to the urban population. See Lin, George C. S. "The growth and structural change of Chinese cities: 2002; and Zhou, Yixing, and Laurence J. C. Ma, "China's urbanization levels: reconstructing a baseline from the fifth population census,"2003.
4. For a "state-led urbanization" argument, see, for example, Chan, Kam Wing, *Cities with Invisible Walls* 1994; Fan, Cindy, "The vertical and horizontal expansions of China's city system," 1999; Chan, Roger, and Zhao X. B., "The relationship between administrative hierarchy position and city size development in China," 2002. For a recent elaboration on China's urbanization in the era of market reform, see Lin, George C. S., "Reproducing spaces of Chinese urbanization: New city-based and land-centered urban transformation," 2007. For a comprehensive review of the studies of Chinese cities, see Ma, Laurence, "The state of the field of urban China: 2006; and Ma, Laurence, "Urban transformation in China, 1949–2000, 2002.
5. A Chinese planning official, Li Jinkui, coined the term "urbanization of the state" (*guojia chengshihua*). But he used it narrowly to refer to state control over land supplies and circulation. In this book, I have expanded the term to include physical, political, and ideological dimensions of local state urban projects, and suggested that the local state is urbanized in all those dimensions. See Li, Jinkui, "Chengshi shuaixian xiandaihua zhiyi—zhongguo hexie chengshihuade guanjian suozai" (Questioning the urban priority in modernization: the key to harmonious urbanization in China), 2005.
6. Abram, Philip, "Notes on the difficulty of studying the state", 1988, Corrigan, Philip, and Derek Sayer, *The Great Arch: English State Formation as Cultural Revolution*, 1985.
7. Grzymala-Busse and Jones Luong have put it concisely in their work on Eastern European transition economies. They maintained that the post-socialist state is not about dismantling of the state, but a process of state-building. It is not "transitory," but processes of state "formation." State formation is defined as

"elite competition over the authority to create the structural framework through which policies are made and enforced." The question is what kind of elites are competing, and how they compete. See Grzymala-Busse, Anna and Pauline Jones Luong, "Reconceptualizing the state: lessons from post-Communism," 2002. This concept is also built on Foucault, Michel, "The Subject and Power," 1982.

8. Oi, Jean, "Fiscal reform and the economic foundations of local state corporatism in China," 1992.

9. Burawoy, Michael, "The state and economic involution," 1996.

10. Delaney, David, *Territory: A Short Introduction*, 2005; Delaney, David, *Race, Place and the law 1836–1948*, 1998.

11. The local state is often treated as "institutionalized avenues of conflicts and compromises to minimize the risk of unpredictable crises." See Hinsley, F. H., *Sovereignty*, 1986.

12. Hinsley, *Sovereignty*, pp. 142–3.

13. State regulation is carried out through zoning, which is one of the most important territorial authorities of the local state, and a territorial strategy of municipalities in the United States and in many other modern capitalist societies. See, for example, Makielski, S. J., Jr., *The Politics of Zoning*, 1966.

14. Lefebvre, Henri, *The Production of Space*, 1991; and Lefebvre, Henri, *The Urban Revolution*, 2003.

15. Smith, Neil and Cindi Katz, "Grounding metaphor: Towards a spatialized politics," 1993.

16. Simmons, James and Larry Bourne, "Defining urban places: Differing concepts of the urban systems," 1978.

17. Walker, Richard, *The Country in the City: The Greening of the San Francisco Bay Area*, 2008. Hanlon, Bernadette, Thomas Vicino, and John Rennie Short, "The new metropolitan reality in the US: rethinking the traditional model," 2006. For a classic discussion of the complexity of American metropolitan regions, see Teaford, Jon, *City And Suburb: The Political Fragmentation Of Metropolitan America*, 1979.

18. Ma, Laurence and Gonghao Cui, "Administrative changes and urban population in China," 1987; Lin, George C.S., "Peri-urbanism in globalizing China: A Study of new urbanism in Dongguan," 2006; Zhou, Yixing and Laurence Ma, "China's urbanization levels: reconstructing a baseline from the fifth population census," 2003; Zhou, Yixing and Laurence Ma, "China's urban population statistics: a critical evaluation," 2005; Kirkby, Richard, *Urbanization in China*, 1985.

19. Chan, Kam Wing, "Misconceptions and complexities in the studies of China's cities," 2007.

20. See Liu, Junde, "Zhongguo zhuanxingqi tuxian de 'xingzhengqu jingji' xianxiang fenxi" (An analysis of jurisdictional economy), 2004.

21. Agnew, John, *Place and Politics*, 1987.

22. Agnew, *Place and Politics*; Cresswell, Tim, *Place: A Short Introduction*, 2004; Cresswell, Tim, *In Place/Out of Place*, 1996; Massey, Doreen, *Space, Place and Gender*, 1994; David Harvey, "From space to place and back again," 1993; Pred, Allan, "Place as historically contingent process," 1984; Geraldine Pratt, "Geographies of identity and Difference 1999; Mitchell, Don, *The Right to the City*, 2003; Smith, Neil, *The New Urban Frontier*, 1996.

23. Gilles Deleuze and Felix Guattari discuss territorialization and reterritorialization, see Deleuze, Gilles and Felix Guattari, *A Thousand Plateaus* 1987. My use of the term "deterritorialization" is different from Deleuze and Guattari's in the sense that I do not see deterritorialization and reterritorialization as necessarily two spontaneous and interconnected processes. When it comes to the interconnectedness between physical, sociopolitical, and discursive dimensions of territoriality, and when it comes to territorial processes at the collective instead of individual level, especially where collective action is concerned, I do not find an automatic connection between deterritorialization and reterritorialization at the same or different scales. Rather, my focus is on the mechanisms of territorialization and deterritorialization, and I emphasize that reterritorialization is not guaranteed at the moment of deterritorialization. Neil Brenner suggests that deterritorializations on one scale or at the same time entail re-territorializations on other scales, or at other times in his discussion of the state in the process of globalization. Again, my point here is to expand from state territoriality to civic territoriality, and to expand the concept beyond the realm of the state. See Brenner, Neil, "Beyond state centrism?," 1999.

24. Lake, Robert, "Negotiating local autonomy," 1994; Defilippis, James "Alternatives to the New Urban Politics," 1999.

25. Castells, Manuel, *The City and the Grassroots*, 1983.

26. Ewing, Kent, "China goes back to the land," 2006. Phan, Pamela, "Enriching the land or the political elite?" 2005.

27. Hsing, You-tien, *Making Capitalism in China: The Taiwan Connection*, 1998.

Part I

Redevelopment of the Urban Core

Chapter 2

Municipal Governments, Socialist Land Masters, and Urban Land Battles

In June 2000, a district chief in Changsha, the capital of Hunan Province, took me on a tour of the city. He repeatedly referred to the land under the direct proprietary control of the district government as "his land." Knowing my background in city planning, he also asked for suggestions on developing "his" 500 mu here and "his" 1200 mu there.[1] Before the city tour, I had attended a luncheon with him and two urban planning officials, a government banker, an architect, and a local developer. The district chief tried to persuade the developer to abandon a project for a high-density mixed residential-retail complex on a corner lot in the city center. He said the district government had plans to build a landmark government office tower on the highly-symbolic site. But the developer, who was connected with the military, said there was no way for him to change the plan now that the foundation work had already started. The district chief was clearly disappointed, ending the luncheon without the customary round-the-table-toasting. So, as he ticked off his prized possessions of land during the city tour after luncheon, I realized his control over urban land, nominally under his jurisdiction, was, in fact, far from total. The urban government's territorial authority and land control must be earned as much as granted.

This chapter[2] tells the tale of land-centered accumulation politics in the core area of large metropolitan cities like Beijing and provincial capitals like Changsha, Jinan (capital of Shandong Province), and Nanjing (capital of Jiangsu Province).[3] These cities host multiple state authorities, including high-ranking ones, within their jurisdictions. For example, Beijing hosts both central government and municipal government institutions, and Changsha provides space for provincial and municipal governments, as well as some central government units. For municipal governments, the presence of the high-ranking state and provincial agencies in its jurisdiction is a mixed blessing. It is a political privilege, for sure. Yet the presence of state units that are not under the jurisdictional authority of the territorial government presents a significant challenge. There is considerable tension between the functional (*tiao*) and territorial (*kuai*) state systems, and the urban core areas of these cities, where the state agencies concentrate and where the land commands the highest commercial values, are at the center of the drama. Competition for premium land in the urban core is fundamental for the territorial government to consolidate its jurisdictional authority. Land competition also transforms the high-ranking functional state units, such as military units, from land users to formidable contenders in the new property market. Land redevelopment in urban centers has thus become the site for the restructuring of the *tiao-kuai* matrix of the state power.

The backdrop to this drama is the state's urban-land tenure. Although constitutionally enshrined, the state's ownership of land has remained unclear in its actual implementation. The law does not specify who within the state sector might represent the state, legitimately exercise ownership rights, and profit from land rent. As rapid urban expansion fueled an upward spiral in the commercial value of urban land in the 1990s, especially in the core areas, intra-state competition over the exercise of ownership rights intensified.

Two sets of state actors are most active in this intra-state competition for land. The first consists of the territorial local government and its leaders. While the State Council has nominal ownership rights over all urban land in China, territorial governments have regulatory authority over land-use planning, immediate access to state-owned urban land in their jurisdictions, and local knowledge. In this chapter, I focus on the municipal governments, with reference to district governments at times.[4] A second set of state actors comes from vertically organized functional state agencies that dominated the *tiao-kuai* power matrix under the command economy. These consist of central-level government agencies, party and military units, utility providers, universities, research institutions, large hospitals and state-owned enterprises (SOEs). These state units are physically located within the jurisdiction of municipal governments, while being subject to the vertical administrative control of the *tiao*.[5] As representatives of the central state, they have exclusive use and management rights over the land they occupy. Since the 1980s, they have expanded their use rights over land granted under the socialist system to *de facto* ownership rights in the new land leasehold market, becoming what I call "socialist land masters."

The land-centered politics of the urban core therefore unfolds as an intra-state battle over land by these two sets of state actors—municipal governments and socialist land masters. Their land battle, in turn, conditions municipal leaders' strategies toward territorial consolidation and market regulation.

Socialist land masters

The role of socialist land masters must first be placed in the context of the development industry in China. The Chinese Development firms have wide-ranging ownership and management structures. Officially, there are two types of development firms: "primary" and "secondary" developers, defined by their access to land. Those that have direct access to land are "primary" developers; those that do not are "secondary" developers.

Municipal or district governments and state agencies in charge of construction establish primary development companies. They are granted official authority to initiate the process of land-use rights transfer from current land users, such as state-owned factories or rural villages, to other users for new projects. They also have the financial responsibility to turn the so-called "raw" land into "cooked" land, which entails relocation and compensation negotiation with current land users, as well as invest-ment in site clearing and infrastructure installation to prepare the site for new construction. After the primary developers "cook" the "raw" land, they turn over the parcels to the land bureau of the municipal government. The land bureau then lists the parcels under municipal registration to affirm the municipality's land rights, and auctions these rights out to secondary developers.

Operating alongside legitimate primary developers, in a sizable adminis-trative gray zone, are other state actors that do not possess formal or full authority to engage in such 'primary' development activities, but do so anyway through various means. Socialist land masters are among the most active and powerful in this gray zone.

Under the socialist land-tenure system in the prereform period, a variety of urban land users, including SOEs, military units, and others listed previ-ously were allocated land through administrative channels according to central capital investment plans. These state institutions were subject to the vertical *tiao* budgetary and personnel control that was largely beyond the reach of local governments. As urban land users, they not only held the use and management rights over the land they occupied, but acted as *de facto* owners who could make decisions about exchange and transfer of the land they occupied. Several socialist legacies give these socialist land masters two major advantages in the current round of competition for control over urban land.

The first of these is locational advantage. The socialist land masters, especially the industrial enterprises, often occupy premium land in the heart of cities. Motivated by the idea that the socialist city should be a production center and not a consumption center, economic planners allocated centrally located land to high-profile SOEs in the 1960s and 1970s. By the early 1980s, industrial enterprises and warehouses occupied about 30 percent of the core area in Chinese cities, a percentage far higher than in most capitalist cities at the time.[6] For example, about 5 percent of the total urban area of Beijing municipality, the core of the city was home to 55 percent of Beijing's state-owned factories.[7] In Shanghai, nearly 60 percent of the state-owned factories were located in the central part of the city, and almost 70 percent of industrial workers worked and lived there in 1982.[8]

A second advantage these socialist land masters enjoy is simply the quantity of land they control. In the past, because the *danwei* (work unit) functioned as the primary channel for social-welfare distribution, land was allocated not only for factories, warehouses, and office structures, but also for employee housing, health clinics, day-care centers, and schools. The logic of soft budgetary constraints also meant that SOEs and other state *danwei* bargained hard for more land than they could use because land came at little cost.[9] These entities might occupy several city blocks. On the eve of the establishment of the land leasehold market in 1988, *danwei* compounds occupied large portions of urban cores.[10] Ten industrial bureaus in Shanghai, for instance, controlled more than a quarter of the city's industrial land in the 1980s, and established themselves as super land masters in the 1990s.[11]

When the pace of urbanization was slow and land rights were rarely transferred for profit, such a system of urban land control posed few problems. But the emergence of an urban land-lease market in the 1980s marked a dramatic shift. Rapid industrialization, urban expansion, and economic diversification have greatly intensified the competition over land in the urban core.

The land leasehold market, formally established in 1988, effectively separated land-use rights and ownership rights. Though ultimate state ownership remained unchanged, land-use rights could now be legally transferred as land leases tradable in the market by negotiation, tender, or open auction.[12] Urban land has thus become commodified, even if de jure privatization of land remains outlawed. By creating market-like competition for land, and opening up the possibility to profit from rising land

1. Traditional courtyard housing encroached by new buildings in inner city Beijing (June 2004)

rents, the commodification of land spurred socialist land masters into action. They established land-development companies, and expanded their rights to include the rental and transfer of land under their control.

The socialist land masters' large land reserves in the center of the city are now paying off. As a low-risk strategy, many of them simply transfer land-use rights to commercial developers and profit by collecting rent. One analyst estimated in 2001 that only a minority of the land development companies in Beijing, about 1200 out of 4000 plus, actually engaged in development projects.[13] The rest sold their land-use rights to commercial developers who did not otherwise have access to the premium land parcels. An informal network of land brokers has emerged to facilitate land circulation in cities. Among the successful brokers are former staff members from land-owning state units, and officials with connections to relevant government agencies.[14]

Enterprising and resource-rich socialist land masters have further expanded their land reserves by consolidating land parcels from many different work units under the same administrative head, or by using insider connections to purchase additional land from SOEs facing bankruptcy. Strong financial backing by the vertical *xitong* has made such land accumulation possible. Thus, throughout the 1990s, ambitious land masters built up land reserves by leveraging the *xitong* system's financial power and by assembling, parcel-by-parcel, large tracks of premium urban land through intra-state transactions. One of the largest development group companies in Beijing, Capital Land, has seven listed companies; one of them is listed on the Hong Kong Stock Exchange. The general manager of Capital Land, Liu Xiaoguang, who is seen as a guru in Beijing's real estate circle, is the former vice chair of Beijing's Economic Planning Committee, which had the authority to approve land development projects. In 2003, Capital Land claimed to have land reserves of 450,000 sq m, the largest holding in Beijing.[15]

As a result, nominal state ownership of urban land has not prevented the emergence of a highly parcelized pattern of land control and management under various socialist land masters. The fragmentation of land control has its roots in the planned economy, but takes on new meaning in the context of a commodified and competitive urban land system in the post-reform era. In the 1990s, the socialist land masters would become the most formidable players in the urban land market, and the major challengers to municipal governments' regulatory capacity and territorial consolidation projects.

Municipal government territorial consolidation strategies

Since the early 1990s, urban governments across China have adopted strategies to consolidate their control over urban land. These include the promotion of Western urban land economics against socialist land allocation doctrines, establishment of new government agencies to streamline land management, and urban redevelopment projects devised in the name of "modernization." I call these City Rational and City Modern strategies.

The city rational strategy

A horizontal, territorially oriented urban land management regime began to emerge in the late 1980s, symbolized by the establishment of the Ministry of Land Management in 1986. Local bureaus of land management were established in ensuing years, and were placed under the supervision of municipal, district, and county governments. The local bureaus were granted authority to prepare annual land-use plans, allocate quotas for farmland conversion into non-farm uses, issue permits for land conversion, and monitor land-lease sales.[16] In 1998, a revised *Land Management Law* stipulated that all administratively allocated land parcels must first be transferred to the municipal government before being leased out to developers. With these provisions, municipal governments were formally recognized as the exclusive representative of the state in exercising the right to transfer land and to profit from its commercial use.[17]

However, legal recognition of municipal government's authority over urban land does not guarantee the successful exercise of such delegated authority. It is politically risky for municipal authorities to initiate direct confrontation with powerful socialist land masters over illicit land deals. Instead, municipal governments have sought doctrinal legitimation from Western urban planning guidelines. The argument advanced is that urban planning is fundamentally about realizing the exchange value of land in the market and about allocating land in market-efficient ways. Accordingly, the land that yields the highest rent should be used for activities that generate the highest market value. Since there is a rent gradient from the urban center to peripheral areas, centrally located land lots should go to the highest bidders who can generate the highest value from the land.[18] High rent-generating projects are usually real-estate ventures like luxury hotels and condominiums, retail boutiques, and office-retail complexes, not mammoth communist-style factories with belching smokestacks.

Since the late 1980s, Chinese urban planners have been trained in schools using American city planning textbooks.[19] Because the principle of efficiency in urban land use dovetails with the development discourse in contemporary urban China, the new generations of city planners have enjoyed the political support of municipal government leaders. Together, municipal officials and city planners argue that money-losing state factories and nonprofit institutions like schools and hospitals should be relocated away from the city center to make room for banks, hotels, retail shops, high-end commercial housing, and office towers. The rapid growth of the service sector in many large cities in the 1990s has added urgency to address the problem of suboptimal use of urban land.[20] China's city planners often compare New York, London, and Tokyo to large Chinese cities to drive home the idea of inefficient land-use patterns in socialist cities, and they echo municipal officials' calls to correct the situation through a more "efficient" use of urban land based on exchange value.[21]

The 'city rational' idea also finds its expression in zoning, which specializes and separates land uses for different categories of urban activities. Modern urban planners argue that the *danwei* land-use pattern fragments land and wastes precious resources, and that the mixed land use of industrial, residential, commercial, and service in *danwei* compounds makes it costly to provide adequate public facilities, which often require a large area devoted to relatively uniform types of use in order to achieve economies of scale. Also, the mixed land-use pattern in large *danwei* compounds makes it impossible to establish a proper land rent gradient for the city as a whole. The planners urge tearing down the walls of the *danwei* compounds and integrating them into a unified urban land planning and zoning system coordinated at the municipal level.[22] In short, in the city rational project, municipal governments adopt the doctrines of efficiency, centrality, and spatial sorting embodied in capitalist land-use planning to strengthen their position against socialist land masters in the competition for premium urban land.

The city modern strategy

Another way municipal officials try to take the city back from socialist land masters is by initiating redevelopment projects in the old neighborhoods of the urban core. For decades, many old neighborhoods in Chinese cities have suffered from a host of problems including high residential density, deteriorating and increasingly unsafe structures, inadequate sanitation facilities and kitchenettes, and nonfunctioning neighborhood sewage systems. To modernize, municipal governments across China have launched massive urban redevelopment projects in urban core areas since the early 1990s. They have established their own land development companies, and/ or used land as equity shares to partner with commercial developers in undertaking such projects.

But *danwei* compounds in the urban center are off limits to municipal urban planners. Municipal officials are blocked from entering the gated and guarded compounds. They find it difficult to conduct land surveys and to gather updated information on land use and land transfers. Residents in such compounds, most of whom are employees, form a tight-knit community and are often reluctant to cooperate with municipal officials and planners. *Danwei* leaders, who answer to their supervisors in the vertical system, resent what they perceive as unwarranted outside intervention from lower-ranked municipal and district government officials.

So municipal officials avoid *danwei* compounds backed by powerful land masters, and instead initiate urban renewal projects in neighborhoods that are not attached to large state units. As developers supported by the municipal government tear down old structures and build new ones, the municipal government redraws the physical boundary of its authority and reclaims its proprietary and regulatory power over valuable urban land. Redevelopment projects usually start with land surveys and an official designation of some buildings as "unsafe" (*weifang*). Then follows the demarcation of "redevelopment zones," land-value appraisal, title verification, and cadastral registration. Detailed plans for land use and redevelopment are made for each redevelopment zone. Licenses are issued for land-use conversion, real-estate development, construction, marketing, and sales of the projects. Each of these seemingly mundane administrative procedures serves to reinforce the municipal government's control over the marked land, and the process of its commercial development. The redevelopment does not change the nominal ownership rights of the land by the state. Yet, it affirms the municipal government's proprietary rights and reinforces its regulatory authority over clearly marked urban space and defines the reach of municipal authority.

Through this process, the municipal government attains proprietary rights over specific and clearly marked urban land parcels. One immediate consequence is that it becomes a signatory to leases with developers. Through land surveys and cadastral registration, it updates its records of individual land parcels, and legally incorporates them into the urban land management system. The claim to proprietorship, more accurate information, and regulatory authority reinforce one another in stablishing the municipal government's firm control over the urban space. By the end of the redevelopment process, if everything goes smoothly, the municipal government will have a clearer inventory of the land it "owns." It can then decide which parcel can be sold or exchanged with whom, at what price. Transaction and development can be taxed accordingly.[23]

For the municipal government, urban redevelopment is about demolishing the old urban spatial structure and installing a new one under municipal management. It is both a spatial and political project aimed at territorial consolidation. Through this process of modernizing the city, the municipal government tries to reclaim control over valuable urban land.

The rush to develop urban land generated a property crisis in the mid-1990s. After Deng's historic visit to Shenzhen in the spring of 1992, "development fever" swept the country. Not only did building in urban core areas intensify, a huge amount of farmland on the urban fringe was converted to nonfarm uses. Construction booms at the urban core and fringe created property oversupplies. By the end of 1993, it was estimated that 30–50 million sq m of built floor area was vacant nationwide. Another 50,000 ha hectares of land were undeveloped.[24] In 1994, Premier Zhu Rongji announced an austerity policy, severely cutting the sources of real-estate finance. Many booming coastal cities were left with skeleton hotels, office towers, and half-finished condominiums.

The crisis in the real-estate market in 1994 proved to be a turning point in the urban land battle. Municipal officials blamed socialist land masters and the fragmentation of the land supply for the excesses of the real-estate bubble. Municipal policy analysts reported that the oversupply of property was created by "too many suppliers without a central coordinator in the market."[25] The first step toward a solution was to identify a "coordinator," or market regulator. The municipal government, as the newly designated manager of state-owned land, so the argument went, was eminently suited to play such a role. In what follows, I outline the municipal government's market regulation strategies and their contradictions, starting from a sketch of the property market.

Municipal government market regulation strategies

The development industry and the property market

Primary and secondary developers are the main producers in the development industry. Though only primary developers are entitled to legally transfer land lots from original users and develop them, socialist land masters also build on lots they occupy in the urban core, and then expand to the urban fringe, where they negotiate directly with villages and build new factories and commodity housing. In other words, many socialist land masters are illicit primary developers. Land and territorial struggles between municipal leaders and socialist land masters in urban cores, as outlined earlier, can be seen as the battle between two types of primary developers, one legitimate versus one illegitimate, yet powerful.

Aside from the primary developers, there are a large number of secondary developers. Secondary developers only have the authority to engage in projects on already "cooked" land. They can be established by any type of government unit or private investor. In the case of governmental secondary developers, finances are derived from bank loans, the budget of the state unit, transfers earmarked for other expenditures, funds collected through their own employees, and/or contractors' shares in the project. They build housing or commercial projects on lots they occupy or obtain through networks, and come to depend on the projects to provide employee housing, additional workspace for the growing unit, and rental income to boost their own revenues. It is not uncommon to find hundreds of such development firms operated by various units under a single municipal government. Their internal coffers (*xiao jinku*) are inaccessible to municipal-level officials. For example, there were 623 development companies established by agencies under Beijing municipality in 1995; 108 of them were owned by state *danwei*, and 485 were owned by various municipal agencies across regulatory, service, and public-enterprise divisions.[26]

Secondary developers also include private firms that have little direct association with governmental agencies. In the Pearl River Delta in the south, where the private sector is prosperous, there are quite a few large private developers who started real-estate ventures in the early 1980s building commercial housing on low-cost rural land in the urban fringe. They obtained cheap land through connections with rural cadres. They also adopted Hong Kong developers' prepayment scheme, in which homebuyers put down a large sum as down payment before construction began. This practice significantly lowered the entry threshold for small developers, and eventually helped some to grow big by the end of 1990s. In cities like Beijing, Jinan, and Zhengzhou, and central cities like Changsha, Nanjing, and Wuhan, private development firms were much smaller and fewer. They became visible only in the early 2000s, during the housing boom. Many of these firms were established by former managers at state-owned development companies or former officials from planning and land management bureaus.[27] While private developers in the south started by building joint ventures with rural cadres for land supplies, their northern counterparts tended to keep strong roots in the state sector where they gained professional experience and political connections.

The distinction between primary and secondary developers and between state and private sectors, however, is not always fixed or clear. Most primary developers, legitimate and illegitimate, tend to keep land parcels they have cooked and become secondary developers engaging in project production and sales at much larger profit margins. In other cases, private secondary developers collaborate with municipal or district governments to gain access to well-located raw land parcels and take the lead in site clearing and relocation negotiation, like primary developers.

The inextricable entanglement of the state, semistate, and private sectors in the development industry was made more complex in the late-1990s, when both primary and secondary developers were restructured. A large number of primary developers turned into shareholding companies with multiple shareholders, including central ministries, local governments, and foreign investment institutions. Some went public, and are listed on stock exchanges in Shanghai, Shenzhen, and Hong Kong. Many have their new shareholding structure only partially separated from state shareholders.[28] Smaller state agency-sponsored secondary development firms were privatized through open sales, management buyouts, employee shareholding, and through mergers and acquisitions.[29] At the urban fringe, some villages also recollectivized their land and financial resources to engage actively in the expanding urban real-estate market (see Chapter 5).

The restructuring of the development industry was undertaken for a host of reasons. Among them was the pressure brought by central policies aimed at restructuring SOEs to improve efficiency, and separate government units from their profit-making operations. Also, the more robust among state-sponsored firms pushed for restructuring to gain greater independence. Other factors included the need to diversify sources of finance, including funds from international institutional investors, and the failure of small- and medium-sized township and village manufacturing enterprises, which then sought new business opportunities in real estate. The diverse set of reasons behind the restructuring set firms on equally diverse paths of reform that cannot be understood simply as "privatization." Out of this mixed bag of reasons came complex outcomes that contributed to a more intertwined and convoluted relationship between the state and the private sector.[30]

Further, the development industry has its own sets of complexity. Long product cycles, the need for large amounts of capital, unpredictable policy changes in zoning, finance and taxation, and fluctuation in other speculative markets make the development industry especially risky. As a risk-alleviation strategy, development firms often diversify their project portfolios and establish multiple independent project-based companies. These project-based companies may have multiple investors, again with diverse ownership backgrounds. For example, an upscale shopping mall in Beijing may have a consortium of investors: the municipal Bureau of Commerce, which occupied the site originally; a Hong Kong developer responsible for project design, planning, and management; the investment company of the district government where the mall is located; the development arms of another municipal government unit, and a primary contractor from Hangzhou responsible for construction as well as a significant portion of the operation capital for the project. The diversification occurs in both directions, as individual firms diversify their investment portfolio to spread risk, and individual projects take investment from multiple stakeholders as a means to share risk. Diversification brings a highly decentralized structure to the industry as a whole, compounding the complexity of the industry in Chinese cities. A high-level manager at one of the largest development firms in Beijing admitted that his company, despite its "leading" position in the industry, contributed only about 3 percent of the total floor area under construction in Beijing between 2002 and 2004.[31]

The diversification of actors in the development industry has occurred in parallel with a growing complexity and specialization in the division of labor among firms. In addition to the standard collaboration between the financial institutions and development firms, development networks also include land brokers, loan brokers, companies specialized in relocation negotiation, planning and design firms, construction contractors, interior contractors, and marketing and sales agencies in both first-hand and second-hand markets. These firms, which also vary in ownership structure and size, are embedded in the web of the development industry. Their behavior and strategies are informed as much by the scale and scope of the firm as by its ownership structure.

Also important in China's development industry is the role of individual urban residents, who play the dual role of consumers and investors in the housing market. More than 70 percent of the real-estate development in China today is in housing.[32] Government housing policies that abolished welfare housing and made mortgages available to urban homebuyers have also been crucial to the expansion of housing production and consumption. High demand for housing for its use value is coupled in the Chinese context with high household saving rates and limited investment channels, which raises the exchange value of housing. Housing as a form of investment and venue for speculation adds an important dimension to the fragmented real-estate market. The dialectical nature of housing, which embodies elements of risk-taking speculation and long-term financial and personal security, continued to draw individual and institutional buyers and ramped up property prices, especially in major metropolitan regions. In the housing-centered property market, investors, producers, and consumers have generated a milieu of investment and speculation, based on the shared expectation of high returns and optimism over the continuous growth of urban economies and the property market.

In short, underpinning China's state-land tenure is a fragmented system of land supplies. Parallel with the commodification of land is a highly

2. Housing trade show in Beijing (August 2004)

decentralized development industry. And, along with urban expansion come players of diverse backgrounds in the real-estate market. The diverse backgrounds of market actors reduce the analytical potency of the state/private dichotomy, and raise the question of how a regulatory regime operates in such a market. If state agencies also participate in the market, what kind of regulatory logic is at work? And how does such logic shape municipal governments' regulatory strategy and affect their regulatory capacity?

Land-market regulation in Chinese cities takes on two salient features. The first is the mutual reinforcement of city governments' regulatory capacity and proprietorship of land. The second is the overlapping strategy of market regulation and state-agent discipline.

The market monopoly strategy

The objective of urban redevelopment is to reclaim urban land parcels in piecemeal fashion. But municipal leaders' ambitions go beyond mere possession of land pieces. They wish to become super landlords, who own, plan, sell, develop, and regulate all land in the city. Many municipal government officials I have met agreed that territorial governments should be made the "real landlords" of their cities. For them, proprietorship is the guarantee of full regulatory control over land use and access to land rents in a fragmented and increasingly commodified urban land system. There was a palpable sense in my interviews with officials that power originates in the possession of measurable, usable, and tradable land parcels under their jurisdiction.

Land is essential to local accumulation through its direct connection with government revenue. As revenue transfers from the central government have been drastically reduced in the new budgetary regime of fiscal decentralization, municipal governments rely on locally generated revenue to cover infrastructure construction, government overhead, social welfare, education, and other expenditures. In this context, land-derived revenue streams become especially important, as they provide direct and increasingly significant contributions to the local state's coffer. It is estimated that land-derived revenue accounted for 30–70 percent of total revenues for most municipal and submunicipal governments in the late 1990s.[33]

Land revenue comes from two sources. The government-as-regulator derives revenues from taxes and surcharges on land appreciation and transactions from various development projects. The government-as-proprietor collects receipts from direct land-lease sales and from renting government-built industrial and commercial structures. The latter source of revenue is more stable than the former because of tax evasion and avoidance. It also costs less to collect revenue from direct sales or rents than from taxes and surcharges. Most importantly, revenue from lease sales is outside the formal state budgetary system, and is thus fully retained in the local coffers.[34] As a result, local budgetary autonomy has come to depend on land-derived revenue, especially receipts from land-lease sales.

To facilitate effective accumulation through land, city governments have sought to centralize land supplies and land-lease transactions. In 1996, Shanghai established the Center for Land Development, which was to function as a land bank for the city. The land bank would purchase land-use rights, negotiate a profit-sharing plan with current users, and put the land parcels in a reserve for resale on the market in open-land auctions or through public tender. A successful land bank could help municipal governments centralize land supplies and coordinate land management and planning.[35] In addition, municipal governments hoped to reap a larger share of the land rent, and establish systematic bookkeeping practices for land taxation.

This attempt at centralized land supplies was in alignment with the recent central government policy. In 2001, the State Council announced a national policy to set up Centers for Land Reserves.[36] In May 2002, the Ministry of Land and Resources issued the No. 11 Ordinance, which made open-land auctions and public tenders mandatory for commercial development projects. In the open-land auction and public tenders organized by municipal Centers for Land Reserves, developers have to pay the official rates for land leases, which are on average eight to ten times higher than privately negotiated prices.[37] Open auctions also mean higher compensation rates for relocated residents, larger down payments, and fixed payment schedules.[38] Developers also have to comply more strictly with land-use regulations, like the density measure called the Floor-Area Ratio (FAR), which is critical to profit margins and to controlling land-use density. It sets upper limits on the total floor area that can be built per unit area in a particular site and land-use zone. The higher the FAR, that is, the larger the maximum floor area permitted in a given parcel, the greater the potential profit will be for the developer. Stricter FAR regulations and other similar measures impacting land prices, development costs, and profits, led to the No. 11 Ordinance being called a "land revolution."[39]

The integration of a municipal regulatory regime and proprietorship serves the dual purpose of unifying the territorial order and consolidating the land-centered regime of accumulation under municipal leaders.

The effectiveness of this strategy of regulation through monopoly is paradoxically conditioned by the integration, rather than the separation of the role of the state and market. Also, municipal leaders' own financial and political capacity sets limits to the success of such a strategy.

An example of this can be found in the case of the so-called "8–31 Cut-off." In 2004, a new national policy was announced in which the government threatened to reclaim land parcels that were leased, but were either not paid for or undeveloped for more than two years. Under the plan, the municipal Land Reserve Centers were to put these reclaimed land parcels up for open auction. The deadline for the municipal government to reclaim these land parcels was set for August 31, 2004. But the "8–31 Cut-off" was a lot of bark and little bite. In a newspaper interview days after the cut-off, the director of the Beijing Center for Land Reserves openly admitted that it was still difficult for the municipal government to reclaim these land parcels. Even if an agreement could be reached between land leaseholders and the municipal government, the cost of reclaiming land was often beyond the means of the municipal government. Regulations required that if the reclaimed land parcel had already been cleared, the municipal government must compensate the developers who carried out the preliminary work to clear the site, including costs associated with compensation and relocation of evicted residents, leveling the land, and installing power and water. It was also politically risky to try to reclaim parcels held by developers with high-level connections. The director said the municipal government had neither the administrative, financial, nor the political clout necessary to see the policy through.[40]

The mediocre results of the drive to centralize land supplies through the land bank led city governments to ramp up their efforts. Instead of solely relying on regulatory institutions like the Land Reserve Centers, they moved to control the more profitable segment of land development. In November 2002, the Shanghai Municipal Government announced the establishment of the Shanghai Real Estate Group Company. It was to be the largest developer in Shanghai. The company was established by the municipal government headquarter and the Shanghai Communist Party Committee to merge the municipal land bank with development firms established by municipal government agencies. A press report described the Shanghai Real-Estate Group Company "the super aircraft carrier" in Shanghai's property market to be deployed in battle against the "great alligators"—the powerful socialist land masters and their developers.[41] In 2007, the Beijing Municipal Government followed suit with similar grandiose plans.[42] In reality, however, the establishment of the Shanghai

Real-Estate Group Company was followed by highly publicized scandals over land deals and the removal of government and party leaders, including Shanghai Party Secretary Chen Liangyu. Both chen and his developer ally, Zhou Zhengyi were imprisoned.[43] Although there was no direct linkage between the group company and the scandal, it nevertheless damaged the credibility of the municipal government's market monopoly project. It is too early to tell whether Beijing's attempt will be more successful in placing the municipal government at the top of the heap in Beijing, one of the largest and most active property markets in China.

Municipal leaders' market monopoly strategy also faces challenges on the ideological front. In the new policy discourse of heralding a modern, service-oriented government, the municipality is expected to be an impartial market regulator, not a stake-holding market participant. As mentioned earlier, numerous large socialist land masters were transformed into shareholding companies over the past decade, and now identify themselves as private firms. Some small- and medium-sized private developers have also become more visible in the property boom of the 2000s. The new private sector, consisting of former socialist land masters and their development firms and smaller developers, now complain about the municipal government's active involvement in land and real-estate markets. They cite conflicts of interest, as the municipal government assumes a dual role as market participant and regulator. In addition, municipal governments find themselves accused of violating the "natural law of the market."[44] The contentious entanglement between municipal governments and development powers continue, with the municipal Land Reserves Centers and municipality-run development companies functioning as bargaining platforms and tools for market monopoly.

The state agent discipline strategy

The mutual reinforcement of regulatory authority and land proprietorship, and the dual purpose of regulation and accumulation in the market monopoly strategy, as outlined earlier, are inseparable from the second feature of the city's regulatory regime, namely the overlapping logics of market regulation and local-state agent discipline.

The two most important elements in China's land regulation are oversight of land-use rights transfers and of conversion of land from agricultural to nonfarm uses. Most projects need approvals on both counts. Land-use conversion is regulated through a quota system that allocates land down the jurisdictional hierarchy from the provincial government to townships.

Those at the higher levels often take the lion's share of the quota, leaving little to rural townships at the bottom. Consequently, most projects in the rural area are illegal, as townships convert farmland to nonfarm uses well in excess of their quota allowance (see Chapter 6).

Throughout the 1980s and 1990s, authority to approve transfers of land-use rights laid in different levels of the local government, including the townships. Lower-level governments retained authority over smaller land tracts, while higher-level governments made decisions over larger ones. The fragmented authority over approvals increased bureaucratic inconsistency and provided space for maneuver. For instance, low-level governments often divided a large tract of land into several smaller pieces in order to avoid the scrutiny of supervisory governments. This process was streamlined since the early 2000s, when lower-level governments' authority to transfer land rights was abolished. But this reform did not immediately create greater coherence within the regulatory regime. Power to approve land-rights transfers at the municipal level remained scattered among several government agencies, depending on the type of land in question, the current users, and the type of new project. These agencies, moreover, sometimes have contradictory interests or mandates, as between the bureaus of land management and urban planning, which belong to separate vertical chains of command or *xitong*. The land management bureau takes orders from the Ministry of Land and Resources, while the urban planning bureau answers to the Ministry of Construction. The land management bureau carries the mandate over farmland preservation and growth control, while the urban planning bureau is under constant pressure from municipal leaders to plan for growth. The land management bureau produces annual land-use plans, and allocates quotas for farmland conversion accordingly. The urban planning bureau produces yet another set of plans for urban expansion, with often exaggerated growth projections. Both sets of plans are legally binding. While the two agencies share authority to approve land conversion and development at different stages of a project, conflicts in their mandate often lead to inconsistencies in land-use regulation.[45] Disagreements prolong the process of project approval and create legal–administrative gaps in land regulation, and allow developers to play one bureau against the other in bids for unlicensed construction and illegal projects. The disagreements are not always principled, either—they are known to compete with one another to issue permits to their respective client developers.[46]

Adding to the challenges facing city leaders, below the municipal government are district governments and county governments. Almost all submunicipal governments have their own development companies and many have more than one such setup. Shanghai, for example, is known for its powerful district governments, which hold premium land in the central districts of the city. The Shanghai Municipal Government delegates authority to the district government over land use, including the right to make land use and urban development plans, approve development projects, negotiate land-lease sales, and sign leases directly with developers. The district governments are allowed to retain as much as 85 percent of the total revenue from land-lease sales.[47] As a result, district leaders have aggressively taken on new development projects. Each has tried to create its own downtown for premium commercial land rents, embarking on ambitious projects to turn old neighborhoods into new commercial complexes. Thus, Shanghai and other large cities now boast multiple "Central Business Districts" (CBDs) built by competing district governments, some of which do not reflect the municipality's development plan. This type of competition persistently threatens to undermine the property market by creating a glut of office or condo space. Internal fragmentation also tends to debase the municipal government's territorial ambition to unify land supplies under the municipal leadership. Therefore one critical tool of regulating the property market is to trim cadres' formal authority over land, and intensify the scrutiny over cadres' Formal authority over land, and intensify the scruting over cadres' illicit operations in the property market.

However, the combined measures of market regulation and cadre discipline have created new dilemmas for municipal leaders. The municipal leader's multi-purpose market regulation aimed at territorial consolidation and effective accumulation often run at counterpurposes. The need to discipline local cadres over land conversion and transfer is often compromised by the need to maintain growth and overall GDP performance. Municipal leaders publicly condemn disorder in the land supply, but they nevertheless rely on impressive urban construction projects and the GDP figures they generate to stay in the good graces of their supervisors.

Implementation of the No. 11 Ordinance in Beijing is a telling example of this dilemma. In 2002, when national policy demanded open auctions and public tender of land parcels for commercial development projects, most municipal leaders allowed some *kouzi*, or exceptions to the new rules. In Beijing, the Municipal Government left open four such *kouzi*, allowing privately negotiated land-use rights transfers for four types of projects. These included building in the green belt zones, small town construction on farmland in the urban periphery, reconstruction of unsafe housing (*weifang gaijian*), and high-tech industrial parks. As it turned out, most development projects fell into one of the four categories and were supported by suburban counties or municipal districts. Thus, most land leases in Beijing continued to proceed through closed-door negotiation rather than open auction.[48] Shanghai permitted similar exceptions.[49] Hence, the overlapping logics of market regulation and local cadre discipline frequently led to compromises on both fronts.

In short, the market monopoly regulatory strategy was compromised by municipal leaders' political and financial capacity, and the dual strategies of market regulation and cadre discipline was undermined by political legitimation rooted in growth.

Urbanization of the local state

How does the land-centered urban politics in China differ from the land politics in Western capitalist cities, if at all? The capitalist "urban growth machine" in US cities, for example, is driven by a coalition of local politicians, private developers, and local media and professional groups. This growth coalition is built on the bedrock of the ideology and institutions of private property ownership, and private developers seem to play a dominant role.[50] In Chinese cities, under state-land tenure, the driving force of the urban growth machine is competition and coalition among different segments of the state, while other sectors are much less prominent than in the American case. But my intention here is not to compare two opposite models of socialist "state-led urbanization" and capitalist "market-led urbanization." Rather, I focus on the territorial politics between different sets of state actors and their embrace of political, administrative, and market logics in the struggle for control of land. I would reframe the question from "does the state play a dominant role in China's urbanization, and how?" to "how does urbanism, as a physical and ideological construction, shape and become shaped by the dynamics of local state-building in Chinese cities?"

The mutually constitutive processes of urban construction and local state-building can be discerned in several areas. First, land development shifts the object of political bargaining between the central and local states. The land-centered regime of local accumulation in the reform era differs from the regime of accumulation under the planned economy. Under the planned economy, urban politics was primarily a struggle over budget allocations divvied out through the vertical *tiao* system by planners in Beijing or provincial capitals. But land, as the new object of urban-resource competition, is eminently local. The immobility of land and its physical attachment to the territory makes competition over land an inherently local affair. Land gives local-state actors an incomparable leverage in this new round of resource competition and bargaining.

Second, land development is decisive for the local state's consolidation of territorial authority and exposes the contentious nature of local state-building processes. In their competition with socialist land masters over urban land control, municipal leaders' success depends on their political capacity to deal with socialist land masters from above. In their attempts to centralize and regulate the fragmented local-land market and development industry, success depends on their regulatory capacity to monopolize the market and discipline lower-level state agents. Land development has therefore become the arena of local state-building.

In the literature on local states in post-Mao China, local-state power is often treated as a natural outcome of top-down fiscal and administrative decentralization policies.[51] But the translation of centrally granted power into the actual exercise of territorial power is largely missing from the literature. The concreteness of land and territory help to reveal the contentious process of decentralization, which, as a grand policy scheme, does not guarantee expanded local-state power. While municipal governments enjoy the delegated authority to manage urban land and coordinate the land market, it remains an open question whether municipal governments will be able to convert such delegated authority into the effective exercise of territorial power. In this process, municipal leaders face challenges and opportunities to define and defend the boundaries of their territorial power, and to test and build their governing capacity. Thus, land development is the arena for, yet not a guarantee of, local state-building.

Urban development projects expose the contingencies in local state-building processes while also conditioning their results. In this sense, the local state does not necessarily "lead" the process of urbanization, but rather, the local state itself is urbanized. As landed politics dominate the municipality, urban land agendas become the primary preoccupation of municipal leaders. They consolidate their power base through land reserves and urban construction projects, establish their political identity as urban builders and promoters, and build political legitimation through urban modernity, construction-based GDP growth, and city image making. Despite the conflicts and competition for land among various state actors in the city, urbanism seems to have provided a unifying ideology for the political elite.

But what about those who are excluded from the urban fortune, and whose exclusion is a necessary component of urban accumulation? In the past decade, urban agendas have not only dominated state politics, but have set the parameters for the relationship between the state and society. The relentless pursuit of accumulation in the 1980s and 1990s exposed municipal governments to mounting challenges to their legitimacy as social protectors.[52] A new challenge, beginning in the early 2000s, came from the growing numbers of residents affected by urban redevelopment projects. In Chapter 3, I turn to the contentious politics between the urbanized municipal government and dispossessed residents in the core of Beijing.

Notes

1. Interview CS0002, Changsha, June 2000. I *mu* equals to 1/6 acre.
2. Portions of this chapter appeared in Hsing, You-tien, "Land and Territorial Politics in Urban China," *The China Quarterly*, No. 187 (2006): 575–591.
3. Unlike North American inner cities, which experienced decline in the 1960s–70s and partial recovery in the 1980s–90s, urban cores in China's large metropolitan centers remained economic and political centers in the reform era.
4. Each municipality is divided into districts. For example, in 2003, Beijing municipality had eighteen districts, four of them in the city core. Shanghai municipality has twenty-three districts, ten of them in the city core.
5. See Xiaobo Lu and Elizabeth Perry (eds). *Danwei*, 1997.
6. Ho, Samuel and George Lin, "Non-agricultural land use in post-reform China," 2004: 765.
7. Zhou, Yixing and Meng Yanchun, *Beijingde jiaoquhua jiqi duice* (Suburbanization and policies in Beijing) 2000: 141.
8. *Shanghai chengshi guihua* (Shanghai's City Planning), (Shanghai: Shanghai Municipal Bureau of Urban Planning, 1998).
9. For an analysis of land squandering by urban industries during early socialist industrialization, see Fung, Kai-yu, "Urban sprawl in China: Some causative factors," 1981.
10. For an account of urban *danwei* construction activity, see Lu, Duanfang, Remaking Chinese Urban Form, 2006.
11. Huang, Chiling, "*Gaige kaifang zhong Shanghai dushi duti fazhan yu dushi kongjian zaijiegou*" (Urban land development and urban space restructuring in Shanghai during economic reforms), 1997. According to a 1998 survey of 17 major cities in China, industrial land still occupied 22 percent of total urban land. Industry still occupied 25 percent of Shanghai's urban core, 17 percent of the urban core in Beijing, and 28 percent in Suzhou. See Cao, Jianhai, *Zhongguo tudi gaoxiao liyong yanjiu* (Studies of efficient use of urban land in China), 2002: 105–107.

12. Article 10, Clause 4, "Provisional Regulations on the Conveyance, Granting and Transferring of the State Land's Use Rights in Cities and Towns," enacted by the State Council, May 1991.

13. Zhang, Wenhao, "*Beijing tudiye chushi*" (Land masters in Beijing), 2002: 41.

14. Interviews BJ0301 (a real estate development consultant), Beijing, June 2003; BJ0309 (general manager of a large development company with an SOE background), Beijing, July 2003.

15. Interview BJ0320 (a top manager at one of Capital Land's subsidiaries), Beijing, July 2003. See also, Xie, Ju, "*Shouchuang sanwen*" (Three questions about Capital Land), 2003. By 2004, the total land area, including developed projects, according to Capital Land, was 2.1 million sq m, compared with 4 million sq ft (or 371,600 sq m) of the floor area of the former New York World Trade Center.

16. In 2003, the land management system was restructured. The Ministry of Land and Resources and its provincial branches reclaimed from local governments much of the authority to approve land-lease sales and farmland conversion. It is too early to tell how effective the reinstallation of the "vertical management" system is. Interview BJ0319 (a high-ranking Ministry of Land and Resources official), Beijing, August 2003.

17. See Wu, Fulong, "The new structure of building provision and the transformation of the urban landscape in metropolitan Guangzhou, China," 1998.

18. See Alonso, William, *Location and Land Use*, 1964.

19. I hosted more than half a dozen such delegations while teaching at the University of British Columbia School of Community and Regional Planning from 1992–1996.

20. Lin, George C.S., "Towards a post-socialist city?" 2004.

21. Cao, Jianhai, *Zhongguo tudi gaoxiao liyong yanjiu*, 2002: 108.

22. Interviews BJ0302 (an urban planning professor and consultant), Beijing, August 2003; BJ0303 (a senior Beijing Urban Planning Committee member), Beijing, August 2003.

23. Interview BJ0303 (a senior Beijing Urban Planning Committee member), Beijing, August 2003. The surcharge amounted to 5–10 percent of total construction costs.

24. Mo, Chengshun, '*Hainan fangdichan paomo*' (property bubbles in Hainan) 2003.

25. Interview BJ0311 (a high-ranking Beijing Land Reserves Center official), Beijing, August 2003.

26. Wang, Zongli et al. (eds.), *Beijing fangdichan* (Beijing Real Estate), 1996: 147.

27. Interview BJ0404 (former general manager of one of China's largest development companies, who then started a development company in Beijing), Beijing, August 2004.

28. Cooper, Mary Comerford, "New Thinking in Financial Market Regulation," 2008.

29. There are also foreign investors and developers in major metropolitan centers like Beijing, Shanghai and Guangzhou, as well as in emerging markets like Chongqing. In the 1990s, foreign developers were mainly overseas Chinese from Hong Kong who concentrated investments in the Pearl River Delta and

later in Shanghai. They formed partnerships with local developers and governments on high-profile commercial projects like hotels and office towers. As the real-estate sector heated up in the late 1990s, international investors from Japan, Singapore, the United States, and Europe poured in. Except for a handful of firms, most are not developers, but are investors who see the booming real estate sector as an opportunity to diversify investment portfolios. A select few of Hong Kong developers, such as Li Ka-shing and the New World Group, received considerable media attention for their high-profile and sometimes controversial projects in major Chinese cities. Large domestic developers boasted of their partnerships with international investors for financial reasons. But most foreign developers played a secondary role in the highly localized real-estate market in China. See Hsing, You-tien, 'Foreign capital and local real estate development in China,' 2006.

30. China economists and political scientists disagree over whether the state sector has contracted as a result of privatization and enterprise restructuring. It is nonetheless clear in the real-estate sector that state actors continue to play important roles and firms of the nonstate, semi-state, multistate and state-owned varieties have taken on increasingly complex ownership structures. For discussion of ownership structures of other sectors, see Corinna-Barbara, Francis, "Quasi-Public, Quasi-Private Trends in Emerging Market Economies," 2001. For a recent review of China's privatization and the creation of a hybrid ownership system, see Lin, Chun, 'Against Privatization in China,' 2008. See also Naughton, Barry, *The Chinese Economy: Transitions and Growth*, 2007. Guo, Sujian, "The Ownership Reform in China," 2003; Yang, Dali, *Remaking the Chinese Leviathan*, 2004. For an earlier discussion, see Nolan, Peter and Wang Xiaoqiang, "Beyond Privatization," 1999.

31. Interview BJ0309, Beijing, August 2004.

32. Interview BJC 0406, a high-ranking official of the Ministry of Land and Resource. Beijing, August 2004.

33. See Ho, Samuel, and George Lin (2003), "Emerging land markets in rural and urban China," 2003.

34. In 2002, the central government demanded that 40 percent of the land appreciation tax be incorporated into the state budgetary system and be shared with the state treasury. But a municipal land management official claimed that he "did not know any city that had followed the new rule," and he felt it would be difficult for the central government to enforce that rule. Interview TJU0301 (a high-ranking Tianjin Municipal Land Management and Planning Bureau official), Berkeley, May 2003.

35. See Ren, Po, "*Beijing yuhui zhilu*" (The winding path that Beijing took 2003); Ren, Po, "*Chengshi tudi zhimi*" (Secrets of urban land) 2003.

36. "Reinforcement of state landed assets management," State Council, April 2001.

37. Interview BJ0309, Beijing, August 2003.

38. Interview BJ0311 (a high-ranking Beijing Land Reserves Center official), Beijing, August 2003. While land-use right transfer fees through individual negotiations can be paid in installments phased over many years, auctioned land parcels require a much larger initial investment (35 percent of the total amount) at the time of lease signing.

39. Tang, Zheng, "*8–31 da-xian*" (The 31 August deadline), 2004.

40. Cao, Shengjie and Lu Shangchun, "*Hepingli beijie erhao: nanyi kaizhang de chaoshi?*" (Hepingli North Street No. 2), 2004.

41. Li, Shufeng, and Po Ren, "*Shanghai tudi chubeizhi zhuanxing*" (Transformation of Shanghai's land reserve system 2003); Cao and Lu, "*Hepingli beijie erhao,*" 2004.

42. "*Beijing guotuju yu longduan yiji kaifa, zhengfu kaifashang zaiban maoshu*" (Beijing Land Bureau plans to monopolize primary land market; Government and developers play cat and mouse game). 29 April 2007. Online. See <http://xinwen. haozhai.com/news-68013.html>, accessed May 21, 2009.

43. Chen Liangyu was sentenced for 18 years. "*Shanghai yuanshi wei shuji chen liangyu yishen beipan 18 nian*" (Former Party Secretary of Shanghai Chen Liangyu was sentenced for 18 years). 11 April, 2008. online. See <http://news.sina. com.cn/c/2008-4-11/153715338337.shtml> accessed May 21, 2009. Also see "*Zhongguo fubai diyian: Zhou Zhengyi yaochu Chen Liangyu?*" (The No. 1 corruption case in China: Zhou Zhengyi gave away Cheng Liangyu?), *Shijie caijing baodao* (*World Finance Report*), 29 September 2006. Online. See <http://finance. icxo.com/htmlnews/2006/09/29/951830.htm> accessed November 27, 2007.

44. Interview BJ0404, Beijing August 2004; Ren, Zhiqiang, *Renren pingshuo* (Ren's commentaries on real estate), (Beijing: Zhonghua gongzhang lianhe chubanshe, 2003). Ren Zhiqiang is a real estate guru in Beijing, and General Manager of a development company established by the Xicheng District Government of Beijing.

45. Interviews SZ9701 (a high-ranking Shenzhen planning and land use bureau official), Shenzhen, July 1997; TJU0401 (a high-ranking Tianjin municipal official), Shenzhen November 2004; SH0401 (a planning professor and consultant in Shanghai), Shanghai December 2004; CD9701 (a high-ranking Institute of Urban Design and Planning official in Chengdu), Chengdu, July 1997; GZ0301 (a high-ranking Guangzhou district Urban Planning Bureau official), Guangzhou, January 2003 and June 2004.

46. Interview BJ0309 (general manager of a large development company with an SOE background), Beijing August 2003.

47. Huang, Chiling "*Gaige kaifang zhong Shanghai dushi tudi fazhan yu dushi kongjian zaijiegou,*" 1997: 72.

48. Cao, Shengjie and Lu, Shangchun "*Hepingli beijie erhao,*" 2004.

49. Yuan, Mei and Xiang Zhang, "*Shanghai tudi tunji zhimi*" (Secrets of land hoarding in Shanghai), 2005.

50. See Logan, John and Harvey Molotch, *Urban Fortunes*, 1987; Altshuler, Alan, "The Ideologies of Urban Land Use Politics," 1996.
51. For a review of the studies on China's state, decentralization, and the local state in post-reform China, see Baum, Richard, and Alexei Shevchenko, "The state of the state," 1999.
52. Here legitimacy is understood as contested processes of justifying political authority claims. For a review of the legitimacy issue in China's transformation, see Shue, Vivienne, "Legitimacy crisis in China?" 2004.

Chapter 3

Grassroots Resistance: Property Rights and Residents' Rights

In June 2006, I met a technician from a state enterprise in Beijing, who was one of the major organizers of the so-called Grand Litigation of Ten Thousand Plaintiffs that took the Beijing Municipal Government to court in 2000 for illegal demolition of inner-city homes. In his early fifties, Lao Shi¹ was sharp and eloquent. He recounted in detail the protest actions he had undertaken since his own home was demolished in 1996. Lao Shi had taught himself law and helped many other displaced residents sue the government, which had put him on the government's blacklist. During periods of high political tension, as during the annual meeting of National People's Congress and Political Consultative Conference every March, Lao Shi was under surveillance twenty-four hours a day. Policemen have even escorted him on his long commute between his new home and work. I asked Lao Shi if he was afraid of what might happen to him. He replied: "No. Why should I be afraid? I do not disrupt social order and I have been following the law. Everything I did was legal. It is the government that has violated the law."

This chapter is about activists like Lao Shi and their strategies for self-protection in the process of urban redevelopment. The politics of land-centered accumulation in the core of large cities presented in Chapter 2 is made more complex by the vigorous politics of distribution initiated by displaced urban residents. These city residents organize themselves to challenge municipal governments' attempts to monopolize urban land, and to decry neglect of the state as a social protector at the moment of violent destruction of homes.

Again, municipal governments' legitimation dilemma is tied to state land tenure, which is assumed to be a defining feature of state socialism. In fact, state land tenure was never formally legalized during the Mao era. The stipulation that "all urban land belongs to the state" did not enter China's

Constitution until 1982. Subsequently, with the establishment of the land-lease market in 1988, the state's land tenure was further reinforced through its monopolistic authority over land acquisition and circulation. The legalization of the state's land tenure and the state-controlled process of land commodification in the 1980s were followed by accelerated urban growth and skyrocketing land prices in the 1990s, hence urbanizing the local state, and fortifying the land-based regime of accumulation.

Local accumulation projects dependent on land acquisition and development have spawned twin legitimation dilemmas for urban governments. The first legitimation dilemma stems from the ambiguity of state land tenure amid market transition. Under state socialism, private property was socialized through political campaigns, not legislation, and did not present a legitimacy issue at the height of state socialism. That situation began to change, when, beginning in the 1990s, urban governments and their development branches benefited enormously from skyrocketing land rents. Widespread social protests began to challenge urban governments' abuse of their underdefined authority to represent the state's claim over urban land and the monopolization of land rents.

The second dilemma posed by the land-dependent local state mode of accumulation arises through the process of land acquisition, one defined by physical destruction. Social activism escalates at the moment of physical destruction of places. Large-scale land acquisition to clear space for urban mega-projects cannot proceed without abrupt and massive destruction of homes, jobs, and communities. In the desperate pursuit of rapid accumulation through wholesale destruction, urban governments have been reluctant to take responsibility for social protection.

The twin legitimation dilemmas have generated two types of housing protests in large cities: property rights protests and residents' rights protests. Property rights protestors were private homeowners in the prerevolutionary era, whose property was appropriated by the Beijing Municipal Government. In the 1990s, these former homeowners launched protests against the municipal government to demand property restitution. They framed their grievances historically. Under state socialism, they were excluded from welfare housing because of their status as members of the pre-Revolution propertied class. During the period of market reforms, they were excluded again from the land-lease markets because of the state monopoly over land rent. Property rights protesters demanded that the government repay its historic debt and restitute their former property. Beijing's property rights protesters were successful in recovering their family homes after years of struggle. While their success has significant

3. Destruction in Jinan (December 07)

implications for other types of grassroots mobilization in China, it is important to note that their rare success was limited by the sterilization and bureaucratization of their rights claims.

Residents' rights protests emerged out of the process of massive destruction in the absence of social protection. The protagonists in this case are called *chaiqianhu*, which means literally "evicted households whose homes were demolished." This group of protesters included property owners and tenants. Unlike property rights protesters, who shared a class identity as property owners, *chaiqianhu* protesters shared a territorial identity as urban residents. Residency was the physical anchor for the quotidian support networks of job, family, community, and urban services—the life-worlds—of city residents. Physical destruction of homes was thus destruction of the life-world of *chaiqianhu*. Based on such framing, protesters demanded reconstitution of their life-worlds in the city. Central to their demands were not merely legal rights over private property, but also social rights to a livelihood.

Urban housing protests have been explosive in the inner city. Neighborhoods have high population densities with long-term resident complex land-use patterns and ownership rights entanglements. Inner-city areas are also highly coveted for redevelopment because of their premium location and high commercial value. Residents in the urban core have been among the most vocal in challenging the legitimacy of urban governments and the land-based regime of accumulation. In this chapter, I focus on property rights protests and residents' rights protests in the core of Beijing in the 1990s and 2000s.

Property rights protest

The group that best represents property rights protests in Beijing is comprised of *biaozhunzu* homeowners. *Biaozhunzu*, which means literally "standard-rent housing," refers to rental housing at municipal government-imposed standardized rents. These houses were privately owned in the prerevolutionary era and subsequently confiscated by the municipal government and turned into public housing managed by municipal housing agencies[2].

The socialization of private homes dates from the late 1950s, when the number of state agencies and employees in Beijing grew rapidly and the municipal government undertook a series of measures to meet the growing housing demand. In the 1960s, as the socialist construction campaign heated up, the State Council announced, "all private-state joint ventures should be reconstructed as SOEs, and capitalists' interests should be totally abolished."[3] Party officials likened privately owned homes to private enterprises and set out to reform both under the banner of socialist reconstruction, or *gaizao*. The policy of socializing private property and the subsequent Cultural Revolution politicized property ownership and radicalized the campaign against private ownership.[4]

During the Cultural Revolution, Red Guards posted red signs on the doors of private homes that read: "Order: Private homeowners should submit their deeds. Those who disobey this order shall be killed without exception." Private homeowners handed over their deeds to avoid further harassment and humiliation by Red Guards. Upon submitting their deeds, they received small wooden plaques, acknowledging that they had relinquished their property, which they would hang on the front door, hoping to keep the Red Guards away. Nevertheless, many were subsequently forced from their homes and from Beijing after struggle sessions.

As a result of political campaigns during the Cultural Revolution, a third of Beijing's housing stock, about 510,000 rooms of courtyard-style housing belonging to over 80,000 families was converted into rental housing and came under the management of the Municipal Housing Bureau.[5] Homeowners, if lucky enough to stay in their own homes after the struggle sessions, were forced to give their tenants the larger and brighter main rooms of the houses, while they were forced to move into the darker, smaller, damp, and north-facing rooms previously used by servants. Socialization of private property was thus completed through political marginalization, social ostracization, and moral degradation of private homeowners.

Historically framed grievances over double exclusion

In 1983, at the onset of market reforms, the Beijing municipal government announced a policy to return houses to their former owners. But the restitution policy had a catch: current tenants had the right to continue living in the units while paying government-imposed standardized rents, which were between 5 and 10 percent of market prices. The term *biaozhunzu* was adopted at this time.[6] The owner and tenant were to sign a government-issued standard lease that specified the rent rates but not the duration of the lease.[7] *Biaozhunzu* owners felt the municipal government's restitution policy offered only nominal property ownership without the substance of ownership rights, namely the right to use, dispose of, and profit from their property.

Biaozhunzu owners grievances ran deep. Under socialism, their status as private property owners was a political stigma that also deprived them of welfare housing allocation. Neither their work units nor the municipal housing bureau felt responsible for their housing. As a result, housing conditions among *biaozhunzu* homeowners were among the worst in Beijing in the prereform era. The 1983 restitution policy raised hopes but did not provide homeownership in any substantive sense. Compounding the resentment, *biaozhunzu* owners were denied the profits generated from their property, as land values in the urban center skyrocketed in the 1990s and the municipal government and its development arms reaped windfall profits from inner city redevelopment. The dual exclusion from socialist welfare housing in the 1960s and 1970s and from the property market in the 1990s enraged the *biaozhunzu* owners.

In the late 1990s, the pace and scale of inner-city redevelopment began to accelerate. Large areas of traditional courtyard housing within the second ring road in Beijing, where most of the *biaozhunzu* housing was located, were demolished. The demolitions alarmed *biaozhunzu* owners in two ways. First, according to the municipal government's relocation compensation scheme, *biaozhunzu* tenants who lived in houses to be demolished were offered 100,000 to 200,000 yuan per household in relocation compensation and some received relocation housing elsewhere. *Biaozhunzu* owners, however, most of whom lived elsewhere, were entitled only to monetary compensation for the building materials of the house, and not for the land. Nor were they entitled to relocation compensation because they typically did not live in the house that was to be demolished. In other words, while tenants were entitled to relocation packages, owners were granted much less compensation in the event of demolition. Second, demolition essentially eliminated *biaozhunzu* owners' property rights. Most *biaozhunzu* owners had submitted their titles to the Red Guards during the Cultural Revolution, so the only proof of ownership was the house itself. The restitution policy gave owners renewed legitimacy and raised expectations that they would be vindicated with full ownership rights, as long as the house existed. But once the house was razed, the only evidence of their property rights claims disappeared. While the *biaozhunzu* owners' grievances originated from the socialist past and intensified during the initial phase of market reform, it is the contemporary process of massive destruction of old homes that triggered a sense of urgency to fight back.

Strategies

Collective action did not take shape until the late 1990s, after half the original *biaozhunzu* housing had been demolished. Discouraged by rent-control provisions favoring tenants, many *biaozhunzu* owners had abandoned their houses or sold them to the Municipal Housing Management Bureau for as little as 150 to 200 yuan per room. Consequently, half of the 510,000 units fell under direct control of the Housing Bureau and were demolished to make way for redevelopment projects. By the late 1990s, with land prices skyrocketing, the stakes involved in losing a house had grown much higher for the remaining *biaozhunzu* owners.

Encouraged by the emerging political discourse of the rule of law, and the drafting of the Property Rights Law, *biaozhunzu* owners began to demand recovery of their family property. Legitimacy, they claimed, was granted by the government's restitution policy, and their goal was merely policy implementation. They began their protests by filing lawsuits individually against tenants. The 1983 restitution policy had stipulated that if tenants or their spouses had allocated housing elsewhere, tenants must return the *biaozhunzu* rental units to the original owners. The tenants' adult children were to move out of the units as well. Many *biaozhunzu* tenants had other housing allocated by their work units. But very few volunteered to give up and move out of their *biaozhunzu* housing because of the low rent and the prospect of earning up to 200,000 yuan in compensation if, or when, redevelopment came to the neighborhood. Tenants were discreet about their allocated housing elsewhere in order to keep their cheap rental units.[8]

The burden of proof to disqualify tenants fell on the homeowners, leading some to visit tenants' *danwei* to inquire whether their tenants had allocated housing elsewhere and to spy on tenants and their family members. But even when they managed to collect sufficient evidence for litigation against their tenants, tenants would plead in court that their allocated housing elsewhere was too small or inadequate. These conditions often exempted tenants from the rules regarding the return of their rental units to the original owners.[9] As a result, very few *biaozhunzu* owners won cases against tenants.

Biaozhunzu owners came to realize that in order to reclaim their property, they needed to change their approach; individualized legal actions would not work. They decided that the key to resolving their problem was to point to the municipal government's commitment to provide relocation housing for their tenants and thereby to pressurize the municipal government to force tenants to vacate their houses.

They launched their first collective action in February 2001 through the *xinfang* (writing petition letters) and *shangfang* (visiting government agencies) mediation channels with three initial demands. These were: an increase in rental rates and an eventually lifting of the rent cap; inclusion of owners in the relocation compensation package; and use of government funds to relocate the tenants and full restitution of homes to their original owners. Over a period of four years they insisted on "lawful resistance," visiting various government offices[10] and writing letters and petitions regularly. They also organized themselves into several *shangfang* groups and would go to every prescheduled weekly or biweekly visitor reception day at different government agencies.

Biaozhunzu owners' persistent *xinfang* and *shangfang* actions were complemented by some less common forms of protest. They submitted an application to organize a Private Property Owner Association and twice requested permission from the Public Security Bureau to hold street rallies involving several hundred people. As expected, none of these applications was approved,[11] but the message seemed, nonetheless, to have gotten through. The protesters managed to attract media coverage and support from activists, artists, and academics who were concerned about the historical preservation of the courtyard housing in inner-city neighborhoods. In August 2001, the Beijing Municipal Government announced that *biaozhunzu* homeowners were entitled to 15 percent of the total relocation compensation. With additional pressure, the rate was subsequently raised to 20 percent. "It was like a tube of toothpaste," one activist said. "Each time you squeeze it, you get a bit more."[12]

Conditional success

By the end of 2002, pressure on the Beijing Municipal Government to resolve urban conflicts began to mount. The increasing frequency and scale of urban protests had slowed redevelopment projects, causing inner-city protests to become not just a legitimation but an accumulation issue as well. Beijing's city leaders began to take steps toward resolving urban social conflicts and made the restitution of *biaozhunzu* homes a priority. In 2003, a new policy entitled owners to full relocation compensation equal to what *biaozhunzu* tenants received. *Biaozhunzu* owners were emboldened by this success and pressed their case further, extracting more concessions from the municipal government, including a rise in rent rates and eventually the lifting of the rent cap.[13]

In addition, between 2002 and 2003 more than a dozen guidelines were issued by various municipal agencies to district offices responsible for financing and building relocation housing for *biaozhunzu* tenants. Some of these guidelines were issued by high-level offices, such as the Municipal Government Office, which have the authority to coordinate tasks and assign responsibilities to various functional agencies. Other guidelines were issued by individual functional departments that dealt with operational details, such as deriving the formula for calculating relocation compensation, or for determining the eligibility of tenant families for various compensation and subsidy packages. Seven *biaozhunzu* protest representatives were even invited to participate in a "communication meeting" with government officials organized by the Municipal Office of Letters and Visits. The purpose of the meeting was to review the *biaozhunzu* owners' suggestions on restitution policies. A public-relations coup for the municipal government, the move also delivered concrete results for *biaozhunzu* owners.

Between September 2003 and February 2004, the first groups of *biaozhunzu* tenants moved into relocation housing built by the municipal and district governments, and 4000 *biaozhunzu* homeowners, including the protest representatives, were handed back full possession of their houses. In 2004, the municipal government listed the restitution of all *biaozhunzu* homes on its list of "Fifty-Six Concrete Tasks" that it would prioritize that year. The government also announced it would spend 2 billion yuan in housing subsidies and relocation housing for *biaozhunzu* tenants in order to persuade them to move out of *biaozhunzu* units and return the homes to their previous owners. By the end of 2004, a total of 13,095 units, or 95.7 percent of *biaozhunzu* homes, had been returned. The term *biaozhunzu*, according to the media, "had entered the history books."[14]

Biaozhunzu owners' actions have been the most successful urban protest recorded in Beijing to date. But their success must be qualified and contextualized. Since 2000, at the beginning of each year, the Beijing Municipal Government has announced a list of "concrete tasks" for the year. While most of the tasks are desirable improvements to the urban environment, they are also highly visible, performance-oriented, well-defined, and confined projects. While these projects are spread widely over policy areas, their associated costs are relatively low compared with the political gain they provide for municipal leaders. The restitution of *biaozhunzu* houses, as one of the Fifty-Six Concrete Tasks of 2004, was listed side by side with other programs like providing more public Internet booths and wi-fi access under the "Digital Beijing" campaign, building more public toilets, and abolishing bicycle license fees.[15] The results of these programs can be measured in quantitative terms, itemized in achievement reports, and converted to points in municipal leaders' performance evaluations. Selection of the "key tasks" automatically marginalizes other pressing issues in the city, and achieving predefined targets effectively closes the case on the issue at hand. Thus, once the *biaozhunzu* matter was ticked off as accomplished, other related issues of property rights ceased to hold legitimacy and restricted, subsequent pursuit of the issue. Such conditional success can be illuminated by two more episodes of property rights protest in Beijing.

The *biaozhunzu* homeowners' successful movement occurred at about the same time as the failure of another group of protesters, called *jingzufang* owners. *Jingzufang*, which means "state-managed rental housing", was socialized in the 1950s and 1960s under "policy opinions" and political campaigns. *Jingzufang* homeowners also suffered political marginalization under socialism and were enraged by their exclusion from socialist welfare housing and from the property market under the reform. They too sensed the threat of the loss of their houses as the redevelopment bulldozers approached, and hoped to regain possession of their family property.

But, unlike the *biaozhunzu*, which was a local policy specific to Beijing, socialization of *jingzufang* was part of a national campaign and was implemented in large cities throughout China. Under the socialization policy, all private homeowners were to lease their houses to the state, and the state would reallocate the houses to tenants, hence the term "state-managed rental housing."[16] While the state was responsible for maintenance and kept 60–80 percent of the rental income, homeowners received the rest of the rent. During the Cultural Revolution, private ownership was heavily politicized and private property owners were morally condemned. The Housing Management Bureau stopped paying rents to *jingzufang* homeowners at that time, citing capitalist exploitation. The halting of rent payments to homeowners was further supported by several central policies that stripped *jingzufang* homeowners' entitlement to rental income, and of their rights to request the return of their houses. Their rights to use, dispose of, and profit from property were effectively abolished. Like *biaozhunzu* owners, *jingzufang* owners were also excluded from welfare housing under state socialism. But the reforms of the 1980s brought explicit central policies affirming the state's ownership of *jingzufang*.[17]

In short, the main difference between *biaozhunzu* and *jingzufang* lies at the root of their political legitimacy at different levels of the state. *Biaozhunzu* was legitimized by socialist ideology and imposed by political campaigns during the Cultural Revolution. Much of the system's legitimacy faded with the market reforms and the official reassessment of the Cultural Revolution in the post-reform era. On the other hand, *jingzufang* as a national policy has enjoyed systematic endorsement by central authorities even after market reforms began. The political legitimacy of the *jingzufang* system was affirmed by a series of central policies that established state ownership in increasingly explicit language.

The central government's endorsement of state ownership of *jingzufang* provided the legitimacy for local states to exercise authority over prime tracts of real estate in Beijing. The municipal Housing and Property Management Bureau subsequently established Housing Management Centers at the district levels. These financially independent Housing Management Centers had strong incentives to monopolize the process of inner-city redevelopment. They sought to remove residents, clear sites, and sell the land-use rights to developers for high-yield commercial projects. Because of the proclaimed state ownership of *jingzufang*, business-minded officials of Housing Management Centers could negotiate relocation compensation with the current tenants of *jingzufang* to make them move.[18] Many of the tenants were long-term state employees with extensive connections in Beijing's bureaucratic networks; some were high-ranking government officials in influential state agencies. Because they had lived in *jingzufang* units for two or three decades and many had made investments by building additional rooms in their courtyards, the tenants had come to view rental housing as their own. When some moved out of their old neighborhoods in the 1990s, they leased out the house, further complicating the property rights entanglements of *jingzufang*. Meanwhile, officials at the Housing Management Center would not bother to involve the pre-Revolution *jingzufang* owners in the negotiation process, since their rights were not officially recognized, nor were they physically occupying the houses in most cases.

The entanglement of proclaimed state ownership, local state agencies' interests in these tracts of prime real estate, and well-positioned tenants made it exceedingly difficult for *jingzufang* owners to pursue restitution of their houses. Yet, encouraged by the successes of *biaozhunzu* owners, *jingzufang* owners began to mobilize in the early 2000s. They adopted similar protest strategies as *biaozhunzu* owners, including a shift from individual litigation against tenants to collective visits and petition letters to government agencies, soliciting media attention, and allying with professionals and preservationists. Nevertheless, the restitution of *jingzufang* was never put on the Beijing Municipal Government's policy agenda, and the collective actions did not bring them any closer to recovering their property.

The marginalization of the *jingzufang* issue and the failure of *jingzufang* owners' mobilization serve to illustrate the limits of *biaozhunzu* mobilization as well. The *biaozhunzu* issue was confined to a particular group of residents in Beijing, whose experience could not be transferred to other groups with similar grievances and demands. Nor did the success of *biaozhunzu* protests represent a challenge to a property rights regime that gives state representatives the dominant position. On the contrary, it was because of the bureaucratization and sterilization of the issue that *biaozhunzu* owners won their houses back.

The limits of *biaozhunzu* protesters' success could also be seen in their inability to sustain their action. After initial success, *biaozhunzu* protestors tried to expand their agenda from property restitution to a more complete set of rights over the houses they now owned. *Biaozhunzu* homeowners, who had just moved back to their inner-city homes after years of struggle, found themselves under threat of losing their homes once again. In the mid-2000s, with the 2008 Olympic Games approaching, housing and land prices in Beijing continued to soar, triggering a renewed frenzy of demolition of old houses in the inner city. In response, *Biaozhunzu* owners launched a new campaign demanding land-use rights certificates, and a clarification of "land-use rights".

Under China's state land-tenure system, land users have use rights, but not ownership rights. Private homeowners' property rights are limited to ownership of the house. As for the land underneath the house, the owners have only "use rights". While the substance of homeowners' land-use rights was left ambiguous, the issue was neglected and exploited by urban government officials. During the first twenty years of inner-city demolition for redevelopment, compensation for dislocated households was calculated on the basis of relocation costs for tenants and building materials for owners. The value of the land was not included. Low compensation helped reduce the cost of premium land parcels in the urban core to about 1–5 percent of their market value.[19]

Biaozhunzu owners perceived the immense gap between the compensation they received and the value that the land commanded in the market as immensely unfair. They demanded to expand their rights over the land, not just the house. Opting to eschew a head-on confrontation with a fundamental constitutional stipulation, they confined their demands to clarification of land-use rights. But they argued that use rights included the right to dispose of the land and the right to profit from land sales. In other words, by avoiding explicit mention of de jure ownership rights over land, private homeowners chose to expand the meaning of "use rights" to include de facto ownership rights. Notwithstanding this rhetorical strategy, the protesters posed a direct challenge to the legitimacy of the land-dependent regime of local accumulation. Because it touched upon the core of the mode of accumulation, the new battle proved to be much tougher.

The first step toward the clarification of land-use rights is the affirmation of such rights. According to the *Land Management Law*, the Land Management Bureaus are supposed to issue land-use rights certificates to legitimate land users. Former *biaozhunzu* homeowners were entitled to such certificates, but found that the municipal government was reluctant to issue the critical certificates. Without the certificates, the homeowners were in a weak bargaining position when it came to negotiating demolition and relocation compensation. As of 2006, only about 200 homeowners, including the protest representatives, out of 40,000 legitimate private homeowners, received land-use rights certificates. There was still a catch. On the certificate, the type of land-use rights needs to be specified, and there are only four legally recognized categories to choose from: administrative allocated land, leased land, land as an equity share, and rental land. None of the four fits the case of *biaozhunzu* houses. Officials of the municipal Land Management Bureau first filled the blank with "administrative allocated land". But administrative allocated land can be taken back by the state whenever the state claims it. Additionally, small print on the certificate indicated that the land-use rights certificates could not be used as collateral for bank loans. *Biaozhunzu* owners protested again through letters and visits. At the end the Land Management Bureau and the owners settled on a compromise that left the land-use rights box blank.[20]

Their predicament reveals the limits of the *biaozhunzu* mobilization's initial success. As they moved from recovering their family property to challenging the foundation of the land-dependent regime of local accumulation, property rights protesters joined a broader quest for residents' rights to the city.

Residents' rights mobilization

Land-dependent local accumulation is built on the local state's acquisition of land. But land acquisition, to borrow an expression from Mao, is not a dinner party. It involves physical destruction of places and the brutal removal of residents from their life-support systems of home, work, community, and urban services. To meet GDP growth targets, local government leaders are eager to remove all "obstacles" as quickly as possible to make way for new development projects financed by loans. The destruction of large numbers of inner-city houses also guarantees the demand for new, low-cost homes built on the periphery of the city, thus closing the circle in the metropolitan-wide "economy of demolition".

The ruthless destruction of homes and liquidation of communities has been justified through legal and rhetorical measures that place redevelopment projects under "old and dilapidated housing reconstruction" programs, infrastructure construction, or commercial projects for the "public interest". The faster the rate of construction, the faster the destruction; the faster the destruction, the more drastic the measures employed; and, the more drastic the measures, the greater intensity of the grievances on the part of households whose homes are demolished. Between 1990 and 2004, more than half a million households were relocated in Beijing.[21] They were called *chaiqianhu*, which means literally "evicted households whose homes had been demolished". Beginning in the mid-1990s, *chaiqianhu* began to take action against eviction and demolition. Unlike the property rights protesters who shared a common background as property owners, the ownership status of *chaiqianhu* protesters was more diverse. A sample survey of 600 *chaiqianhu* protesters found a 4:6 split between tenants and property owners.[22] Unlike *biaozhunzu* homeowners, what the *chaiqianhu* protesters had in common was not ownership, but the experience of abrupt and frequent brutal destruction of their livelihoods and the consequent instability in their lives. Their collective identity was based on residency in the city and the loss of territorial attachment. Moreover, unlike property rights protesters who framed their grievances historically, *chaiqianhu* protesters framed their grievances, demands, and resistance strategies territorially.

Here, "territorial" refers to control over resources and people in a place. While the state is the usual subject of territorial power in the literature on geopolitics, I emphasize here that territory and territorial power can also be shaped by social actors. Place-based collective identity can be sharpened and activated in the process of resisting the state's territorial dominance, and those engaged in this resistance have territorial tools and strategies to assert their rights to the city.

Territorially framed grievances over life-world destruction

One of the most common grievances of *chaiqianhu* protesters concerns "unfair relocation and demolition compensation." This seemingly straightforward framing has at least two territorial implications.

The first implication of *chaiqianhu* grievances concerned the location of the demolished house in the compensation calculation. As presented earlier, under state ownership of urban land, building materials used for the house were compensated for, but the land was not. If the house to be demolished was privately owned, the staff of the Demolition Office would use the official compensation calculation guidelines that converted the total floor area, the number of electricity outlets, the size of wells in the courtyard, the materials used in the roof, floor, walls, and so on into monetary equivalents and offered cash compensation in a lump sum. In this formulation, the houses were treated as territorially detached and locationally homogeneous structures. The exclusion of land value in the calculation significantly reduced the total compensation payment. With the increased demand for land and rampant speculation in the city, the municipal government could sell the land for as much as a hundred times higher than the compensation paid out to home-owning *chaiqianhu*.

Home-owning *chaiqianhu* saw the immense gap between the compensation they received and the market value of the land as hugely unfair. For them the issue was not just about compensation for the structure of the house, but the change in land value due to the locational advantage of the land on which their house was built. They felt that they had been denied potential profits from the land due to the government's deliberate exclusion of the locational factor in the calculation of compensation. The issue of the location in relocation compensation were crucial to the conflicts between local development powers and *chaiqianhu*.

Another territorially framed grievance was the issue of relocation. In the 1990s, *chaiqianhu* were compensated with relocation housing in designated locations, but the relocation housing was mostly in remote, semi-rural areas; and relocatees had no choice of where they would be relocatees. For the Demolition Office, allocating relocation housing was administratively and economically expensive—the practice was prone to disputes and prolonged negotiation. Beginning in the early 2000s, compensation in kind was largely replaced by cash compensation, which was justified as following the market principle and providing greater choice in relocation destinations. But cash compensation in a market-like economy did not provide greater choice. The majority of *chaiqianhu* wanted on-site relocation or relocation within the general area of their original homes. But skyrocketing property values in the inner city made on-site relocation prohibitively expensive for most. As the city continued to expand, relocation housing affordable to *chaiqianhu* was located farther and farther from the city center. The long distance between the old and new homes destroyed *chaiqianhu* life-worlds and was at the heart of their grievances about relocation.

In their remote relocation sites, housing conditions were frequently substandard. Basic utilities like running water and drainage were often not functional. There were also reports of polluted groundwater that caused serious illness. Residents would ride pedal-powered carts two to three hours each way to retrieve clean water from city water sources. Moreover, the abrupt uprooting changed every aspect of family life and caused physical separation between family members. The majority of *chaiqianhu* were in the middle-low to low income group. By the late 1990s, higher-income residents, who worked in well-endowed *danwei* or private enterprises, had already moved out of dilapidated inner city neighborhoods. Those left behind were mainly retirees, workers of stagnant state *danwei*, low-skill and low-pay service workers, and street vendors. Proximity to the city center was important for them and their family members to find odd jobs. Moving to the remote outskirts meant commutes up to three hours each way between home and work. The commutes were made worse by poor bus service and congested traffic between the urban center and remote suburbs resulting from rapid urban sprawl. Consequently, many *chaiqianhu* lost their jobs as a result of relocation, and became a new class of urban poor.

For inner-city elderly retirees, the loss of medical care was a devastating blow. Retirees were assigned services at public hospitals in the city center, up to two hours away by bus from the relocation housing. For school-age children, if they were to continue attending city schools, where education quality tends to be better, the choice was between a long commute accompanied by an unemployed adult or staying with relatives in the city, and living separately from their parents. Families were often forced to live separately because members found housing, jobs, and schools in different parts of the city. Long-term neighbors were also moved to different relocation housing projects, dismantling the social support network for inner-city *chaiqianhu*.

The scene at relocation housing projects is demoralizing, with unemployed middle-aged men and women and elderly retirees idling outside their shabby buildings in the dust amid unpaved roads and semi-completed projects. Even when residents were relocated on-site, the housing provided was invariably of poor quality, mismanaged, and congested. For these people, relocation has created new urban slums.

There were also people who refused to move because they considered the relocation compensation insufficient and the process unjust. Police would take them, often by force, to cheap hotels, or they would take up rental housing on short-term leases, or stay with relatives for short periods of time. Many evicted households were simply not relocated. They turned into urban drifters. According to Fang (2000), by 1998, there were already more than 100,000 people in Beijing removed from the inner city who had not yet been resettled.[23] In 2005, a major inner-city redevelopment project in the *Dashilan* (or *Dazhalan*) and *Qianmen* areas created about 20,000 *chaiqianhu*. With the limited cash compensation they received, most of the *chaiqianhu* could not afford to buy new homes in the same area, and ended up renting temporary housing nearby. The sudden surge of housing demand produced by the large number of home demolitions in a short period of time created a crunch in the housing market, pushing rents higher, and causing more people to join the ranks of urban drifters. In Beijing, these urban drifters are sometimes referred to as *da-you-fei*, a term evocative of flying pests.[24]

Relocation housing projects create a different type of uncertainty for *chaiqianhu*. Many of those who were forced to move to the designated relocation housing in the remote urban outskirts had to pay additional out-of-pocket funds for larger units than the compensation packages would provide. However, much of the relocation housing on the peri-urban areas, while cheaper, was illegally built by rural village and township development companies on protected farmland (see Chapter 6). These illegal relocation housing projects had neither gone through the legal procedures for land-use conversion from agricultural to nonagricultural uses, nor through the procedure for land tenure transfer from village collectives to the state. Thus, village and township developers could not obtain planning and construction permission for the project, and could not provide legal title papers to *chaiqianhu* homebuyers. Many *chaiqianhu* discovered to their chagrin that their new homes were illegal only after they had moved in. Some of these illegal relocation housing projects were subsequently demolished under a national campaign to recover and preserve farmland. Because land that has previously been a building site cannot be easily converted back to farming, such demolitions are mostly symbolic, but they directly affect the *chaiqianhu*. Some became *chaiqianhu* a second time after being

4. Half-destroyed inner city neighborhood in Beijing (August 2004)

evicted from their relocation housing. Others were misled into believing that the new homes in the peri-urban zones could be exchanged for houses in the inner city, only to find out later that they did not possess the legal ownership of their new homes. To top it all, they owed rent, property management fees, and contract violation fines to the development companies for the new homes.[25] Most *chaiqianhu* refused to pay the rents for the relocation housing and were taken to court by the development company. As the litigation proceeded, banks froze their accounts and a new round of struggle over housing began.

The destruction of life-worlds was further aggravated by brutality and violence. Under political pressure to achieve GDP growth and financial pressure to pay off debt-financed redevelopment, urban government leaders sought to accelerate the pace of destruction in order to build and sell the land faster. The pressure often escalated into harassment and physical violence. Residents who refused to accept compensation offers were frequently visited by staff from the Demolition and Relocation Office, followed by repeated harassment, including the cutting off of water, power, heat, gas, telephone lines, and even roads. Elderly residents were reported to have died of heart attacks, seizure, and stroke at the shock of witnessing their homes and neighborhoods demolished. Physical confrontations between wrecking crews and *chaiqianhu* were common. Those who tried to stop bulldozers were routinely arrested and detained by police.[26]

If residents refused to budge, more violent measures were employed, including the use of mechanical diggers to reduce parts of the house to rubble and to smash furniture while residents were out. In other cases, home were broken into and demolished in the middle of the night. In extreme cases, residents were blindfolded and taken from their homes by force. When the blindfolds were removed, the only thing the residents saw was the rubble of their former homes. Thugs and migrant workers from other regions were hired to do this work, making it difficult to identify the individuals involved and take legal action.[27] A special term was given to this practice: *yeman chaiqian*, meaning "savage demolition and eviction." China Central TV repeatedly reported instances of *yeman chaiqian* in Beijing and other cities.[28] A newspaper commentary described the violent demolition and forced eviction as "worse than the Red Guards' beating, smashing, and looting (*da-za-qiang*) during the Cultural Revolution."[29]

Public condemnation of *yeman chaiqian* has been accompanied by a counter discourse condemning those who resist demolition as stumbling blocks on the road to progress. *Chaiqianhu* have been repeatedly mocked in popular and official discourses and affixed the pejorative terms *dingzihu*, or "nail households," and *lanluhu*, or "tigers blocking the road." *Chaiqianhu* are presented as uncooperative and opportunistic negotiators for higher compensation and are accused of sacrificing the public interest for personal gain, and even of causing housing price hikes. By this reasoning, the *dingzihu* deserved the harsh measures that the government used against them and were comparable to tax evaders, unlicensed vendors, and illegal builders.[30] They were blamed for failures in policy implementation and social disorder. Based on this framing, government officials justified the oppression of *chaiqianhu* as merely "pulling out the nails" (*bading*) or "crushing the nails" (*zading*).[31]

The use of violence weakened the resolve of many *chaiqianhu* hold-outs and intimidated others. Furthermore, once *chaiqianhu* were physically removed from their homes and the material existence of the houses disappeared, chaiqianhu lost the anchor of their rights claims, making it more difficult for them to take legal action against developers.[32]

The violent destruction of houses was also systematically used by development powers to accelerate compensation negotiations with *chaiqianhu*. Monetary compensation for relocation is based on property value appraisals conducted by appraisal agencies that were inclined to produce biased appraisal reports in favor of the Demolition and Relocation Office, thus lowering the amount in compensation packages. Many *chaiqianhu* felt that appraisals were inaccurate and relocation compensation unfair, and took the Demolition and Relocation Office of the district government to court. The court would order a reassessment of the value of the property in question in order to examine the compensation package. To carry out the property value reassessment, however, the physical existence of the property is crucial. Yet, city policy allowed demolition to continue even as disputes between *chaiqianhu* and the Demolition and Relocation Office were pending.[33] This policy gave office staff a strong incentive to bulldoze houses under dispute as quickly as possible. Even if a *chaiqianhu* won the case after lengthy judicial procedures and obtained a court order to reassess the value of the property in dispute, the house was often already razed, making it impossible to reassess the value of the house and recalculate the compensation. Physical destruction of the house was therefore sufficient to persuade even the most stubborn nail households to move.

Strategies

In the early 1990s, *chaiqianhu* would protest unfair compensation and forced evictions individually. They took the district government, developers, and the Demolition and Relocation Office to court. They also wrote letters and visited government agencies to lodge complaints. But most of these individual protests proved ineffective. Some *chaiqianhu* began to organize collective litigation against government agencies. By the mid-1990s, there were already hundreds of litigation groups composed of thousands of litigants.

Chaiqianhu grievances were diverse, ranging from unfair property appraisal, underpayment or discriminatory compensation payment, inadequate relocation housing, destruction of personal property, and physical injury. Some litigants made demands for material compensation. Others sought to resolve the conflicts at the roots, by demanding clarification and redefinition of land-use rights. Still others protested imposed relocation plans, and demanded the right to choose their place of residency. Contestation over compensation was sometimes resolved through under-the-table negotiations between Demolition and Relocation Office staff and individual *chaiqianhu*. The secretive deal-making generated distrust among *chaiqianhu* and eventually undermined their solidarity. In the latter case, those who insisted on redefining land-use rights on principle rejected better compensation packages offered by the Demolition Office staff or the developers.

Despite the diversity in grievances and demands, *chaiqianhu* in different neighborhoods have adopted similar strategies to protect their residents' rights. In what follows, I outline three mobilization strategies. These strategies have had both discursive and legal significance. They also have strong territorial implications. The first strategy concerns sustaining rights claims over razed homes; the second concerns delegitimizing eviction and relocation programs; and the third concerns the building of cross-neighborhood mobilization networks.

Strategy I: sustaining rights claims[34]

The first type of strategy employed by *chaiqianhu* involves sustaining rights claims over inner-city homes that had been razed. This was organized around the issue of address changes on the residents' identification cards. In 2005, the central government initiated a renewal of Resident

Identification Cards nationwide. Citizens were required to apply for new ID cards with their current address on them. In Beijing, relocated *chaiqianhu* were requested to register their new addresses on the new ID cards. But protesters refused to do so, insisting that they would only use their old address.

Chaiqianhu protesters argued that the ID card is a legal document, and everything on the card had to be legal. But their new homes were the result of the government's illegal destruction of their homes and forced relocation. They never recognized the new homes as their real homes. They feared that conceding to the new address on the new ID card would be a de facto recognition of the legitimacy of government-sponsored demolition and relocation. By insisting on keeping the old address on the new ID card, *chaiqianhu* protesters showed their association with and their rights to the old homes, even if they had already been razed and turned into office towers and luxury condos.

The insistence on keeping the old address that no longer physically existed was not just a discursive strategy. It also had a legal implication. *Chaiqianhu* felt that precisely because of the physical disappearance of the house, they needed a legal document as evidence of their residency in the location to legitimize their cause. Lacking titles and deeds, ID cards were the only legal documents they had. They turned to the identity card law and its implementation guidelines to find that their situation did not fit any of the conditions listed in the guidelines for change of address on new ID cards. After challenging officials of the Registration office, some *chaiqianhu* received new ID cards with their old addresses.

The dispute over address change on the new ID card signifies *chaiqianhu's* efforts to sustain their rights claims over their long-term residence in the inner city. While redevelopment powers attempted to erase any association that former residents may have retained with their old homes, *chaiqianhu* strategized to keep the past alive and maintain the presence of the disappeared. The discursive politics of memory and territoriality became intertwined with the legal implications of the dispute.

Strategy II: delegitimizing eviction programs

In addition to striving to sustain rights claims over their old homes, *chaiqianhu* protesters have also tried to delegitimize the new homes. Litigation over rent payments for relocation housing is exemplary of this strategy. Before moving to their relocation housing, many *chaiqianhu* were promised by relocation officials that the relocation housing units were offered in exchange for their old homes. But, as mentioned earlier, it was not until they moved to the new homes that *chaiqianhu* discovered that they did not possess legal ownership of the new homes, but instead owed rent, property management fees, and contract violation fines.[35]

Most relocated *chaiqianhu* refused to pay. They argued that the rent could only be paid to legal owners, but the development companies had obtained the land illegally and could not produce legal proof of ownership. Following the same logic, the *chaiqianhu* claimed that the entire process of demolition and relocation was illegal, and that their refusal to pay rent for the relocation housing was simply an act to end the chain of illegal actions of the government and its allied developers. A protest leader pushed the argument even further by saying that "if a *chaiqianhu* paid the rent for housing that was illegally built, then the *chaiqianhu*'s action became illegal."[36]

Again, the discursive strategy to delegitimize development powers carried legal implications. Many *chaiqianhu* who refused to pay rent were subsequently taken to court by the developers of relocation housing. Developer-initiated litigation in turn opened the gate for *chaiqianhu* to enter the judicial system, which had excluded *chaiqianhu* litigants since 1995. By being taken to court by developers, *chaiqianhu* could gain a foothold in the legal system as a defendant. Once the court accepted the case, *chaiqianhu* could reverse their status from defendant to plaintiff, and sue the government-sponsored developer for land-rights violations and demanding adequate compensation. *Chaiqianhu* used litigation to shift their position from reactive defendants to proactive challengers of the land-dependent local regime of accumulation.

Chaiqianhu rights claims over their old homes and their strategic rejection of their new homes was inseparable from their demand for residency rights and defense of life-worlds in the city. By the early 2000s, litigation over rent payments had spread throughout the city, and increasing numbers of *chaiqianhu* had been drawn into lawsuits as individual defendants. These *chaiqianhu* had a strong incentive to learn to protect themselves in court, and became the core members of an emerging cross-neighborhood campaign of mass legal education in Beijing.[37]

Strategy III: cross-neighborhood mobilization networks

The national campaign to promote the rule of law that began in the 1990s provides certain legitimacy to citizens' gatherings under the name of "mass legal education." Several *chaiqianhu* activists and legal professionals established the Center for Mass Legal Education in Beijing in 1996 and organized numerous mass legal education meetings. These meetings were held in neighborhoods facing demolition and in newly built relocation housing complexes. Meetings took place on weekday evenings or during the day on weekends, and attracted up to 100 participants each time. At the meetings, self-taught activists would deliver lectures on the issues that were directly relevant to the audience's immediate concerns, including laws related to demolition procedure, compensation calculation, and land-use rights. Lectures were often followed by heated discussion.

The meetings provided more than information and education. They also served as mobile and decentralized nodes of mobilizational networks. Along with the legal education campaign, activists organized an unprecedented collective litigation with 10,357 plaintiffs to sue the Municipal Land, Housing and Property Management Bureau in 2000.[38] Known as *wanren dasusong*, or "Grand Litigation of 10,000 Plaintiffs," the suit included fifty-seven subgroups from various districts and neighborhoods in Beijing.[39] This cross-neighborhood network continued to expand, despite the fact that the Municipal Court never accepted their case. The seven representatives of *wanren dasusong* have continued to take the case to the Municipal Court every year since 2000. They also undertook another collective action dubbed the "grand petition and revelation" (*wanren dajubao*), getting over 30,000 signatories in 2003, and another "grand revelation" on a similar scale in 2005. In the latest "grand revelation" letter addressed to Communist Party leaders, the CCP Disciplinary Committee, and the National People's Congress, the protesters demanded a redefinition of land-use rights and residents' civil liberties. They condemned official corruption in land deals and singled out Beijing's party secretary between 1997 and 2002, Jia Qinglin, who ranked fourth in the pecking order of the CCP Politburo in 2002, as the individual responsible for the corruption that led to the plight of *chaiqianhu* in Beijing.

At the height of their mobilization, particularly at the outset of the "grand litigation," legal education meetings were held daily in various neighborhoods. After initiation of the litigation and later of the "grand revelation," representatives held information meetings to explain the litigation and revelation letters, and to report to followers on the progress of the case. They would also analyze the shifting political climate and its possible impact on their case. After the initial lectures, activists were often invited back for further discussion. These meetings helped disseminate legal information, educate followers, and raise consciousness and expectations. The face-to-face meetings were also important for recruiting followers and building group identity. The mobile, irregular, and fragmented nature of their network seemed to have allowed the activists to continue meeting without the authority's active repression.

By 2003, the number of cases of violence against *chaiqianhu* reportedly dropped, and the scale and pace of demolition in the inner city slowed. It is difficult, however, to establish a direct causal link between *chaiqianhu* mobilization and these signs of changes. Nor can we predict with great confidence that *chaiqianhu's* legal mobilization will blossom into a full-scale urban social movement that promises "qualitative change in urban system, local culture, and political institutions," as defined by Manuel Castells (1983).[40] Moreover, Beijing *chaiqianhu* protesters have couched their demands and strategies in terms compliant with the state-delineated legal order, risking what radical legal scholars would consider imprisonment within the state-sponsored ideology of law as the basis for legitimacy, and that the activists risked losing their political imagination. So what promises did Beijing's housing protests bring, if any, and what is the territorial implication of their protest?

Civic territoriality in the inner city

As discussed in Chapter 1, I call social actors' collective struggles to build their own territoriality at both the physical and discursive levels *civic territoriality*. I emphasize that territoriality, when seen from below, is as much a tool of resistance as of dominance. While the local state uses urban construction to consolidate its territorial authority, societal actors use territorial strategies for self-protection. Civic territoriality brings society to the center of territorial politics, and sees territoriality as the platform of social activism.

In inner-city Beijing, *chaiqianhu* protesters have framed their grievances and demands in territorial terms. Their place-based identity is sharpened and activated in the process of forced eviction and in the face of the loss of livelihood. Place-based identity in turn is translated into grievances and demands framed around location and relocation. The location of old homes in the inner city, where land values continue to increase, is crucial to protesters' demands for fairer relocation compensation. The relocation causes grievances because of the brutal rupture of livelihoods once the residents are forced to move to designated relocation sites far away from urban services, social support networks, and jobs.

Place-based identity is also a part of the discursive and legal strategy for protesters' collective actions. The controversies over address change triggered by the ID card renewal program, as well as the rent payment litigation are all examples of *chaiqianhu* protesters' employing territorial strategies to delegitimize forced evictions and to assert their entitlement to inner-city homes and neighborhoods.

The territorial consequences of these strategies are found at the organizational and discursive levels. In the case of the "Grand Litigation of 10,000 Plaintiffs" and the "Grand Petition and Revelation," legal actions functioned as a basis for cross-neighborhood networking in Beijing. Although the network was loosely organized and the legal education meetings moved from neighborhood to neighborhood, it is likely that the mobile and irregular nature of the network has sustained it without inviting repression. The decentralized, mobile network could well be a territorial effect that helped to sustain the collective action.

At the discursive level, the territorial effect is in the politics of rights redefinition and recognition. While pre-Revolution private homeowners won back their homes, they began to push a more fundamental agenda of land ownership instead of home ownership. Meanwhile, *chaiqianhu* protesters, including homeowners and tenants, framed their demands not just as property ownership rights but as residents' rights to the city, thus broadened legal claims for property rights to a moral claim for residents' entitlement. Their efforts went beyond the prevalent, state-sponsored legal order, reflecting the beginning of a changing discourse in the 2000s. Capital accumulation through dispossession and livelihood destruction is no longer hidden behind a billboard that reads "development is the absolute principle." Nor is massive urban displacement unanimously viewed as a historical necessity on the path to higher modernity. Inner-city activism and its version of civic territoriality have put forth a territorial agenda toward redefining the state-dominated property rights regime in the inner city and recognizing urban residents' rights to the city regardless of their property ownership status. Civic territoriality, therefore, is an integral part of the quest for citizenship rights. The mobilization for property and residents' rights in Beijing is central to what T. H. Marshall has outlined as civil and social citizenship rights.[41] By focusing on the territorial dimension of the framing and strategies of housing protestors in Beijing, I hope to demonstrate the connection between urban and citizenship struggles.

For sure, resistance is not the only form of societal self-protection or the only way to build civic territoriality. In Chapter 5, I introduce a different type of civic territoriality not built on confrontational resistance, but skillful negotiation, which helps strengthen villagers' territorial autonomy. In addition, the optimistic conclusion that I have drawn in this chapter is not always applicable to other types of grassroots resistance. In Chapter 7, I further examine the process of deterritorialization of dispossessed peasants in the remote rural edge of the metropolis.

Notes

1. Fictionalized name. Interview BJS0602, Beijing, June 2006.
2. In this section on *biaozhunzu* protests, I have used interviews conducted by Bi Xiangyang, recorded in his doctoral dissertation. See Bi, Xiangyang, *Cong caomin dao gongmin: dangdai Beijing dushi yundong* (From the Masses to Citizens: Contemporary Urban Social Movement in Beijing). Ph.D. dissertation, (Beijing: Sociology Department, Tsinghua University, 2006). I also am indebted to Professor Shen Yuan, Dr. Bi Xiangyang, and Shi Yunqing for sharing insights and information, and for helping me set up interviews for the rest of this chapter.
3. *Zhongfa* (1966) Document No. 507.
4. According to Bi, Xiangyang (2006), in the early 1950s, the Beijing Municipal Government issued new titles to the city's private homeowners to allay concern over the newly installed communist government, whose reputation at the time triggered fears of imminent confiscation of private property and even wives. In the late 1950s, when the regime began to stabilize, a series of measures was used to socialize private homes.
5. Wu, Chenguang, *"Beijing biaozhunzu sifang de jiejue zhidao"* (Ways to resolve the problem of *biaozhunzu* private homes), 2003.
6. In 1983, it was 0.11 yuan/sq m. In 2000, the rent was raised to 3.45 yuan/sq m. It was subsequently raised to 10 yuan/sq m in 2002, and 35 yuan/sq m in 2003, still much lower than the market rates of 80–200 yuan/sq m for mediocre quality courtyard housing in the inner city.
7. See "Beijing Municipal Government Rules for returning private homes that were taken over during the Cultural Revolution" (1983) and "Decisions made at the 26th meeting of the leading team of private home return policy" (1983), quoted in Bi, Xiangyang, 2006.
8. Tenant couples would even file for divorce in order to keep their *biaozhunzu* units.
9. Department of Marketing in Municipal Housing Management Bureau, Document No. 409.
10. Such as the Municipal Housing Management Bureau, the Municipal Office for Answering Letters and Receiving Visitors, the Ministry of Construction, and its Department of Real Estate. They also filed petitions to other related government agencies at both national and local levels.
11. In 2001, *Biaozhunzu* activists proposed to establish the Beijing Private Property Owner Association. They sent applications to the Municipal Land and Housing Management Bureau and the Civil Affairs Bureau, but were rejected. In 2002,

they filed an application with the Public Security Bureau to hold a 480-person rally, with the protest slogan in the application: "Implement the Constitution, Return Private Homes." This was the first such application in Beijing since the Law on Assemblies, Processions, and Demonstration became effective on 31 October 1989. Several leaders were called by public security officials for questioning several times and were verbally abused by them. The activists believed that because their protests were lawful, and their request was protected under the Constitution and other laws; they were harassed by the public security, but were never arrested. See Bi, Xiangyang *Cong caomin dao gongmin*, p. 253.

12. Bi, Xiangyang *Cong caomin dao gongmin*, p. 242.

13. It was raised to 10 yuan/sq m in March 2002, then to 20 yuan/sq m in March 2003. The rent cap was to be abolished in December 2003. See Beijing Municipal Document No. 37, "Opinions on resolving the problems related to rent rates of *biaozhunzu* housing in Beijing Municipality." The municipal government made the increase in rent rates possible by subsidizing the rents through Municipal Housing Funds and making individual tenants' *danwei* pick up part of the bill.

14. Hong, Yanjie and Yang Baochuan, "212 *hu biaozhunzu sihu jinqian xinju*" (212 *biaozhunzu* private homeowners moved into new homes today), 2004; Guo, Yan, "*Jiejue 20 nian yiliu wenti, yiwanduo hu banchu biaozhunzu sifang*" (A 20-year historical problem resolved; more than 10,000 tenants moved out of *biaozhunzu* housing), 2005.

15. "*Beijingshi 2004 nian 56 xiang shishi sheji baixing shenghuo jiuda fangmian*" (Nine areas of everyday life are covered by Beijing Municipal Government's 56 concrete tasks of 2004), January 7, 2004. Online. See <http://news.xinhuanet.com/newscenter/2004–01/07/content_1263576_1.html> accessed May 27, 2009.

16. The national policy to socialize private industrial and commercial enterprises in 1953 was extended to landed property in 1955. The Policy Opinion was issued by the No. 2 Office of the Central Secretariat.

17. Jiang, Yun, *Chanquan jieding de quanli shijian: yi jingzusifangzhu de weiquan huodong wei gean* (Rights practice in property rights confirmation: A case study of rights protection of *jingzufang* private home owners), 2006.

18. Housing management centers and developers do not necessarily demolish the old houses and build new ones. Under the growing demand for traditional courtyard housing in the late 1990s and early 2000s, they renovate well-preserved old houses and sell them to foreign expatriates and rich locals at a premium price. Interview BJ030, Beijing, August 2003.

19. Traditional courtyard housing in designated historical preservation areas is worth 3 to 4 million yuan, and some were worth over 10 million yuan per unit. The maximum compensation ranged between 200,000 and 400,000 yuan. In another case, a courtyard home of more than 600 sq m was estimated at 30 million yuan because of its antique wood window and door frames, posts, carved stone statues, and antique roof tiles. But the owner was promised

440,000 yuan as compensation. See Bao, Limin *"Laoren chi xianfa dizhi chaiqian shi xu—chaiqianhu fangguanju gezhiyici"* (The incident of the old man holding up the Constitution to resist demolition continued, *chaiqianhu* and the Housing Management Bureau each has a story), *China Youth Daily*, April 12, 2004. Online. See <http://house.focus.cn/news/2005–03–18/62239.html>.
20. Bi, *Cong caomin dao gongmin*, pp. 256–60.
21. Zhou, Le, *"Dui Beijing dongqian da guimo weijiufang gaizaode sikao"* (Thoughts on massive urban redevelopment in Beijing), 2002. Qin, Wen, *"Beijing weifanggaizao jinru weixunhuan shidai"* (Redevelopment in Beijing enters a new period of "microcirculation"), 2005; *Beijing Statistical Reports*, 2003, 2004, 2005, Beijing Municipal Bureau of Statistics.
22. Interviews BJ0304 and BJ0605 (social researchers), Beijing, June 2006.
23. Fang, Ke, *Dangdai Beijing jiucheng gengxin: diaocha, yanjiu, tansuo* (Contemporary conservation in the inner city of Beijing: Survey, analysis, and investigation), 2000, pp. 38. The availability of cheap hotels, short-term rental and relatives' homes might explain the relative invisibility of homelessness in Beijing. The very harsh treatment of drifters by city patrol teams also keeps many of them away from the "key areas" of the city.
24. Nan, Xianghong and Ma Jieting, *"Chule Qianmen daona anjia?"* (Where to after moving out from Qianmen?), 2006.
25. Liu, Zhiming, *"Chaiqian chai de rangren xinhan"* (Demolition chills people's hearts), 2003.
26. Interviews, BJ0507, Beijing, June 2005; BJS0602, Beijing, 2 June 2006. Wang, Wei, *"43jian pingfang lingchen zao yeman tuiping"* (43 housing units were razed to the ground after midnight), 2005; Wang, Xiaoxia, *"Shehei chaiqian: Beijing yi jumin shenye zaobang bei yiweipingdi"* (Gangster-involved chaiqian: a civilian home was razed to the ground at the deep night), 2003.
27. *"Mingxing qiye jiao de shehei zhilu"* (Star entrepreneurs in gangster-involved demolition), *China News Week* (*Zhongguo xinwen zhoukan*), No. 14, 18 August 2003. Online. See <http://news.china.com/zh_cn/domestic/945/20030814/11523253–2.html>. accessed May 20, 2007.
28. Weifa chengqiang shibao: Beijing yeman chaiqian xianxiang jidaizhili (Illegal violence: Brutal demolition in Beijing urgently needs a solution), China Central TV, November 5, 2003; Chaiqianhu beikun weifang jin yiyue yeman chaiqian chaidaole shenmo (Chaiqianhu stuck in dangerous house for almost a month: what have demolition projects demolished?), China Central TV, May 26, 2004.
29. Jian, Xia, *"Chaiqian, haishi jiaofei?"* (Is it demolition or attacking bandits?), 2004.
30. *"Sun! Kao dang zhuanye chaiqian dingzihu laizhifu"* (Shame! Getting rich by being a professional *chaiqian* nail household), *Huaxi City News*, November 1, 2004; Guo, Qiang, *"Zeyang yifa chaiqian jiucheng gaizhao de dingzihu fangwu?"* (How to legally demolish the houses of *chaiqian* nail households?), 2004. In a "letter to the editor," one reader writes: "If they want to die, the government shouldn't stop them. They are just acting!" and "every common home buyer is paying for

the *chaiqian* nail households." Online. See <http://house.focus.cn/msgview/895/10524965.html>, accessed December 15, 2006.

31. An economist at Beijing University suggested that in order to redevelop the inner city at a lower cost and efficiently, the government should accelerate the pace of redevelopment projects and acquire the land before people have fully developed their consciousness of property rights. Wang, Yuesheng, *"Ruhe zouchuchaiqiande liangnan jingdi"* (How to resolve the dilemma of *chaiqian*), 2005.

32. Interview, BJS0602, Beijing, June 2006. Liu, Zhiming, *"Sushi fufu: shei chaile wode fangzi?"* (Mr. and Mrs. Su: who tore down my house?), 2003.

33. "Regulations of Management of Urban Housing Demolition and Relocation in Beijing," Beijing People's Government Ordinance No. 87, November 1 2001. The principle stated in the policy was that demolition and vacating the land could be done prior to dispute resolution.

34. Information of this strategy is from Shi, Yunqing's unpublished study of Beijing's chaiqianhu. Shi, Yunqing, 2006, Department of Sociology, Tsinghua University, Beijing.

35. Liu Zhiming, *"Chaiqian chai de rangren xinhan."* (Demolition chills people's hearts), 2003.

36. Interview, BJS0602, Beijing. June 2006.

37. Interview BJS0602, Beijing, June 2006. Also, many some of the plaintiffs of *wanren dasusong* did little more than following the protest leaders. They would sign their names on collective litigation documents, and expected the leaders to represent them and to do the rest. But those prompted by rent-payment litigation and brought to court as defendants tended to be more active. They participated in mass legal education meetings, had stronger associations with *wanren dasusong* groups, and became a major force in the "Grand Petition" and "Grand Revelation." This observation was made by Shi Yunqing of the Sociology Department at Qinghua University, Beijing, in September 2006.

38. Interview BJS0602, Beijing, June 2006; and Bi, Xiangyang, *Cong zaomin dao shimin* 2006. In the "Grand Litigation," the common ground they found to accommodate both property owners and tenants with a diverse range of grievance and demands was to sue the Municipal Land, Housing and Property Bureau over a procedural flaw. According to the Letters and Visits Guidelines (*xinfang tiaoli*), government agencies are obligated to respond to petition letters within thirty days of receipt. The representatives first sent a letter to the bureau, requesting recognition and affirmation of residents' land-use rights, and for relocation compensation to be calculated on the basis of the value of land, not just the house. Unsurprisingly to the petitioners, the housing bureau did not respond to the petition letter after thirty days. The representatives consequently sued the bureau for violating the guidelines and demanded a written response from the bureau to their petition letter.

39. For discussion of the use of social networks in China's recent urban social mobilization, see Shi, Fayong and Cai, Yongshun, "Disaggregating the state:

networks and collective resistance in Shanghai," 2006. What I found in Beijing is that social networks based on family, long-time neighbors and co-workers seemed to be more useful within individual districts or neighborhoods, but cross-district networking and recruiting requires more active mobilization beyond the existing social networks.

40. Manuel Castells suggests that an urban social movement is "a conscious collective practice originating in urban issues, able to produce qualitative changes in the urban system, local culture, and political institutions in contradiction to the social interests institutionalized as such at social level." See Castells, Manuel, *The City and the Grassroots*, 1983, p. 278.

41. Marshall, T. Humphrey, *Citizenship and Social class*, 1992.

Part II
Expansion of the Metropolitan Region

Chapter 4

Metropolitan Governance, Real-Estate Projects, and Capital Accumulation

In August 2004, I met with the director of the Bureau of Land Management of a rural county under Beijing Municipality. The county was incorporated into a municipal district three years earlier, and had recently completed a new expressway connected to central Beijing. The new district was in the news at that time for its successful land-lease sales through open auction to one of the largest and most aggressive development companies in China. The development company had bought 77 acres of land from the district for 905 million yuan, an unprecedented sum, to build luxury "villa" in this sleepy agricultural district. I asked the director why the developer had invested in his district. The director responded candidly: "Who'd want to deal with the troublemakers in Beijing's old hutongs if they can easily find much larger pieces of land here?" I pressed him on who the troublemakers were in Beijing. He replied, "Of course, it is those danwei and hutong old residents who play tough when bargaining for relocation compensation." Then he added, "Everyone knows it is easier to deal with peasants than urbanites."[1]

In this chapter I shift the geographical focus from the urban core to the urban fringe of the metropolitan region. In the urban core areas, the type of land in question is state-owned land. At the urban fringe, the battle is mainly over rural land owned by village collectives. In the urban core, the leading contenders for land parcels are socialist land masters and municipal governments. At the urban fringe, competition occurs between urban governments at the municipal and district levels and rural governments at the township and village levels. While the reconfiguration of the socialist *tiao-kuai* power matrix sets the parameters for land politics in the urban core, China's longstanding rural–urban tension frames the land politics at the urban fringe.

China's rural–urban divide, which is reinforced by the household registration, or hukou system, is a well-documented legacy of the communist regime.[2] There is also extensive literature on the transformation of the rural–urban divide in the post-Mao era. While rapid rural industrialization helped to reduce the rural–urban divide in the prosperous areas of the Pearl River Delta and the lower Yangtze River Delta, the overall rural–urban income gap has grown nationwide, especially since the 2000s.[3] While observers paid much attention to the increasing rural-urban gaps in post-reform China, the tension between the rural and urban government has been largely neglected. I believe that such tension has become a critical axis in China's territorial power restructuring since the 1990s and at its crux is the massive conversion of rural land at the outskirts of the city especially in industrialized areas.[4]

In this chapter, I examine the race between rural and urban governments to convert and develop farmland. While rural governments rode on industrialism and thrived on small and scattered development zones in the 1980s–1990s, urban governments have been consolidating its control over the rural hinterland and launched mega urban projects at the urban fringe in the 2000s. The shift from industrialism of the 1990s to urbanism of the 2000s signifies the formation of an urban-dominant territorial governance system in China, reinforcing the urbanization of local states and their politics.

Urban dominance in territorial governance and land control

During the Maoist era, China's urban and rural areas were governed by separate systems. Within each province were municipal governments that administered only the urban areas of prefectures and counties.[5] Since the majority of the Chinese population and most of the country's land were rural at the time, prefectures and counties commanded greater influence than municipalities over rural resources.

This rural-oriented territorial governance underwent a reversal to an urban-centered system in the early 1980s. Based on the principles of comprehensive regional planning and rural–urban integration initiated in 1982, provincial governments began to convert rural counties and prefectures to urban status by upgrading their territorial ranking or merging them with existing municipalities.[6] When a prefecture is merged into a municipality, rural counties (and the townships under them) that were previously under prefectural administration enter the jurisdiction of the newly created municipality.[7] These new prefecture-level municipalities are, in fact, city regions that include urban centers and vast rural hinterlands within their jurisdiction. The key element of the jurisdictional restructuring was to place the rural hinterland under the administrative authority of municipal governments in a system called "*shi guan xian*" (city-governing counties) or "shi dai xian" (city-leading counties).[8] The hierarchical supervision in China's territorial and bureaucratic system gives the municipal government increased personnel and budgetary autonomy from the supervising provincial government, as well as commanding authority over its rural hinterland and subordinate rural governments at the county and township levels. Higher-ranking municipalities, including the provincial-level municipalities of Beijing, Shanghai, Tianjin, and Chongqing, as well as provincial capitals like Changsha, Zhengzhou, and Nanjing have also converted rural counties into municipal districts and incorporated large areas of rural hinterland with the jurisdiction of the municipalities.[9] Figures 4.1 and 4.2 show the large proportion of rural hinterland under the jurisdiction of large municipalities like Beijing and Nanjing.

"Regional integration of rural and urban areas" has thus shifted the control over rural resources from rural to urban governments. Of these resources, land is the most critical. Urban government control over rural land is further reinforced by a set of legal and administrative institutions. First is the regime of land tenure. The Constitution of People's Republic of China stipulates that urban land belongs to the state and rural land to the collectives; yet, the state retains ultimate claim over "all land in China." The *Land Management Law* further stipulates that the state can requisition any land when it is in the "public interest."[10] Under this principle, those who represent, or claim to represent the state, such as urban governments and state *danwei*, are able to requisition rural land. Although collective land requisitions need to be based on the "public interest," the lack of definition of "public interest" has been taken not as a constraint, but as an excuse of land grabs. In the name of the public interest, urban governments are able to expropriate farmland to build commercial housing complexes, industrial zones, wholesale and retail markets, golf courses, and amusement parks.[11]

A second institutional basis for urban governments' control over rural land is their monopoly of the land market. When China's land-leasehold market was formally established in 1988, a clear distinction was drawn between ownership and use rights. The latter was given a price tag and a fixed period of leasing. But the land-lease market applies only to state-owned land. Village collectives are not allowed to lease rural land to outside investors.[12] Rural land can be leased out only after it is transferred to state ownership through an urban government. The transfer from collective to

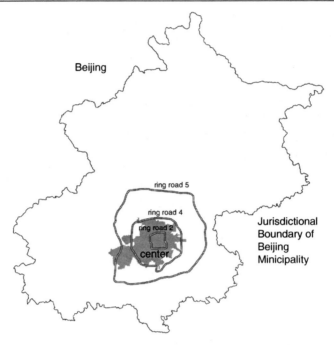

Figure 4.1 Large areas of rural hinterland under Beijing Municipality. Cartographer: Darin Jensen

state land involves lengthy approval procedures and premium fees paid to land management bureaus. And only village collectives, not individual villagers, can initiate land-lease sales.

Parallel to the legal institutions regarding land rights is a new land management regime that emerged in the mid-1980s. A new Ministry of Land Management was established in 1986. Local Bureaus of Land Management were established in the ensuing years. The bureaus at the municipal and district levels are formally recognized as the exclusive representatives of the state in land management.[13] The bureaus are granted authority over farmland conservation and are accordingly granted authority to prepare annual land-use plans, set quotas, and issue licenses for farmland conversion. They are also empowered to requisition and transfer land from collective to state ownership and to monitor land-lease sales.

At the center of land management are quota allocations for farmland conversion. The Ministry of Land Management draws national annual land-use plans and allocates quotas for farmland conversion to individual provinces. Provincial land management bureaus allocate the quotas

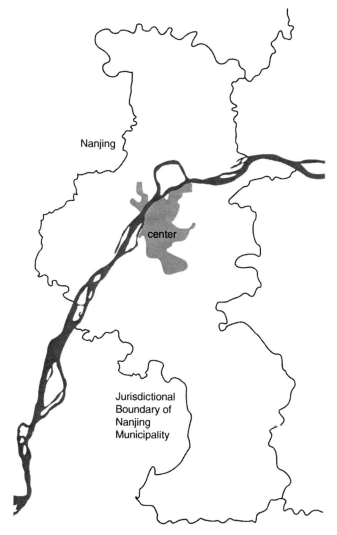

Nanjing

center

Jurisdictional
Boundary of
Nanjing
Municipality

Figure 4.2 Large areas of rural hinterland under Nanjing Municipality. Cartographer: Darin Jensen

down the territorial hierarchy to subprovincial local governments. Urban governments bargain with their supervising government agencies for larger quotas, while townships at the bottom of the hierarchy are usually left with little allocation for farmland conversion. This system, in turn, renders rural governments' farmland conversions automatically illegal in most cases.

Finally, urban governments have the authority to draw legally binding urban development plans. These plans are drawn on the basis of population and economic growth projections, which are often inflated. Inflated growth projections, in turn, help to legitimize urban expansion into rural land, to justify the incorporation of large areas of collective land into planned urban areas, and to freeze land-use conversion by townships and villages. Urban governments therefore come well-equipped for the battle over rural land.

Land battles have gone through two stages and can be characterized by two types of land development. In the 1990s, rural land conversion was dominated by *kaifaqu* (development zones) projects aimed at industrial development. Since around 2000, the new model has been the *xincheng* (New City), which is a much larger mixture of residential, office, and retail space at the fringe of the city. These two types of development reflect the changing territorial politics at different stages of rural land conversion.

Development zones in the 1990s and their predicaments

"Development zone," or *kaifaqu*, was the buzzword of 1990s China. In 1992, Deng Xiaoping's "southern tour" to Shenzhen, the first Special Economic Zone in China, was widely interpreted as a green light for deepening market reforms. Deng's visit to Shenzhen triggered a nationwide "development zone fever." It was estimated that by 1993 there were over 6000 *kaifaqu* nationwide, occupying 15,000 sq km of rural land, exceeding the total built-up area of all the cities in China.[14]

Modeled after the Special Economic Zones,[15] *kaifaqu* were said to aim at promoting rural industrialization, foreign investment, and technology transfer, as well as job provision. The *kaifaqu* fever of the 1990s reflected a highly decentralized pattern of industrialization in China's countryside that was paralleled by the development of the so-called Township and Village Enterprises (TVEs). The TVEs are collective enterprises owned and/ or managed by townships and villages, which were much acclaimed as the engine of the first wave of growth in the post-Mao period. More than half of the *kaifaqu* were initiated and developed by rural governments at the county, township, and village levels for their TVEs.

The geography of *kaifaqu* establishments echoed the pattern of industrial decentralization. Located in villages and towns, they fell under the control of rural governments and were highly dispersed. To develop them, villages and townships converted farmland and built industrial estates and residential complexes for rent, or illegally sold land-use rights to outside developers. The race to convert farmland into *kaifaqu* by rural governments was so fierce that it was dubbed the "land enclosure movement" by commentators in the media and policy circles.

In 1994, responding to signs of an overheated economy, Premier Zhu Rongji launched fiscal austerity programs and tried to cool the development zone fever. Subsequently, the Ministry of Land and Resources took various actions, including a six-month freeze on farmland conversion in 1997. These measures seemed to have slowed the pace of the "land enclosure movement" by the end of the 1990s. But, beginning around 2000, a renewed and even stronger wave of development zone fever gripped China.[16] This time, the scale of the development zones was considerably larger, from 1 to 3 sq km in the early 1990s to 10 to 20 sq km. By 2003, the total area designated for development zones nationwide was estimated to have reached 36,000 sq km, compared with 15,000 sq km in 1993.[17] Lin and Ho (2005) reported that of the 18,100 hectare of illegal land conversion and sales recorded in 2002, 76 percent were undertaken by state agencies and collectives.[18] As to the illegal authorization of land conversion, county governments were responsible for nearly half of the total, while townships and villages were responsible for 11 and 31 percent, respectively.[19] Po Ren (2003) suggests that the so-called new land enclosure movement (*xin quandi yundong*) of the early 2000s was predominantly initiated by governments at the county level, and especially the township level.[20] By 2002, among the 3837 registered *kaifaqu* in China, 68 percent were approved by local governments at the municipal, district, and county levels, and more than half were operated by townships and villages.[21]

Over time, the economic and political viability of the *kaifaqu* strategy was brought increasingly into question. According to the Ministry of Land and Resources, in the 900-plus provincial-level *kaifaqu* nationwide, only 13.5 percent of 2 million hectare of designated *Kaifaqu* area was actually developed.[22] In other words, more than 85 percent of the converted and vacated land was "baking under the sun." These were only the official figures. In interviews, county and township planners and leaders admitted that some of their *kaifaqu* were not included in the official data.[23]

The demise of *kaifaqu* must be understood in the context of the changing economic and sociopolitical discourse of the late 1990s and early 2000s.

First, *kaifaqu* were not the effective growth generators that local governments had expected. The mid-1990s saw waves of industrial restructuring in rural China. The widely heralded small- and medium-sized TVEs with low technology and capital thresholds began to lose their advantages in increasingly competitive domestic and international markets. Many TVEs turned into financial liabilities for local governments and many went bankrupt.[24]

As the small manufacturers, who were the major tenants in *kaifaqu* began to decline, local governments and developers found it increasingly difficult to attract outside investors. In response, local governments would offer land for free in exchange for an investment commitment. The political logic was that land-lease sales and development projects in *kaifaqu* could boost local GDP growth figures and help local leaders' performance evaluations. But the final result was stagnant local government revenues and swollen local government debt.[25]

In other words, while selling *kaifaqu* land cheap was politically advantageous in the short term, it was an ineffective approach for local accumulation and eventually became a political liability. In the media, local government leaders were criticized for their myopia and the immense losses in state assets as a result of their reckless offers of rural land at extremely low prices. Failed *kaifaqu* dotted the countryside.

One might have expected that such ineffective accumulation tactics would have sent local governments back to the drawing board to revise their strategies. Yet, the economic factor alone was hardly sufficient to induce change. Another driving force came from the changing sociopolitical discourse at the turn of the millennium that began to stress the "three agricultural problems" and the central policy of land-oriented "macroeconomic adjustment and control."

Rural unrest triggered by land grabs was on the rise in the early 2000s due to violent and forced eviction of peasants and unfair compensation. In July 2002, a township head of Hubei Province, Li Changping, wrote an open letter to Party Secretary Wen Jiabao to reveal three interrelated agricultural problems: decline in agricultural output, deterioration of rural villages, and destitution of peasants. The letter triggered a wave of public discussion in the media and intellectual circles about peasants' desolation, local cadre corruption, and social injustice, after decades of relentless growth at the expense of peasants. The "three agricultural problems" were then placed at the top of the central government's policy agenda under the new Hu Jintao-Wen Jiabao regime. In addition to the concern over social instability in rural areas, the central government and party leaders were alarmed by the connection between massive farmland loss and national food security, as well as the enormous loss of state assets through low-level cadres' illicit farmland conversion and land-lease sales.

Land issues also gained political momentum through the discourse of "macroeconomic adjustment and control." In 2000, a new run of macroeconomic expansion began in the wake of the 1997 Asian financial crisis. The upturn of the early 2000s was generated mainly in the real estate sector.[26] After *danwei* housing was abolished, real-estate markets, especially the commodity-housing sector, grew at 30 percent a year and became the engine of growth in many cities. The rapid expansion of the early 2000s soon raised central leaders' concern over a possible overheating of the economy. In 2003, as GDP growth reached 10 percent, another run of macroeconomic adjustment began.[27]

As in earlier occasions, the central leadership announced a series of macroeconomic policies to try and cool the economy. But this round of macroeconomic contraction differed from earlier similar moves in important ways. For the first time, land was brought in as a primary policy tool for macroeconomic adjustment. Along with the other tools of monetary and fiscal control, such as tightening credit for property development projects and second homebuyers,[28] control of land supplies was considered a fundamental cure for excessive investment. This land-focused macroeconomic adjustment and control method was followed by a series of policies and government actions.

In March 2004, the Ministry of Land and Resources and the Ministry of Supervision jointly announced the No. 71 Document, which stated that privately negotiated land leases would be invalidated and, if leasing fees were not fully paid and official development approvals not obtained by August 31, 2004, the land parcels in question would be reclaimed by the state to be put in the land reserve.[29] Farmland conversion and land-use plan revisions were frozen for six months.[30] Following this, a decision from the State Council was passed that tightened control over farmland conversion and transfer through more rigorous approval procedures. Premier Wen Jiabao announced the decision in a nationally televised conference in December 2004.[31] The Ministry of Land and Resources subsequently announced eleven supplementary ordinances, announcements, and opinions concerning farmland protection and compensation rates.[32]

In addition to policy announcements the central government took a series of actions against the chaotic development. The authority to approve farmland conversion and lease sales was transferred from rural to municipal and provincial governments at the end of 2003.[33] In 2004, the Ministry of

Land and Resources and six other central agencies sent joint work teams on land auditing tours to various provinces and municipalities. The organization of a joint force of seven ministries was unprecedented. Rural *kaifaqu* were the main target of the central government's investigation campaign. Land parcels that were leased out but not fully paid for, not officially approved, or not developed within two years were taken back to the state land reserve system. The action resulted in the abolition of 4813 *kaifaqu*, or 70 percent of the 6866 *kaifaqu* nationwide. In terms of land area, about 24,900 sq km, or 64.5 percent of the total area earmarked for *kaifaqu*, was ordered into the state land reserve.[34]

The unprecedented attention given to land issues seemed to have effectively put local officials on alert. A local government official commented: "Once the central government elevates the policy to the level of macroeconomic adjustment and control, we know that they are serious this time."[35] Indeed, the State Council's decision explicitly stated that local government and party cadres would be held responsible for farmland conservation and rational utilization of land.[36] Farmland conservation became a major criterion in local cadres' performance evaluations.[37]

As a result, *kaifaqu* were no longer the embodiment of modernity and of local leaders' political achievements. Instead, they were evidence of the peasants' plight and local cadre corruption. Slogans declaring "development is the absolute principle" and calling for "deepening market reform and improving the material conditions of people's lives," which were frequently seen on the walls of *kaifaqu* in the 1990s, were replaced by new slogans demanding "growth management" and "rational utilization of land." As the new whipping boy in official discourse, *kaifaqu* were easy targets for attack.[38]

In short, the concept of *kaifaqu* lost momentum by the end of the 1990s and was unable to fulfill the task of effective accumulation for local governments. The small and scattered industrial establishments neither contributed to sustainable rural industrialization nor to local government finance. The emerging sociopolitical discourse of "three agricultural problems" and "macroeconomic adjustment and control" also made it increasingly risky for county and township leaders to convert village land for *kaifaqu* projects.

'New Cities' in the 2000s: new players and new strategies

Weakened rural governments and the decline of rural industrialism did not slow down the conversion of rural land, however. In the 2000s, a new set of

5. Zhengzhou New Town (May 2006)

players with greater political and economic clout began to dominate the process of conversion, sale, and development of rural land. These were urban governments at the prefecture or subprovincial levels. In this chapter, I refer to them by the general term "urban government."

As mentioned earlier, urban governments have authority over a hierarchically organized set of jurisdictions that include urban districts and rural counties and townships. In other words, rural governance falls under the authority of the urban government.

For urban governments, the scattered *kaifaqu* of the 1990s and early 2000s represented a major challenge to their territorial authority over the rural hinterlands within their jurisdiction. Many small, rural *kaifaqu* were neither administered by urban governments,[39] nor did they go through the formal approval procedure for farmland conversion and project construction.

The fragmented *kaifaqu* development in the 1990s exposed the urban governments' limited authority over their territory. Yet, as urban populations and economic diversity grew, the need to expand into the rural hinterlands became imperative, not only for industrial growth but also for expansion of all types of urban functions, including housing, commerce, and services. Bolstered by the new discourse against *kaifaqu* and legitimized by new macroeconomic adjustment policies, urban governments came up with a new set of strategies to consolidate rural land for urban expansion.

These new strategies were epitomized by *xincheng* (New City) projects at the urban fringe. While *kaifaqu* were mainly industrial estates, *xincheng* promised a new city built on rice paddies. Because *kaifaqu* were framed in the language of industrialization, the measure of their success was growth in industrial output. By contrast, *xincheng* were carried out as mixed-use real-estate projects to build new urban space for commercial, residential, cultural, and administrative activities. Their success was measured by property value increases. Where *kaifaqu* builders commodified farmland, *xincheng* planners and developers treated the totality of urban space as a commodity.[40]

By the early 2000s, *xincheng* had replaced *kaifaqu* as the buzzword of the era. The *xincheng* fever was encapsulated with a new jargon calling for "*chengshi yunying,*" translated approximately as "urban operation and management." Developers called themselves "*chengshi yunying shang*" (businessmen of urban management). Urban government leaders aspired to follow the principle of urban operation and management to transform the city. But urban government leaders were concerned with more than urban management. *Chengshi yunying* was a version of urban entrepreneurialism, with a clear purpose to "create value in the city." "Value" referred to property values, and the way to create property value was to follow the logic of the real-estate market.[41] Unlike *kaifaqu* builders in rural townships and villages who brokered small pieces of farmland for sale or rent, ambitious urban government leaders have acted as the chief planners and developers of mega-urban projects.

A trio of strategies can be found in *xincheng* projects forming a synchronized set of accumulation programs directed toward place production, place consumption, and place marketing.

Place production: creating locational advantage

The primary logic of real estate is location. Urban governments have long used planning, zoning, and infrastructure investment to create locational advantage and to increase property values in designated places. In urban infrastructure plans, the designation of transit routes and the allocation of urban services (schools, hospitals, sports facilities, parks) all affect property value and the potential for increases in value. Zoning as a tool of modern urban planning is used to define the type and intensity of land uses. Zones that have a strong commercial appeal and high quality of life command high land rents. While new and upgraded transit systems and other urban infrastructure help open up real-estate frontiers and increase property values, zoning stabilizes values.

Urban planning was also popular with rural government leaders in the 1990s. But in the 1990s, planning was employed mostly to justify rural land enclosure for *kaifaqu*, while zoning was mainly a tool to categorize land and put a price tag on parcels.[42] Development plans sought to sell rural land at its current worth instead of increasing the value of land; detailed subdivision plans and coordination were generally absent. In many cases, individual townships and villages would build their own small roads, but the roads were not incorporated into regional transit networks, making it difficult to connect the scattered industrial estates with major urban centers. This led to the failure of many *kaifaqu* projects. Even where *kaifaqu* attracted investment, local governments had little control over the direction of land development once the land-use rights were sold to developers, and local government could benefit little from property value increases after developers took over the land.

In *xincheng* projects, urban planning was approached more proactively and strategically. Old-fashioned economic planning (*jihua*) and urban planning (*guihua*) were replaced by strategic planning (*cehua*), a term borrowed from business management and marketing. Real-estate developers and marketing gurus were hired to advise mayors on directions of urban operation and management. Strategic urban planning is now the *sine qua non* for pioneers on China's new real-estate frontier. As Li Yuanchao, the Party Secretary of Nanjing Municipality candidly pointed out:

> The urban government does not always have control over all urban land; urban planning has thus become the most precious and important resource for the urban government. Good planning is a source of tremendous wealth....Nanjing's Hexi New City Plan has gained attention and attracted investment worth 12 billion yuan.... Urban planning facilitates urban management and improves the level of modernization.[43]

Indeed, Nanjing's Hexi project serves as a good example of city government initiatives to generate locational advantage at the urban fringe. Nanjing was the on-again, off-again capital of imperial China for almost 500 years since the third century, and is now one of twelve "super-large cities" (*chaoda chengshi*) in China, with a population of 7.4 million, as of 2007.[44] Located 291 km west of Shanghai, Nanjing's growth in the 1990s was slower than that of Shanghai and other cities like Suzhou and Wuxi in the lower Yangtze River Delta.[45] In 2001, Nanjing was chosen as the site of the Tenth National Games. Nanjing municipal leaders seized on the opportunity to "wake up the old city that has been asleep for too long."[46] In 2002, the Nanjing party secretary announced the new Hexi *xincheng* development plan on the western bank of Yangtze River, which divides Nanjing into two parts. While the eastern part of the city was highly urbanized, Hexi, literally "west of the river," had long been a backwater. Like Shanghai's Pudong area prior to the 1990s, land in Hexi was undesirable.

With the expansion plan for the Hexi *xincheng*, municipal leaders and planners are determined to transform the image of Hexi to an up-and-coming new city center. Hexi *xincheng* was to become a new urban center, zoned for modern corporate office buildings, public monumental projects like museums, universities, and sports centers, upscale commercial establishments, residences, hotels, and other tourism-convention facilities.

6. Commodity housing in Hexi New Town (May 2006)

The planned Hexi *xincheng* covers an area of 56 sq km, 14 sq km larger than the total area of the old city. Echoing the principle of urban operation and management, the executive chief of the project committed himself to "promoting real estate development and increasing land values."[47] Between 2001 and 2004, a new underwater tunnel for rapid rail transit was built to connect the new city with the old. Another 100 km of roads, thirty-seven bridges, and seven connecting canals were constructed.

Key to Hexi *xincheng* is the strategy to increase the government's share on the newly generated property values. Leaders of Nanjing municipality had learned their lesson the hard way. In the mid-1990s, the government announced plans for several "new cities" with a total area of 94 sq km at the eastern fringe of the city, and to build a subway that would connect the old city center with the new cities. The announcement immediately triggered land battles among developers, who rushed to negotiate joint development projects with villages and townships located along the planned transit line. Land prices rose more than tenfold in one year. Some developers earned windfall profits from commercial housing projects built along the subway line, and the municipal government, which had invested in the transit line, was mocked for "working for the developers."[48] Nanjing municipal leaders were shrewder for the Hexi project. They first drew the general urban development plan and incorporated large areas of village land into the plan. Incorporated rural land was turned into state land and put in municipal reserves. Then the government announced the plan to build Hexi *xincheng* and a second subway line from the old city. The municipal government borrowed heavily to make the initial investment in infrastructure, and announced the transit system to pique investor interest. The initial infrastructure construction made the plan convincing, allowing the municipal government to begin to sell land-use rights along the new line. As most land parcels with good prospects were already in the hands of the government, developers, investors had to go through municipal open land auctions and pay a premium price for the land.[49]

As the opening anecdote of this chapter shows, development sites at the metropolitan fringe save urban governments from becoming mired in land rights entanglements, compensation payments, and high political costs of inner-city redevelopment projects. In turn, the relative ease, low risk, and low cost of appropriating village farmland help city governments accumulate large land reserves. Land reserves are critical to real-estate operations for several reasons. First, land is the most critical raw material in urban development, but supply of land, especially premium land, is highly unpredictable. Large land reserves are a way to minimize risks, and assure steady expansion of *xincheng* projects. Second, the spatial logic is compounded by a temporal concern: reserves allow for the building of multiphased projects over a long period of time. The initial phase of a *xincheng* project may occupy a few square kilometers of land, but a much larger area of land, usually several times larger than that of the initial phase, is normally set aside for future development as property values increase with the growth of investment and population density. Land reserves ensure long-term returns that justify huge initial investments in infrastructure. Banking enough land to accommodate multiphased development projects is crucial for achieving economies of scale in infrastructure provision, construction costs, and property management. Large land areas that can accommodate multi-phased projects make it possible to develop a multifunctional new city with diverse and complementary urban activities. For example, industrial projects attract workers who create demand for new housing; increasing population, in turn, creates demand for more commercial services. Finally, land reserves are integral to project finance. Because most *xincheng* projects are heavily financed by bank loans, reserved land can be used as collateral. In addition, in order to maintain cash flow and manage bank-loan payments effectively, developers need to simultaneously have multiple projects at different stages of the product cycle. Projects currently at the selling stage are used to service loans for projects at the construction stage. This financial strategy can be effective only with sufficient land reserves.[50]

Place consumption: the economy of demolition and relocation

Mass production of new urban space requires mass consumption. As more than 80 percent of the new projects in the 2000s have been primarily residential, sufficient demand for new housing needs to be created. Housing demand is stimulated by policy moves, such as granting urban residency (*hukou*) to rural migrant homebuyers in the city, as many cities and towns did in the 1980s and 1990s, and by abolishing *danwei* welfare housing and providing low-interest mortgages for commodity housing, as has been done since the late 1990s. Massive and systematic demolition of old housing through urban redevelopment also makes purchasing new homes imperative. The causal connection between massive demolition of old homes and the creation of demand for new housing is popularly known as the "economy of demolition and relocation" (*chaiqian jingji*). It is an explicit strategy of "urban operation and management." In a press interview, the executive mayor of Chengdu in Sichuan Province explained his calculation as follows: "Every square meter of housing that I demolish will create a demand of 2.5 to 3.0 square meters of new commodity housing."[51]

In cities like Chengdu, Wuhan and Nanjing, where the demand for new housing comes mainly from local buyers, the volume of demolition and relocation has an immediate impact on the local housing market and housing prices. In Nanjing, for example, in order to guarantee stable demand for new housing projects, the municipal government lowered mortgage rates from 2 to 0.75 percent, and granted Nanjing *hukou* to homebuyers from outside of the city.[52] The government also launched massive housing demolition and relocation in the old city. Between 2001 and 2003, 80,000 homes were demolished. Households received compensation payments ranging from 1000 to 5000 yuan per square meter, which were locked in special accounts earmarked for new home purchases. About 37 percent of the compensation payments went directly to the market for new housing. Although a majority of those relocated could not afford new housing and went to the second-hand housing market, their moves nevertheless helped boost the demand for existing homes and enabled original owners to purchase new housing. Most households relocated from inner-city areas could not afford new homes on-site and were either assigned relocation housing or they purchased new homes in urban fringe areas. In other words, inner-city redevelopment created a demand for new commercial housing at the urban periphery where the *xincheng* projects were located.

A variant of *xincheng* projects, called University Towns (*daxuecheng*), gained popularity among expansionist city leaders, beginning in the mid-2000s. These massive projects incur heavy indebtedness and involve high risks. Despite the "economy of demolition and relocation," the market demand for upscale commercial housing and office space in the urban fringe is quite uncertain. In fact, many *xincheng* projects planned by expansionist city governments, such as Guangzhou's Zhujiang New City failed because of insufficient demand for the large number of posh apartment units far from the urban center. The lack of market demand caused the project to flounder and it became a political liability for the municipal leader.[53]

University Towns have breathed new life into new city schemes. They are, by definition, towns built for universities, most of which are located in large cities. Most universities in China went through a process of campus mergers in the early 2000s under a policy of university consolidation. Minor and specialized universities and colleges were incorporated into the leading universities of the city.[54] Meanwhile, in the 1990s and 2000s came a surge in university enrollment, induced by a policy of self-reliance in university budgets. Campuses lowered the entry threshold for students in order to boost university revenue from fees and tuition. Expanded enrollment was also a result of increasingly competitive job markets and the increase in urban household incomes, which made it more urgent and affordable for parents to invest in their children's higher education. As a result, university enrollment increased from about 2 million in 1990 to more than 15 million in 2005, averaging 14.4 percent growth annually.[55] Large universities also began to devote parts of their central city campuses to commercial development while expanding into the suburbs.

Amid macroeconomic contraction in the early 2000s, education and research were among the few types of land use that enjoyed strong political legitimacy. Building new University Towns of 10 to 20 sq km or more turned out to be a viable territorial expansion strategy. New campuses helped the universities accommodate the swelling numbers of students, the majority of whom live in or around the campus, while the sudden influx of 30,000–100,000 students brought instant life to the new city. By contrast, in conventional new towns, housing projects often remain vacant for an extended period of time. The lack of people and commercial activity in huge, empty new towns can become a political and economic liability, whereas dorms and campus buildings in university towns are politically legitimate, and are immediately filled with students trapped in the urban fringe, far from the city center. College students and staff provide a captive market for commercial establishments. New campus buildings also give providers of power, water, means of transportation, and telecommunication the incentive to invest in utilities and services, making the new university town more livable than many suburban projects.[56]

University towns also face easier relocation negotiations with peasants. In the University Town in Jinan, Shandong Province, which I visited in December 2007, relocated peasants rented out extra rooms in their relocation housing units to students. Unlike the corporatist villagers presented in Chapter 5, whose central location attracts countless migrant workers and entrepreneurs as tenants, university towns are too far from jobs and commercial centers. University students fill the void. Cheap rooms in substandard relocation housing are affordable for college students, and the rents are an important source of income for relocated peasants. In short, university towns enjoy immediate success thanks to large public universities that serve as motivated investors and large numbers of students corralled into the new town. After the initial stage, as students bring life to the new town, investors are attracted to its commercial projects, office parks, and luxury condos in subsequent development phases. Jinan's university town, for example, is a part of a 43-sq km "university and high technology town," which plans to include 12 universities accommodating 240,000 students, high-tech parks, convention and entertainment centers, hotels, residential projects, hospitals, and other commercial establishments.[57]

Place marketing: spectacles and "New Urbanism"

Competition between cities for outside investment is not new to China. *Kaifaqu* projects often offered favorable investment packages to investors, including generous tax breaks, low-cost land, and subsidized utility and infrastructure provision. Most important in the era of *kaifaqu* were aspects mainly tied to production costs, such as investment packages, labor costs, and production-related infrastructure. In the 2000s, with the shift to *xincheng* as the preferred local development strategy, and with the shift in priorities from industrial output to property values, competition between cities became a far more sophisticated operation of image production and city marketing. The new economy, according to the media and business magazines, is an "economy of spectacle," or *yanqiu jingji*. The image of modernity and prosperity that gets public attention is expected to attract investors and visitors, and thus boost property values.[58]

Spectacles can be created by spotlight events like the 2008 Olympic Games in Beijing, the 2010 World Expo in Shanghai, annual international trade fairs in Guangzhou, and high-tech fairs in Shenzhen. These spectacles are systematically exploited. To host the 2010 World Expo, the Shanghai Municipal Government has established a new agency called the World Expo Bureau and a new government-owned World Expo Investment company, and drew up a special Detailed Subdivision Plan of the 6 sq km-plus site for the Expo in central Shanghai, supported by the new Shanghai World Expo Land Reserve Center in charge of land acquisition and lease sales. The excitement over the international event, along with the urban government's commitment of astronomical infrastructure investments, and the removal of 18,000 households and 270 enterprises from the site, which lies in the city center, have triggered a veritable real-estate frenzy. Since 2002, upon announcement of the 2010 World Expo, Shanghai has experienced its largest building boom and property value hikes since the 1980s. Between 2002 and the end of 2004, the average housing price in the city increased by about 60 percent. The real-estate fever was cooled only slightly after the central government started to tighten land and credit supplies in mid-2005.[59]

Similarly, the 2008 Olympic Games in Beijing boosted property values in the western part of the city, where the sports facilities are concentrated. A government official estimated that property values had increased between

20 and 30 percent.[60] Other cities have maneuvered to organize spectacles on a smaller scale, like the 2005 Tenth National Games in Nanjing and Wuhan's 2006 Eighth National Art Festival. Just as the Tenth National Games inspired the Hexi *xincheng* project, the Eighth National Art Festival gave rise to Wuhan's Hangyang *xincheng* project in 2003. Hexi *xincheng* became the hot spot for property sales in Nanjing in 2003 and 2004. The average price of housing more than doubled from 2000 yuan per square meter in 2002 to more than 5000 yuan per square meter in 2004. As prices in Hexi New City rose, the average housing prices in older parts of Nanjing were also boosted.

But major events are one-offs that do not necessarily sustain excitement and investment. Cities require spectacles that provide a longer-term effect on the image of the city as a growth center. Visually striking monumental structures, such as the tallest building in the world, the country, or the region, are a favorite among government leaders, as exemplified by Shanghai's 94-story (460-m) World Financial Center and the twin towers planned by the Guangzhou Municipal Government for its Zhujiang *xincheng* project.

Establishment of Central Business Districts (CBD) is another long-term strategy in the quest for image creation and real estate accumulation. High-density urban cores, where business services and high-end retail is concentrated, enjoy premium land rents, often the highest in the city. CBDs and their high-rise offices have come to symbolize modern business and global connections far removed from the socialist and industrialist past. The image of dense urbanity also appeals to young, urbane professionals, who aspire to live and work in a milieu of cosmopolitan flair and sophistication. Since it takes years to complete a CBD project, the city government begins to cash in on the project early on by making the plan itself a spectacle. Pictures of the mayor shaking hands with brand-name foreign planners and architects in charge of project design are regularly splashed across the front pages of local newspapers and feature on TV programs, against backgrounds of colorful maps showing the promise of the city's future. Cities also race to build glitzy, room-sized models of urban development plans with future CBDs and skyscrapers as centerpieces. The flashy exhibition centers become a part of the urban spectacle, charging high entrance fees to tourists.

The CBD symbolizes modernity and potential property-value increases. More than half the projects in the CBDs are luxury condos, with retail space located at the ground floors. Developers invent new terms, like Central Living Districts (*zhongyang juzhuqu*, CLDs,), Central Cultural Districts (*zhongyang wenhuaqu*, CCDs) for residential projects with private schools or galleries attached, and Recreational Business District (*xiuxian shangwuqu*, RBDs) for complexes with residential space, personal services, hotels, and restaurants.

According to a survey commissioned by the Ministry of Construction, by 2003, thirty-six cities were planning or building CBDs in their *xincheng* projects. Among these cities were Beijing, Shanghai, Tianjin, and Chongqing, ten provincial capitals, including Wuhan, Chengdu, Nanjing, Jinan, and Fuzhou, and large coastal cities like Shenzhen, Xiamen, Dalian, and nine other prefecture-level, and even county-level cities like Xiangfan, Huainan, Wenzhou, and Wuyi.[61] Even projects located two hours' drive from the official CBD are advertised as being located in the "pan-CBD" area. Other projects farther away from the center are referred to as "upper-CBD," "lower-CBD," or "in the backyard of a CBD."

The key word in the CBD fanfare is "central." It refers not only to physical, but also to social and cultural centrality in order to appeal to investors and buyers. It signifies an emerging cultural discourse of "neo-urbanism," often mentioned in Beijing and Shanghai fashion magazines. Displaying all the acumen of capitalist marketers, developers in Beijing pointed out: "Selling houses is not selling a commodity but a lifestyle."[62] And not just any lifestyle, but a new urban lifestyle promoted by design professionals, advertisement agencies, and real-estate developers. The images of a modern urban person are not necessarily homogeneous, as reflected in the diverse names of commodity housing projects, some of which borrow names from luxurious Western resorts like "Seventeen-Mile Drive" of coastal California, while others appropriate traditional Chinese symbols of political and cultural status like Royal Garden. The new housing projects echo and shape the urban dwellers' visions of modern living.

From industrialism to new urbanism

In this chapter, I have focused on the evolution of land politics at the urban fringe from the 1990s to the 2000s (see Table 4.1). Whereas *kaifaqu* represent a high degree of decentralization over land control and the active role of rural governments in the 1980s and early 1990s, *xincheng* projects represent city governments' efforts to consolidate the territorial authority over the rural hinterland in the 2000s.

Based on a chronological and typological analysis, I made two interconnected arguments concerning the relationship between land and state power restructuring in the rural and urban interface areas. The first concerns the shift from parallel systems of rural and urban governance under Mao to

Table 4.1 Comparison of Development Zone of the 1990s and New City of the 2000s

	kaifaqu (Development Zone) of the 1990s	*xincheng* (New City) of the 2000s
Political discourse	Industrialism	Urbanism
Main local state actors	Rural County, Township, and Village governments	Cities at the prefecture level and above
Role of state actor	Collective enterprise managers	Urban promoter and developer
Project type	Industrial parks and small scale housing complex	Mixed-use "new cities" that include residential, commercial and service
Spatial pattern	Small-scale, scattered in rural hinterland	Large-scale, concentrated around urban fringe
Strategy	Offering favorable investment packages and low land prices to industrial investors	Engaging in urban place production, marketing, and consumption
Role of Urban Planning	Passive justification of farmland conversion for industrial uses	Active incorporation of rural land as urban development reserves; creating locational advantage to increase property values
Measure of success	Industrial output and GDP contribution from industrial output	Increase of property price; GDP contribution from real estate and infrastructure investment
Implication for Urban-centered Territorial Governance	Unmanageable decentralization led by undisciplined rural cadres in townships and villages	Consolidation of territorial authority in the hands of large municipalities that function as leading cities of metropolitan regions

urban governments' dominance over rural areas in the post-Mao era. The second suggests that urban governments' control over rural areas is built on land development at the urban fringe through an integrated logic of the state and the market, in which the city government strategizes for territorial expansion are intertwined with real-estate strategies of place production, consumption, and marketing. The result of these dynamics is the formation of new urbanism in post-Deng China.

This new urbanism is more than a real-estate marketing strategy. Compared with Maoist policy that associated urban agendas with industrial production, the new urbanism embraces a regime of accumulation and legitimation founded on land rents. Compared to rural industrialism during the first phase of China's reforms, new urbanism is distinctive in its privileging of place production over industrial production. As city leaders rely on urban expansion for territorial consolidation, accumulation, and legitimation, and identify themselves as city builders and boosters, and as urban construction dominates local development agendas, urban modernity, rather than industrial modernity, has become the hegemonic ideology of the new era.

Yet, urbanism, like any -ism, is more of an orientation of action and ideology than a static condition or achievement. Urbanism facilitates and is facilitated by the changing power dynamics among state actors and their relationship with capital. While not all urban projects succeed, urbanism nevertheless defines and confines the local state. urbanism underlies the political-economic and cultural logic of urbanized municipal government in the urban core, as elaborated in chapter 2. In this chapter, I have outlined the urbanized politics between the rural and urban governments at the urban fringe.

In what follows, I again turn to society. I examine society's response to rapid urban expansion. Diverging from inner city residents' confrontational resistance to displacement, as depicted in chapter 3, villagers at the urban fringe managed to bargain with the urban government and share a piece of the growing urban real estate market.

Notes

1. Interview BJ0405, Beijing, August 2004.
2. For a study of the hukou system and urbanization, see Chan, Kam Wing, *Cities with Invisible Walls*, 1994.
3. For China's rural–urban divide under communism, see Kirkby, Richard, *Urbanization in China*, 1985. The income disparity between rural and urban residents was reduced between 1978 and 1984, then it began to widen. In 2008, the Minister of Agriculture reported that 2007 saw an increase of 9.5 percent of peasants' per capita income, the highest rise since 1985. Yet, the income ratio between urban and rural dwellers also climbed to 3.33:1, or 9646 yuan in absolute terms, the largest since reform began. See Jing, Hua *"chengxiang jumin shouruchaju jinwanyuan"* (Rural–urban income gap almost reaches 10,000 yuan mark), 2008. The China Academy of Social Sciences also reported in its 2008 report on population and labor that the absolute rural–urban income gap increased 12-fold between 1990–2007. Yu, Chengyao, *"2008 nian sanjidu jingji pingshu"* (Economic commentary of the third quarter of 2008, 2008. For a recent review of the complexity of economic inequality in China that goes beyond the rural–urban dichotomy and coastal/inland regions, see Zhou, Yingying, Han Hua, and Stevan Harrell, "From Labour to Capital," 2008.
4. Massive conversion of rural land for urban projects since the 1980s, especially in the eastern coastal regions is well-documented. For a review of land conversion see Ho, Samuel and George Lin, "Emerging land markets in rural and urban

China: policies and practices," 2003. The definition and calculation of China's urban expansion and urban population growth have long been controversial, due to the use of multiple criteria and reporting flaws. For discussion on the complexity, see Ma, Laurence and Gonghao Cui, "Administrative changes and urban population in China," 1987; and Zhang, Li and Simon X. B. Zhao, "Re-examining China's "urban" concept and the level of urbanization," 1998. More recent work suggests that it is safe to accept the figure of 36–40 percent as "urban." That is, between 1980–2002, the urban population grew from 18–20 percent of the overall population to 36–40 percent of the total population, or, about 250 million in total were added to the urban population. See Lin, George C. S., "The growth and structural change of Chinese cities," 2002; and Zhou, Yixing and Laurence J. C. Ma, "China's urbanization levels," 2003.

5. Chung, Jae Ho and Tao-chiu Lam, "'City system' in flux 2004.
6. There are two types of "cities" below the provinces: prefecture-level municipalities with administrative authority over several districts (in urbanized areas) and counties (in rural areas) and county-level municipalities that are upgraded to municipal status mostly after 1986.
7. In 1985, there were 162 prefecture-level cities; by 2005 the number had risen to 283, an increase of 121 in 20 years. The population of prefecture-level cities ranged from 710,000 to 10,750,000 Online. See <http://www.xzqh.org/yange/2003.htm>, accessed on June 1, 2006.
8. For the difference between a "city leading county" and a "city governing county," see Chung and Lam, "'City system' in flux," 2004; and Ma, Laurence, "Urban administrative restructuring, changing scale relations and local economic development in China," 2005.
9. Between 1985–2005, the most notable change in China's territorial organization is the massive increase of the number of municipalities and the decline of rural-based prefectures and counties. During these 20 years, the number of cities increased from 324 to 661, while the number of prefectures declined from 165 to 50. By the end of 2005, 15 provinces and autonomous districts had abolished all prefectures, turned them into prefecture-level cities, and implemented the system of "city leading counties." At the level of counties, there were 2046 counties in 1985, reduced to 1636 by 2005, as a result of annexation by cities or upgrades to become county-level cities. The increase in county-level cities was most rapid during the mid-1980s and mid-1990s, the boom period of rural industrialization. See Zheng, Dingquan, *"Jin 20 nian woguo difang xingzheng quhua de bianhua"* (Changes in local jurisdictions in China in the past 20 years), 2007.
10. PRC Constitution, Article 10. *PRC Land Management Law* (first adopted in 1986, amended in 1988, 1998, and 2004), Article 2.
11. According to a survey of the 200 largest projects in 11 counties of an unidentified province in 1992, only 21 percent of appropriated land was used for public purposes like roads and schools, 5 percent for governmental agencies, and 74

percent for commercial projects. See Lin, Mingyi, Lu Yuejin, and Zhou Zhenglu, *"Shiluan jinjiao chengshihua jingcheng zhongde nongmin jiti tudi chanquan zhidu jianshe"* (Establishing a peasants' collective landed property rights system in the process of urbanization in suburban areas), 2004.

12. Since 2001, several provinces and municipalities, including Zhejiang, Jiangsu, Anhui, Guangdong, and Beijing have selected certain cities and towns in their jurisdictions to experiment with new policies for "rural construction land circulation" without the urban government's interference. See Xie, Wei, Liao Ailing, and Xie Yanjun, *"Beijing tupo tudi guanlifa xianzhi jiansheyundi shidian liuzhuan"* (Beijing breaks away from *Land Management Law*, experiments with circulation of (rural) construction land), 2004.

13. Wu, Fulong, "The new structure of building provision and the transformation of the urban landscape in metropolitan Guangzhou, China," 1998.

14. Yeh, Anthony Gar-an, and Fulong Wu, "The new land development process and urban development in Chinese cities," 1996.

15. For a critical review of the Shenzhen Special Economic Zone, see Cartier, Carolyn, "Zone Fever", 2001, and Wu, Weiping, *Pioneering Economic Reform in China's Special economic Zones*, 1999.

16. Interview BJ0312 (a high-ranking official of the Ministry of Land and Resources), Beijing, August 2003.

17. Yeh and Wu, "The new land development process and urban development in Chinese cities," p. 345. Another feature of this revived development zone fever of the 2000s is that the land use of new zones was much more diverse. They no longer concentrated on industrial projects. Instead, more zones were planned for residential, commercial, and recreational purposes.

18. See Lin, George, and Samuel Ho, "The state, land system, and land development processes in contemporary China," 2005.

19. This was only the official figure. A high-ranking official of the Ministry of Land and Resources admitted that the actual figure was higher than the official one. Interview BJC0312, Beijing, August 2003. Also, a vice director at the Procuratorate in Hubei province stated in his investigative report that the number of unreported cases far exceeded the reported ones. Most of the cases are resolved by fines instead of recovering the land for farm uses. See Xu, Hanming, *Zhjongguo nongmin tudi chiyou chanquan zhidu yanjiu* (Study on Chinese Farmers' Property Rights of Land), 2004, p. 140.

20. Ren, Po, *"Xinquandi yundong molu"* (The end of the "new land enclosure"), 2003.

21. Similarly, according to Liu Neng's survey of villages in Shandong, since 1995 there had been a visible decrease in both state expropriation and individual housing projects in the total farmland conversion to non-farm uses. Yet, township- and village-initiated projects increased from less than 20 percent to almost 80 percent of total converted areas in sample villages. See Liu, Neng, *"Xiangzhen yunxing jizhide yici jiepo"* (An analysis of the mechanism of township operation), 2000.

22. Ma, Hongshou, Zhou Renjie, Xiong Manling, and Su Yan, *"Zhongguo xuyao duoshao CBD?"* (How many CBDs does China need?), 2003.
23. Interviews SHXS9601 (head planner of a town in Shanghai Municipality), Shanghai, May 1996; SHSJ 9702 (a township head in Shanghai Municipality), Shanghai, July 1997; SH9501 (professor and consultant of city planning in Shanghai), Shanghai, April 1995; GZPY980401 (a planning official in Guangzhou), Guangzhou, October 1997, July 2004.
24. Interview SHXS9602 (vice general manager of a township enterprise in Shanghai Municipality), Shanghai, May 1996. See also Shi, Yi, and Zhao Xiaojian, *"Sunan yuyan"* (The tale of southern Jiangsu), 2001; Zhang, Jianjun, *"Zhengfu quanli, jingying guanxi he xiangzhen qiye gaizhi—"* (Government power, elite relationships, and TVE reform), 2005.
25. Luo, Xiaojun, *"Zhejiang chuangzhi"* (Zhejiang's policy innovation), 2005; Mao, Shoulong, *"Cun zhidushang fansi Taole de jue zhaiwu"* (Reflections on the massive debt of Taole,) 2004; Li, Peng, *"Zhongguo difang zhengfu zhaiwu fengxian cheng touhao weixie, chuyu shikong bianyuan"* (Chinese local governments' debts are the No. 1 threat, at the edge of losing control), 2004.
26. Cycles of expansion and contraction have been one of the features of China's macroeconomic policies since the early 1980s. See Naughton, Barry, *Growing out of the Plan*, 1996.
27. Wu, Jinglian, *Dangdai Zhongguo jingji gaige* (China's contemporary Economic Reform), 2003.
28. People's Bank of China, No. 121, Notification of reinforcing credit control of real estate development), June 5, 2003. Online. see <http://www.bifang.com/news/policy-827.html>. accessed on May 5, 2006.
29. This policy was widely referred to as *"ba-san-yi daxian,"* or *"*8–31 Big Cut-off."
30. According to the "Urgent Notification of Strict Regulation of Land Market," three procedures were temporarily frozen for six months: farmland conversion, revision of land-use plans, and adjustment of primary protected farmland.
31. *"Wen Jiabao: yange guanli tudi shi changqirenwu juefei quanyi zhiji"* (Wen Jiabao: rigorous control of land is a long-term task, not a temporary tactic), Xinhua, December 14,2004.
32. Yang, Liping, *"Tudi: hongguan tiaokong disanzhong liliang?"* (Land: the third force in macro adjustment and regulation?), 2005.
33. In 2003, the Ministry of Land and Resources announced a restructuring of the land management system, called the "verticalization" of land management. It was intended to strengthen provincial-level control over land by reclaiming authority over farmland conversion from cities and counties to provincial-level bureaus of land management. It also involved direct appointment of directors of local land management agencies by provincial land management bureaus. Interview BJC0406 (a high-ranking Ministry of Land and Resources

official), Beijing, August, 2004. See also Wang, Fengjun, "*Guotu ziyuanbu de gaige luxiantu*" (Map of reform of the Ministry of Land and Resources), 2004.

34. Dai, Shichao, "*Cuntu cunjin kaifaqu*" (Precious land and *kaifaqu*), 2004.

35. Interview BJ0549 (an official in Land Management Bureau of a county under Beijing Municipality), Beijing, 2005.

36. "State Council's Decision on Deepening the Reform and Tightening Land Management," Xinhua, December 24, 2004. Online. See <http://www.sina.com.cn>, accessed on November 23, 2006. The decision is meant to clarify cadres' responsibility in land management. It says that the central government has the authority and responsibility to regulate the increase of construction land nationwide and local governments have the authority to sell land leases, and are responsible for farmland conservation and rational utilization of land. Most of all, the top leaders of local governments at all levels are directly responsible for farmland conservation.

37. Office of State Council, "Evaluation Guidelines for farmland conservation," *Guobanfa* <2005>, No. 52, 28 October 2005.

38. Yang, Lei, "*Huanbao fengbao beihou*" (Behind the storm of environmental protection), 2005; Yang, Liping, "*Tudi xinzheng: hongguan tiaokong shashoujian*" (New land policies: the teeth of macroeconomic adjustment and control), 2004; Ying, Xue, "*Fangdichan hongguan tiaokong: chengbai xiyu fangjia?*" (Real estate macroeconomic adjustment and control, 2005.

39. Ho and Lin report that of the total farmland conversion for non-farm uses, more than 70 percent took place at the subprovincial, county level. See Ho, Samuel and George C. S. Lin, "Emerging land markets in rural and urban China: policies and practices." 2003.

40. Yang, Liping, "*Ni Pengfei: chengshi pinpai diyixiang*" (analysis of competitive edge: the first report on branding the city· An interview with Ni Pengfei), 2004. This article discusses the "Report on City's Competitive Edge" by Dr. Ni Pengfei of the Research Institute of Finance, Trade and Economics at the Chinese Academy of Social Sciences.

41. Yang, Liping, "*Wang Zhigang: chengshi jingying shi raobukaide*" (Wang Zhigang: We cannot avoid entrepreneurial management of cities), 2004.

42. Urban development plans were drawn on the basis of population and economic growth projections. The growth projection in turn justified annexation of villages and land grabs for future development. Because the projection is often exaggerated, the total area of village land incorporated in the urban development plan is often larger than actually needed.

43. Li, Yuanchao in an interview with visiting members of the American Planning Association. Online. See <http://www.planning.org/china/aboutapa/interview with Mr. LiYuanchao.htm>, September 15, 2003.

44. Chen, Yanping. '*2007 niandi Nanjing changzhu renkou 741.3 wan*' (Nanjing's population reached 7.413 million by the end of 2007), *Jing Ling Evening*

News, April 15, 2008. Online. See <http://policy.xhby.net/system/2008/04/15/010239375.shtml> accessed on June 15, 2009.

45. Po, Lan-chih, *Strategies of Urban Development in China's Reforms*, 2001.

46. For the Tenth National Games, seen as preparation for the Beijing Olympics in 2008, the Jiangsu government spent at least 5.5 billion yuan, or $680 million, building new venues, including a 70,000-seat showpiece stadium. See "Yearender: Gold is not sole goal for Chinese Sports", People's Daily, December 26, 2005. Online. See <http://english.peopledaily.com.cn/200512/26/eng20051226_230824.html>. accessed June 10, 2009.

47. Xu,Wei, Yan Gun, Gu Guo-cai, and Shan Yi-hu, "*Nanjing hexi xinchengqu fangdichan fazhan qushi fenxi*" (Analysis of the prospect of real estate development in Nanjing Hexi New City), 2002.

48. Interview NJ0601 (general manager of a medium-sized development company in Nanjing), Nanjing, May 2006.

49. Fan, Lixiang, "*Nanjing: zhengfu caopan xincheng tiaokong dichan baoli*" (Nanjing: municipal government controls *xincheng* and regulates huge profits), 2004.

50. For land-financed development projects, see *Zhongguo Jingji yanjiu zhongxin* (Research Center of Chinese Economy) "*Tudizhidu, chengshihua yu hongguan tiaokong*" (Land System, Urbanization, and Macroeconomic Adjustment and Control), Beijing University, June 14, 2004.

51. Interview with Chengdu Executive Mayor Sun Ping in He, Zhongping, "*Chengdu mofang*" (Chengdu complex), 2003.

52. Nanjing Municipal Government Document No. 110, "Opinions on energizing the real estate market." See Xu, Wei; Yan, Gun; Gu, Guo-cai; and Shan, Yi-hu "*Nanjing hexi xinchengqu fangdichan fazhan qushi fenxi,*" (Analysis of the prospect of real estate development in Nanjing Hexi New City), 2002, p. 59.

53. Interview GZ0402 (an urban planning professor and consultant in Guangzhou), Guangzhou, January 2003, July 2004. See also Wang, Hao, "*Zhujian xincheng CBD zhilu zaoyu hongdeng*" (Red lights on the road to Zhujiang New City CBD), 2005; and Su, Si, "*Zijin queshi houde zhujiang xincheng xiezilo kaifa lujing*" (Capital shortage and development strategies of office space in Zhujiang New City), 2004.

54. Interviews BJ0304 (a university professor and department chair in Beijing), Beijing, August 2003; SH0401 (a university professor and department chair in Shanghai), Beijing, December 2004.

55. University enrollment in 1990 was 2,063,000 and rose to 15,618,000 in 2005. http://www.stats.gov.cn/tjsj/ndsj/2007/indexch.htm, accessed on September 12, 2008.

56. Interview JN0701 (director of a government-run construction management company in Jinan Municipality who was also in charge of the construction of Jinan University Town), Jinan, December 2007.

57. University High Technology Park brochure prepared by Jinan Western District Construction headquarters, December 2007.

58. Here I follow the analysis of the reciprocal relationship between reality and image in the spectacle by Debord, Guy, *The Society of the Spectacle*, 1995.

59. Tian, Xinjie, *"Shibohui jinru shizhi yunzuo Shanghai chengjian kuaipao"* (The World Expo preparation proceeds, Shanghai urban construction runs fast), 2005.

60. Newspaper interview with Yue Songdong, vice director of the Center for Development Research, State Council, in Guan, Shuang, *"Aoyun shi fangdichan shengyan zuigao ke zengzhang 30%"* (The Olympic Games: A banquet for real estate, estimated growth to be 30 percent), 2005. For a critical review of Beijing's construction for the Olympics, see Broudehoux, Anne-Marie, "Spectacular Beijing: The conspicuous construction of an Olympic Metropolis," 2007.

61. *"Quanguo xingjian CBD, wei Beijing Shanghai gouge"* (The whole nation is building CBDs, but only Beijing and Shanghai are qualified to build), *Beijing Daily*, April 16, 2003.

62. Interviews BJ0404 (general manager of a medium-sized development company in Beijing), Beijing, August 2004; and BJ0406 (general manager of a medium-sized development company in Beijing), Beijing, August 2004.

Chapter 5

Village Corporatism, Real-Estate Projects, and Territorial Autonomy

On December 27, 2006 in Guangzhou, capital of Guangdong Province, I found myself in the office of the party secretary of Shuping Village.[1] Mr. Deng and I met in his spacious office on the ninth floor of a twenty-two-storey building in Zhujiang New City, an emerging new commercial center to which Shuping Village had contributed much of its land. In return, Shuping was granted development rights to a piece of land in the New City. I asked Deng what his goal was as party secretary of the village, which was now called Shuping Sanwan Group Company.[2] A bright-eyed, shorthaired, stocky man in his late forties, his answer was brief and clear: to increase the value of the village-shareholding company from 350 to 500 yuan per share, and to successfully see through the redevelopment of Shuping village.

These two seemingly mundane goals of a village head are not to be taken lightly. The share value that Deng referred to relates to the "shareholding cooperative company" that the village had established on the basis of collective assets, in particular the village's land. The "old village redevelopment" project centered on converting old village houses into commercial projects. Share values of the shareholding company are now central to the livelihoods of the villagers, after 98 percent of the village's land was lost to urban expansion. The redevelopment project is integral to the distribution of profits generated from redeveloping the remaining 2 percent of the village land, which was converted from farmland at the urban fringe to commercial land in the newly developed subcenter of metropolitan Guangzhou. At the heart of Secretary Deng's comment was the critical issue of the place of villages in the growing metropolis and villagers' share of profits from the booming urban real-estate market. These matters, in turn, are directly linked to the village's territorial autonomy under metropolitan governance.

Shuping Village is a "village in the city," or *chengzhongcun*. "Villages in the city" refer to villages at the urban fringe that originally surrounded the city. As the city expands into farmland and urban structures grow around the villages, they become villages surrounded by the city, or villages in the city. Physically, some villages in the city have grown into new subcenters of the expanding metropolitan region. As farmland is converted to urban uses, former peasants continue to live in the residential parts of the village. While villages in the city can be found in most rapidly growing Chinese cities, the largest ones are in major southern metropolitan regions like Guangzhou and Shenzhen. Villages in the city make up more than 20 percent of Guangzhou and 60 percent of Shenzhen's planned areas, and are home to about 80 percent of the millions of migrant workers and entrepreneurs who have flocked to these cities since the 1980s.[3]

Villages in the city are different from neighborhoods in the core of cities like Beijing in at least three ways. First, the latter neighborhoods are built on state-owned land, while villages in the city retain constitutionally recognized collective rights over village land, which gives villagers leverage when bargaining with expansionist urban governments. Second, while old neighborhoods in northern urban cores are steadily shrinking, villages at the fringe of southern cities are moving targets geographically and historically, as the metropolis continues to expand. The village *by* the city today can be the village *in* the city tomorrow. Finally, inner-city neighborhoods in northern cities are well-integrated into the urban governance system through work units and residents' committees, while the governance of villages at the urban fringe remains in the hands of village collective organizations and largely beyond the control of the metropolitan government.

The village in the city represents territorial compromise in the process of metropolitan expansion. Even as villages are swallowed up by large cities, peasants managed to eke out a share of urban wealth through real-estate operations and maintained relative autonomy within the urban territory. In the Pearl River Delta, the villages in the city have organized shareholding companies as a mode of economic and political organization that integrates accumulation and distribution systems within the village. I call this system "village corporatism." Village corporatism differs from state corporatism (Stepan 1978) or local-state corporatism (Oi 1992). While state corporatism takes a top-down approach to resolve legitimation crises, and local-state corporatism focuses on accumulation projects led by local political and economic elites, village corporatism focuses on villagers' initiatives from the bottom-up and covers accumulation and distribution. While state corporatism seems to be an institutional device, village corporatism is historically rooted in the lineage systems of southern villages. Amid rapid urban expansion, corporatist strategies represent an opportunity for peasants to carve out a space of autonomy in the increasingly urban-centered metropolitan governance.

The village in the city

The story of villages in the city starts from the unprecedented pace of urban expansion in southern China, especially in Guangzhou and Shenzhen. Between 1978 and 2003, the built-up area of Guangzhou grew from 87 sq km to more than 240 sq km, a threefold expansion. Shenzhen grew from a village of 2.9 sq km in 1979 to a city of 713 sq km planned area in 2006.[4] The pace of metropolitan expansion was breathtaking, but the puzzle is how the metropolitan government managed to obtain such large amounts of rural land for urban expansion in such a short period of time.

One obvious answer is the application of violent land grabs, which began with the demolition of villages and relocation of villagers. Demolition crews were known for their brutality and intimidation. From time to time, however, enraged villagers attacked demolition crews. Physical confrontation and injury to either side is politically costly. Confrontations also threaten to interrupt the demolition process and slow construction. To prevent an escalation of conflict and facilitate the smooth operation of development projects, local governments began to deploy hundreds of government employees to accompany demolition crews to the sites to demonstrate the government's authority. Hired security guards, armed police officers in armored vehicles, and even helicopters were deployed as a show of force and were made available in case of confrontations. For local cadres responsible for carrying out demolition and forced relocation, the job could be as tense as warfare—and wars are costly, financially and politically.

As it turned out, a more efficient way to obtain rural land was to offer concessions to the peasants. In Guangzhou and Shenzhen, city governments opted to leave a small portion of village land in the hands of villagers as "reserved construction land" (*liuyongdi*) and "reserved housing sites" (*zhaijidi*). To win the cooperation from villages, the government would "return" a certain percentage of the appropriated land back to the village as "reserved land," in addition to cash compensation. In the 1980s, government units that appropriated village land were responsible for providing jobs to landless villagers. For every mu of land, the government unit had to provide 1.5 nonfarm jobs. Villagers at first acquiesced to the "land-for-jobs" scheme, because nonfarm jobs enjoyed higher social status and better and more stable income. With limited education, however, landless villagers often ended up taking on low-skill, and low-paying jobs.[5] They also lost their residential status, which entitled them to village welfare and contract land allocation. Some even lost their homes.

In the early1990s, as the scale and pace of land appropriation picked up, it became more difficult for the government to exchange poorly paid, nonfarm jobs for increasingly valuable village land. At about this time, the scheme to offer reserved construction land was introduced in Guangzhou. Under this scheme, the city government would return a certain percentage of appropriated land to the village. The going rate was 5–8 percent of the total area of appropriated land; it rose to 10–12 percent as real-estate values soared, and villagers became less willing to give up their land. In Shenzhen, the government had to offer 15 percent of reserved construction land for villages to win their cooperation, perhaps due to pressure from above to build an exemplary modern city to suit its image as the first Special Economic Zone as fast as possible.[6]

In essence, reserved construction land is about the distribution of rents rather than the recognition of land ownership. It is not an affirmation of the village's collective ownership, which remains ambiguous in law and easily abused in practice. Instead, it is a piece of clearly marked land that the village can develop as a way to share the fortunes generated by urban expansion. The urban government uses its planning power to rezone the land parcel, so the village can convert it from farming to more lucrative industrial and commercial uses without having to pay onerous conversion fees or being accused of converting land illegally. The government also converts the reserved construction land from its original category as collective to state-owned land so that the village can legally transfer use rights for profit. The trade-off is that the village must consent to the city's claim over the rest of its land. As land values continued to increase throughout the 1990s and the 2000s, and villages in the city continued to profit from the reserved land, the scheme proved helpful in facilitating the city government's expansion plans.

Another part of the package is a deal between the government and individual village households in the form of "reserved housing land," or *zhaijidi*. Reserved housing land was originally established under rural collectivism. While village farmland and infrastructure land were under the control of village collectives, individual households were allocated land for their own housing. Legally, reserved housing land belongs to the collective; in practice, individual households have a claim over their homes and the land beneath. Under the contracting system in the 1980s, when farm-land allocation to individual households could be adjusted periodically, and even taken away from violators of specific policies such as the family-planning policy, reserved housing land was a more certain possession of individual households. During the process of land appropriation in the 1980s and 1990s, the Guangzhou and Shenzhen governments agreed that villagers' reserved housing land would be kept intact. In exchange, the urban governments were relieved of the burden to provide relocation housing to villagers. As a result, unlike villagers facing urban expansion in the north, villagers at the fringe of Guangzhou and Shenzhen could stay in the original village site.

Villagers' territorial strategies

For villagers in the city, the reserved construction and housing lands are governments' promises that have to be materialized through their own actions. Individual households build high-density rental housing on their reserved housing sites, maximizing the floor area on the small lots in order to secure land rights and profit from them. Village collective organizations are authorized to take charge of reserved construction land and seek to develop the land to consolidate their control. This consolidation of control is woven into a general restructuring of village collective organization and a reinforcement of village collectivity.

The village in the city is a physical expression of a territorial pact between villages and city governments, designed to smoothen the process of appro-priation of collective land for rapid urban expansion. As the village collec-tive organization and individual villagers accumulate fortunes from real estate, the territorial autonomy of the village is reinforced by continued occupation of the village site, renewed collective identity with the village, and the evolving self-organization of villagers around their collective for-tunes. In what follows, I elaborate on two facets of the territorial autonomy of villages in the city. The first is at the level of individual households, and is focused on reserved housing land; the second, at the level of the village collective, and is focused on reserved construction land.

Strategies of individual households

Under the land-appropriation plans of the urban government, individual village households were left with a piece of reserved housing land.[7] This policy was to rid the government of the responsibility to provide relocation housing for villagers. Villagers would use family savings and cash compensation from land appropriation to rebuild homes, and rent out the extra rooms to rural immigrants. Immigrant workers were attracted to the centrally located, cheap housing in the villages in the city, while immigrant entrepreneurs rented space on the ground floor to run small shops. Rents then became the major source of income for most villagers in the city.

By 1993, as the nationwide construction fever peaked and a growing number of migrants poured into Guangzhou and Shenzhen, villager-landlords rebuilt their houses up to five or six stories high, violating building

7. Tall buildings on small lots, a Village in the City, Guangzhou (June 2004)

127

codes that set the maximum at three stories or 80 m in height.[8] Urban governments made repeated attempts to control the upward expansion of villages in the city and threatened to demolish illegally built floors. In addition, government leaders in the late 1990s started talking about the importance of redeveloping the congested villages in the city. In the policy discourse, villages in the city had become eyesores and hotbeds for crime and disease.

But the government's threats had a reverse effect. Campaigns of building code reinforcement invariably triggered a rush of construction in the villages in the city. Villagers believed that the faster they built, the greater the immediate profits they could make before the government made good on its threats. In addition, the more they built on reserved housing land, the

8. "Thread-like sky" of Village in the City, Guangzhou (June 2004)

more difficult it became for the city government to launch redevelopment. In 2000, one village in Guangzhou saw ten new housing frames erected in a single night after the municipal government announced redevelopment plans for villages in the city.[9] Many houses reached eight stories tall in Guangzhou, and ten in Shenzhen.

As a result, population densities in the villages in the city became extremely high. In Shenzhen, the average population density of a village in the city by 2004 was 230,000 per square kilometer.[10] In Guangzhou, by 2000, the villages in the city housed more than 3 million people and occupied 80 sq km, or 26.2 percent of the city's built area, with an average density of 37,000 residents per square kilometer.[11] Shuping Village, one of the largest villages in Guangzhou, had reached a population density of 174,450 per square kilometer, about twenty-five times greater than Tianhe (5574 per square kilometer), the fastest growing municipal district of Guangzhou, where Shuping Village is located. The population density of Shuping Village was about 200 times higher than the national average for urban areas.[12] For a comparison, New York County, the most densely populated county in the United States, which overlaps with the Borough of Manhattan, had 27,267 residents per square kilometer as of 2007, about one sixth of Shuping's density.[13]

The high population density of villages in the city left little land for streets and public spaces. Space between buildings became so narrow that they were called "hand-shaking buildings" or "kissing buildings," suggesting that people in adjacent buildings could shake hands with, or even kiss one another from their respective windows. The widest streets in Shuping Village, for example, are 3 m wide; the narrowest is 0.7 m.[14] The narrow streets and tall buildings block most of the sunlight, creating another descriptive term for this type of streetscape: "*yi xian tian*," or thread-like-sky which means that the sky between the buildings is as thin as a piece of thread.

Intensified use of reserved housing land was intended to maximize rental income. This economic logic was intertwined with a territorial logic. Villagers built on the reserved housing land to convert an abstract agreement with the urban government into a material project under their own control. Villagers felt that while their high-density housing might violate building codes, it did not breach the gentlemen's agreement with the urban government. The additional floors might be illegal, they argued, but their attempt to maximize rental income was not illegitimate because they were acting in the same economic spirit as the government and developers. Further, they did not build beyond the boundary of their reserved lots, which they saw as the dividing line between the government's turf and their own. Within their own turf they believed that they should have the final say about the use of the land.[15]

This sense of legitimacy was reinforced by villagers' interpretation of the law. To explain his stand on the issue of legality, one villager used the expression of *"fabu zezhong"* to mean that the law should not, and could not penalize the majority.[16] As long as most villagers, including the village head, participate in the practice, the cause is justified and the majority has justice on its side.

At the same time, the practical effect of the construction rush was to make it more difficult for the urban government to buy back the reserved land.[17] Shuping Village's former village head estimated that it would cost the government more than 2 billion yuan in cash compensation for the total built area of 100 million sq m of Shuping Village. To redevelop all the forty-plus villages in the center of Guangzhou City, the municipal government would need more than 80 billion yuan in cash compensation, more than the cost of the Three Gorges Dam.[18] Redeveloping villages in the city has therefore become prohibitively expensive for the government; and the longer it waits, the greater the increase in land values, making it even more difficult to negotiate with the villagers. The villagers' high-density housing has effectively discouraged attempts to redevelop the villages in the city.

In some cases, villagers' territorial concerns surpassed economic ones, as evidenced by what critics called the "blind construction rush." The locational advantage of housing sites within the village is not even. Buildings that face commercial streets command higher rents because the bottom two floors can be used as commercial space. For those located near the center of the village, far from the major roads and commercial activities, rents tend to be low, and vacancy rates can be as high as 50 percent. Yet, most villagers in the core of the village added floors to their houses regardless of high vacancy rates. Urban planners see this "irrational behavior" as a demonstration of market failure and criticized villagers for their "blind construction rush." Similar construction patterns have also been found in villages that are less well-located. According to a recent survey of villages in semirural areas in the Pearl River Delta, where rental housing was not in high demand, villagers would still borrow and spend 200,000–300,000 yuan to build new housing on their reserved housing land after their farmland was appropriated. Calculations show that, unlike villagers in well-located villages in the city who could recoup their investment within five years, it would take at least thirty years for those in semirural areas to begin to see net returns.[19]

But villagers follow a different logic. They believe that construction on the land is the only way to assert their claim to it. If the government decides to reclaim the reserved housing land, the structures on the housing land would provide the villagers better leverage to bargain for higher compensation. Alternatively, the compensation could make it too expensive and difficult for the government to carry out redevelopment plans in the first place.[20] Tall structures on site helps to prolong the negotiation process, and delay demolition and relocation. Increasing the intensity of land use serves as a form of insurance against government appropriation.[21] A planner pointed out that in the best scenario, it takes two years to complete a relocation negotiation with a village in the city.[22] Normally it takes much longer, if completed at all. The process can stall redevelopment plans for more than a decade, as has been the case in Guangzhou.

Strategies of village collectives

An equal, if not more important factor in the capability of villagers to impede government plans is the village's collective control over reserved construction land, which can be used for much larger real-estate projects.

9. Corporatist village's collective real estate project, Guangzhou (June 2004)

Reserved construction land is managed by the village collective and cannot be divided among village households. It is usually the most important collective asset. It is considerably larger than individual reserved housing land and is usually located along commercial streets, making it suitable for larger commercial projects, such as hotels, restaurants, and retail markets that command much higher rents.

Reserved construction land is crucial to the territorial autonomy of villages in the city for two reasons. First, hotels, restaurants, and shopping malls give the village a physical, political, and economic presence in the expanding metropolis—they are statements of the village asserting its rightful place in the city. Many of the prominent projects are joint ventures between village collectives and large private or government-sponsored developers. These ventures make it more difficult for the urban government to intervene in village business without disrupting the entangled interests of the economy at large.

Second, reserved construction land is pivotal for village self-organization. Management of this collective asset helps restore village leadership weakened by the household contracting system. Profits generated from reserved construction land are also the main source of income for the village and its welfare programs, which reinforce villagers' dependence on the village organization. The reorganization of the village collective to manage reserved construction land and the distributional regime derived from the land reinforce the collectivity, while a reinvigorated sense of the collective helps, in turn, to fortify the territorial assertion of the village in the city.

SHAREHOLDING COOPERATIVE SYSTEM

At the center of village collectivity is the shareholding cooperative system built on nondivisible common property in reserved construction land. Communal land is not new to southern Chinese villages. Lineage corporate land holdings have been a central theme in ethnographic studies of Chinese village organization, especially southern villages. Access to lineage land for settlements and cultivation was an important definition of village membership. Moreover, lineage members are entitled to welfare benefits generated from lineage land. The management of, and power over lineage land holdings was intertwined with power structures of the village, and lineage property was thought to be positively associated with village solidarity.[23] On the eve of the communist revolution, land in many villages in the Pearl River Delta was 30–40 percent communal land under the control of village lineage organizations. Under Maoist agricultural collectivism, communal land was further institutionalized through strong party-state intervention. The household contracting system in the 1980s was revolutionary in breaking down the communal land system and giving individual households control over their own lots. But the practice of household land contracting system varied over different parts of rural China.

As pioneers in rural industrialization in post-Mao China, villagers in the Pearl River Delta began to pool contract land for larger development projects, and to convert farmland to small factories in the early 1980s. Some factories were run by one or several households, while some were village-owned collective enterprises.[24] Urbanization proceeded in a highly decentralized manner as rural industries grew in small towns and villages. In the 1990s, migrant workers and entrepreneurs continued to pour into the delta, looking for places to build factories and to live. Meanwhile, many small-scale rural industries were subject to increasingly fierce competition. Villagers concluded that rather than run the factories themselves, it would be more profitable and less risky to collect rents and let the migrants run the factories. To that end, they began to lease out land parcels or factory buildings to investors and manufacturers from other regions.

To accommodate industrial production and clustering, villagers pooled land parcels into larger industrial estates. Village collectives would "lease back" the contract land from individual households and build industrial estates or commercial housing. In exchange, villagers would receive equity shares of collective-run property. Another source of land supply was large chunks of village collective land not recorded in official cadastral surveys. These were sometimes two, or even three times larger than what was reported to land-management bureaus. The rest was the hidden land that was converted by villages for industrial and residential projects.[25] In addition, villagers pooled funds to build factory structures, roads, and other infrastructure to increase the commercial value of their property. By the 1990s, village shareholding real-estate projects were widespread in the industrialized parts of the Pearl River Delta. When the scheme of reserved construction land was implemented as the result of government land appropriation in the 1990s, it further institutionalized villages' shareholding system for real-estate operations.

Shuping Village can illustrate the role of the village shareholding company and how it has reinforced village collectivity and autonomy in four ways: consolidation of village leadership, brokering of urban governance, balancing of lineage interests and strengthening of collective identity.

CONSOLIDATION OF VILLAGE LEADERSHIP

Shuping is located in eastern Guangzhou. According to the village gazette, the village has gone through several waves of land appropriation since the 1950s and lost 3.3 sq km of land to various state units, including the Guangzhou Municipal government for the mega project of Pearl River New City. By 1996, Shuping village had about 1 sq km of land left. In 1997, under a new municipal policy of conversion of villagers into urban residents at the moment of village land appropriation, Shuping Village was formally abolished and turned into a shareholding company called Sanwan Group Shareholding Company.

The conversion of the village into a shareholding company in 1997 helped restructure the power relationship between the administrative village and villagers' teams, the two tiers of village organization, and strengthened the former.[26] The administrative village is a constellation of several villagers' teams, also known as "natural villages," which follow the village boundaries established since the pre-Revolution era.[27] Prior to the 1990s, under agricultural collectivism and the household contracting system, villagers' teams were the center of resource management and allocation in most villages.[28] Since the mid-1990s, under the policy of centralizing farmland management, administrative villages have been granted greater formal authority in land management to approve farmland conversion for nonfarm uses.[29] The reserved construction land policy furthered the power shift from villagers' teams to the administrative village. More than half of the reserved land and cash compensation for land loss was channeled to the administrative village, while the rest was shared among individual teams.

In the village shareholding system, the shareholding company inherited the two-tiered organization of the village collective, but the administrative village became the largest shareholder, while individual villagers' teams became minor shareholders. Shuping Village's twenty-seven villagers' teams, now called "economic associations," are legal shareholders in the village company. Each economic association contributed to the company a portion of the cash compensation it received from land appropriation, and its reserved construction land to be converted into equity shares of the new shareholding company. Together the twenty-seven associations own 45 percent of the company. The majority shareholder is the administrative village, now called the "allied economic association," which holds 51 percent of the company. The remaining 4 percent of the shareholding company is held by village enterprises formerly managed by the administrative village, and left to be controlled by the allied economic association. The party secretary of the administrative village, who also chairs the allied economic association, is the CEO and Party Secretary of the shareholding company.

The shareholding company helps to affirm the central power position of the administrative village and its leadership. It quantifies power through the number of shares held by each player, and helps to legitimize an unequal partnership between villagers' teams and the administrative village through a nominally fair shareholding system. The Shuping Village shareholding company party secretary argued that the centralized management of collective assets helped to achieve economies of scale and improve distribution between well-endowed and poorly endowed associations. Using this argument, two branches of the village shareholding company were established in 1999 and 2001: a property-development establishment, and an investment operation. Both are organized as shareholding companies aimed at absorbing the reserved construction land and capital that the economic associations still held.[30] Again, the administrative village is the majority shareholder of the two new establishments, and the village party secretary is the main decision maker in the new organization.[31]

BROKERING OF URBAN GOVERNANCE

The village shareholding company also serves as an extension of urban governance. Village leaders act as power broker's between the village and the city, whose expansion has gone beyond the governing capacity of the city government. When the shareholding company was first established and Shuping Village was officially abolished in 1997, the village affairs were taken over by the administrative office of the new company. This was said to be a temporary arrangement, yet, as of 2006, Shuping shareholding company's full-time administrative staff had grown from four to eight, making it the second most important office of the shareholding company, next to the party branch.[32] The administrative office, like the village administration before it, continues to take on the responsibility for family planning, infrastructure planning and construction, land-use regulation, household registration, public health, village security, military recruitment, works of the women's federation, union, overseas Chinese and Taiwanese affairs, civil dispute reconciliation, and letters and visits to higher-level governments. Some tasks have been passed on to the residents' committees under the municipal district government, but overhead and personnel expenses still come from the village shareholding company budget.[33]

Because the municipal government's ambition to expand the city was not matched by its financial and administrative capacity, strong villages in the city have never been fully incorporated into the metropolitan governance system. As a result, Shuping Village's shareholding company continues to oversee local affairs on behalf of the city government. Its role as an extension of the city government helps to stabilize its position in the city, and legitimize its authority within the village.

Within the village, the company is the primary provider of welfare programs. There are two types of welfare programs in Shuping Village: one includes universal coverage for medical care and livelihood support through cash dividends of "welfare shares" allocated to all qualified villagers; the second is need-based, including subsidies for elderly medical care, living expenses and funerals, building nursing homes, day-care centers, kindergartens and primary schools, and provision of scholarships and tuition subsidies for college students.[34] In addition, Shuping Villagers have a priority for better-paid and more secured jobs in village enterprises. Most of the programs are financed by the shareholding company. The collective wealth accumulated from real estate has enabled the shareholding company to provide well for its villagers. As a result, though they are

10. Primary school founded and funded by the corporatist village, Guangzhou (June 2004)

officially urban residents entitled to the municipal social-insurance program, few villagers participate in the programs.[35] Some Chinese sociologists have called this phenomenon the "*danwei*-ization of villages," meaning that the village shareholding company channels welfare goods in the same way that work units did under the planned economy.[36]

While the shareholding company provides for the welfare of villagers, the economic associations are responsible for dividend distribution. Individual villagers hold shares in the association they belong to, but not of the village-wide shareholding company. In Shuping village, 85 percent of individual economic associations' revenue was redistributed as cash dividends. The need to distribute dividends has limited the capacity of most associations to invest in larger accumulation projects. Most associations' enterprises are smaller than those of the village shareholding company and enjoy a slower pace of growth.[37]

BALANCING OF LINEAGE INTERESTS

Scholars generally agree that there has been a revival of lineage organizations in rural China since the 1980s, especially in Guangdong.[38] Yet, it remains controversial whether and how the reemerged lineage organizations have affected village politics.

In Shuping, more than 80 percent of the villagers belong to three surname groups: Li (37.5%), Deng (23.5%), and Peng (14.6%).[39] Since the 1980s, these surname groups and other smaller surname groups have rebuilt or renovated their ancestral halls and invested in revising and updating their lineage history. Prior to the communist land reform, as much as 45 percent of Shuping Village's land was communal land owned and managed by lineage organizations, called "*tai gong tian.*" The communal land was used to fund welfare and community affairs, and formed the economic base of lineage organizations.

There is a correlation between surname groups and team divisions, which were converted to economic associations. In most teams, one of the three major surnames would have higher representation. Villagers of the same surname group are further divided into sublineages. It is difficult to trace whether and how lineage and sublineage organizations have facilitated or complicated village-wide power consolidation across villagers' teams in Shuping Village. But both village leaders and villagers point to the effort to keep a power balance among the three major surnames in the leadership of the village.[40] The three surnames in Shuping Village have followed an unspoken rule to take turns heading the administrative village since the

1960s.[41] Also, all three surnames always held key positions in the village administration. Other researchers have commented that these arrangements helped Shuping avoid conflicts, as is frequently found in villages composed of multiple large surname groups.[42]

It is unclear exactly how the three surname groups in Shuping Village reached a consensus on power sharing. The party secretary mentioned armed conflict among surname groups prior to the communist era, as was common in the rural south.[43] What is clear, though, is that blood connections do not have a pre-determined effect on village organization. Surname organizations can facilitate village solidarity or create internal conflicts. The political role of the lineage depends on the way it is defined and mobilized in the context of territorial power strategies. Blood connections are flexible, as in quasi-blood organizations like village-centered lineage organizations.[44] They are as much historical and geographical as genetic in villages' social organization. Qian Hang (2001), among others, has pointed out the Chinese tradition of alliances between different surname groups in a specific place through marriage and other means.[45] The place-centered alliances of lineage groups collapse the boundary between blood-based and place-based social organizations. In other cases, people of the same surname would establish surname lineage associations across villages. In Shuping, the coalition of major surnames at the administrative village level has worked to both legitimize the leadership of the administrative village and to stabilize village politics.

STRENGTHENING OF COLLECTIVE IDENTITY

The self-organized shareholding system has strengthened villagers' collective identity through two inter-related mechanisms. One is the distributional function of the shareholding company; the other is the shareholder status that reaffirms village membership.

Unlike agricultural collectivism under Mao, which focused on production, real estate-centered collectivism in the village shareholding system emphasizes the distribution of collective wealth. With a large amount of village land being appropriated by the urban government, the issue of fair distribution of what's left over became a matter of survival for villagers. The need to clarify village membership arose in the 1980s and 1990s in the prosperous areas of the Pearl River Delta and the Yangtze River Delta, where there was a large influx of migrant workers into village enterprises and living in villages. Modeled after the *hukou* system, rules were established by prosperous villages to identify who was eligible for welfare benefits, employment guarantees and privileges, consumption subsidies, and, most of all, access and entitlement to collective land. Overall, a village membership is an exclusive privilege granted to those born in the village. Full membership was granted to members of families that settled in the village prior to the revolution, and had subsequently become members of the village's production teams. These full members were awarded contract land under the household contracting system in the 1980s. Full village members thus had a dual identity as land contractors. In fact, access to collective land was the most critical among all membership rights—all other privileges came through land rights.

Because the stakes were high and outsiders often outnumbered locals in wealthy villages, it became a pressing issue to set the boundary between insiders and outsiders. Certain privileges and full village membership were granted to outsiders only under special circumstances, such as for technical talent recruited to village enterprises. In other cases, some villagers were granted urban *hukou* in the 1960s and 1970s after their land was appropriated by state *danwei*. These villagers were able to buy back their village membership.

The shareholding system of the 1990s added a new layer to villagers' membership by marking them as shareholders. Eligible village members were granted shares in their economic association. In Shuping, membership shares were granted to those who had contracted land in the 1980s, and the number of shares was calculated by the number of years of residency in the village since 1966. Although the official regulation of the shareholding system emphasized the labor contribution as the basis of share allocation, the focus of the villages' own calculation was based on the principle of compensating villagers' land loss: welfare shares and employment shares were issued to those who lost their contractual land as a result of urban government appropriation. They could receive additional shares if they had worked in village enterprises prior to the abolition of the village.

The shareholding system, backed by village membership and land contracts, fortifies the boundary of the village collective. While villagers who were born into the village enjoyed shares based on land, employment, and welfare entitlement, "outsiders" were granted only certain types or no shares at all. Partial or nonshareholding village residents included recent migrant workers, villagers who had transferred their agricultural to nonagricultural *hukou* before the 1980s, women married out of the village, those who married into the village but had not yet lived there for three years, and urban youths who had been "sent down" to the village during the Cultural Revolution and stayed on. Some full shareholders could be stripped of their shareholding status; these included criminals, military deserters, and family planning violators and their nonquota children. Partial shareholders or nonshareholders had partial or no rights to village land. The total number of shares of each economic association under Shuping's Sanwan Group Company was fixed on January 1, 1995. The shares allocated since that date could not fluctuate, regardless of births, deaths, or movements by residents in and out of the village. Shares could be inherited (except for welfare shares), but not sold, mortgaged, withdrawn, given away, or inherited by nonshareholding members. Only eligible shareholders could buy additional shares, and there was a cap of forty shares for any one shareholder. In this way, the shareholding system is bounded by a closed membership. The village and the shareholding company define one another, and Shuping Village and Sanwan Group Company become the dual centers of village shareholders' collective identity.

At the center of villagers' collective identity is land. The first layer of such land-centered identity is the shared experience of land loss and the sense of entitlement to compensation for the loss. The second layer builds on the reinforced village membership through which villagers enjoy an exclusive access to profits from the collective's real estate operations. At both levels, the anchor of their identity is the exchange rather than the use value of land. The loss and gain of the exchange value of land in turn frames the way villagers in the city calculate and strategize for the future.

Shuping's shareholding system is a story of village's strategies of affirming its place in the city through the control over collective assets. It legitimizes and stabilizes its position by brokering urban governance and dispensing welfare provisions to villagers. At the same time, it has created a power-sharing scheme among major surname groups that prevents major rifts in the village and strengthens village identity.

Shuping therefore represents a relatively successful story of civic territoriality, defined as the society's struggle over controlling a place. Successful civic struggles over territorial control helps to build territorial autonomy. For the rest of this chapter, I use the case of Shuping to elaborate further on the relationship between space and power from the perspective of the villages at the urban fringe.

Corporatist village's territorial autonomy and its limits

As outlined in Chapter 1, the analysis of the relationship between space and power can begin with building connections among the cumulative layers of location, locale, place, and territory.

At the core of Shuping is the prime location of the village in the expanded center of Guangzhou metropolis. The village real estate and infrastructure construction adds to the location, materializes the presence of the village, and turns the location into a locale. On the top of the locale is the socioeconomic organization of the village, in the form of village corporatism, and the reinforced identity of villagers that turn the locale into a place. The premium and strategic location of the village creates a high-stakes struggle between the village and the urban government. The struggle turns the village from a place into a territory. The village's territoriality is built on spatial strategies to define and defend the interests and autonomy of the village.

One of the most decisive elements in Shuping's territoriality has been its successful resistance to relocation. Compared to displaced inner-city residents in Beijing, corporatist villagers in southern cities have the advantage of staying in the same location. Their territorial control was secured because the physical, social, and emotional place of the village is not only intact, but also has been reinforced over time.

In Shuping, villagers maximize land use by building up on their own reserved housing land. High profits from well-located village collective real-estate projects trigger a process of internal power consolidation and strengthen the village's financial and self-governing capacities, as well as its bargaining leverage with the urban government. The enhanced village welfare and distribution system has also reinforced villagers' identity with the village collective.

Reorganized and consolidated village collectives build high-profile commercial projects in the new metropolitan center. They also invest in roads, schools, sewer systems, power, and water supplies. The village's infrastructure investments also deepen its entanglement with the urban economy through joint ventures, which strengthens the physical and political-economic presence of the village in the new center of the metropolis. The village's social organization and presence turn the locale into a place that Shuping has occupied for over 700 years.[46] That history, presented in Shuping's own gazetteer, helps legitimize the village's moral claim over the place. As the metropolis expands into the village, the villagers' historical and emotional attachment to the village is strengthened by the economic stake villagers come to have, making the village an even more meaningful place for villagers, and a more contentious site. Shuping's territoriality is built in the specific location through this process of place-making, consolidating, and defending. It is a process of building and sustaining the territorial autonomy of the village and hence the village's territorialization.

When successfully territorialized, the villages in the city represent an opportunity for peasants to share in growing urban wealth while maintaining relative territorial autonomy under a regime of metropolitan expansionism. The villages' legacy of lineage corporatist land holdings and collective organization, strengthened by the corporative organization of accumulation and distribution, constitute what I call "village corporatism."

In my formulation, village corporatism differs from state corporatism (Cawson 1986; Stepan 1978) and local-state corporatism (Oi 1992) in several ways. State corporatism is an elitist model focusing on the capitalist state's accumulation and legitimation strategy, while village corporatism takes a bottom-up approach, focusing on society's strategy for self-protection and local accumulation against an extractive state.

Also, state corporatism typically refers to an arrangement of the capitalist state to incorporate the interests of society. Stepan (1978) suggests that corporatism is an elite response to crisis, an attempt by elites who control the state apparatus to restructure the relationship between the sectors of civil society (the national bourgeoisie, and in some cases workers and peasants) and the state. It is not a reflection of the growth of civil society, nor is it the result of social struggle. Rather, corporatism is a policy output, a political structure consciously imposed by political elite on civil society.[47]

Oi's local-state corporatism focuses on the local, rather than the central state. She maintains that local officials in post-Mao China played the leading role in coordinating rural industrialization. Local officials acted as "the equivalent of a board of directors" of a business corporation.[48] In this conception, the integration of political and economic elites in the local developmental state explains China's successful rural reforms in the 1980s. While focusing more on accumulation than distribution strategies of the local state, this model does not include society, either as a social input or a policy output of state corporatism.

Oi and Stepan share a top-down framework in their model of state-dominated corporatism. In Stepan's framework, society is a passive participant, while the political elite, who control the state, respond to crises and impose a set of policies and institutions on society. Oi does not include society in her analysis, focusing exclusively on the political and economic elite operating through the apparatus of the local state.

My alternative view of village corporatism highlights the active role of society in urban social transformation. It takes a bottom-up approach that looks at the process of state-peasant resource struggles, and the way peasants develop strategies of accumulation and distribution when dealing with an extractive local state. In this model, the village is not a passive participant in a corporatism imposed by the state. Instead, the village actively negotiates with the local state to form corporatism as a strategy for self-protection. Village corporatism is a self-initiated strategy against local state-land appropriation. If state-dominant corporatism, according to Stepan, is the state's response to a legitimation crisis, village corporatism is peasants' response to the threat of local state's land expropriation.

Corporatist villages of Southern China also diverge from "urban villages" in the United States and squatter settlements in Latin America. The difference lies in the corporatist villagers' collective territorial claims, reinforced by corporatist organization.

Southern China's corporatist villages differ from the "urban village" in the urban ecology tradition of urban studies. Exemplified by Gans's classic study (1962)[49] of the immigrant community in inner-city Boston, the urban village is a community of immigrants (Italian in this case) brought to the neighborhood through chain migration. Though socially connected, the immigrant residents in inner-city Boston, unlike villagers in southern China, lacked a collective organization legitimized by constitutionally recognized land rights. As individual private property owners and tenants, Italian immigrants in Boston relied primarily on legal institutions instead of collective territorial claims to secure their place in the city.

The corporatist village in southern China, with its well-established economic, social, and territorial base, is also to be distinguished from squatter settlements in Latin American cities, as examined by Manuel Castells (1983).[50] While Latin American squatter settlements are a major driver of urban expansion, the village in the city in China is a consequence of metropolitan expansion. Unlike Chinese corporatist villagers, who are local in the city, Latin American squatters are migrants from the countryside, who have little legitimacy in making claims over illegally occupied urban land. Corporatist villagers in southern China have collective ownership of premium land as their main bargaining chip, whereas squatters in Latin America hold the power of the ballot box as leverage with which to bargain with urban politician patrons. Corporatist villagers in China organize welfare and infrastructure, whereas Latin American squatters, under the populist politics, exchange their votes for the provision of urban services.

In short, compared to immigrant enclaves in North American neighborhoods and squatter settlements in Latin American cities, southern Chinese corporatist villages are distinct by their collectivity, which is composed of highly structured corporatist organizations, valuable collective assets, and a reinforced identity based on prior land rights and present economic benefits. They use their collectivity for protection and to bargain with the urban government and development powers.

The corporatist village's collectivity is inseparable from the villagers' long-term occupation of the place. Unlike urban villagers or squatter settlers, corporatist villagers are not sojourners from overseas or the countryside seeking a place to settle in an alien city. They did not go to the city—the city came to them. Centuries of settlement in the place armed villagers with a strong sense of entitlement to the place that goes beyond legalistic ideas of property rights. Shuping Village, for example, took the initiative to publish a village gazetteer in 2003, allegedly the first village gazetteer in China. Tracing the history of the village as far back as 1273 in the Southern Song Dynasty (1127–1279 CE), the Shuping Village gazetteer opens with a chapter entitled "Natural Geography" containing a list of land parcels appropriated by urban, state, and military units and agencies since 1912. The two-page list details the dates and names of more than a hundred state agencies that had appropriated village land and also informs about the size of each parcel. The villagers' moral stance as victims of land grabs, supported by the weight of history, strengthens the village's territorial legitimacy. The gazetteer also is a telling example of the way Shuping Village uses the power of representation to find its place in Guangzhou's urban history. In Shuping Village's gazetteer, urban development is perceived as a series of land appropriations rather than glorious expansion and growth, as would be the case in Guangzhou's official record.

An actively cultivated sense of entitlement is buttressed by villagers' spatial proximity to the heart of the urban economy. Villagers have long understood the function of markets from selling vegetables in the city and other entrepreneurial undertakings since the 1970s, and they have accumulated bargaining skills through intensive interaction with urban authorities in repeated rounds of land appropriation. As the head of the Shuping Village told me: "I have seen six turnovers of the director of the Land Center of Zhujiang New City since 1994. I know much better about what's going on around here than any of the directors."[51]

However, corporatist organization is not without pitfalls. First, rigorously guarded village boundaries are powerful mechanisms of social exclusion. Migrant workers from other provinces have contributed significantly to the village corporation, but live and work as second-class members of the village. This social exclusion has given rise to a new class division in prosperous corporatist villages.[52]

Second, the village shareholding company runs expressly for profit. The sustainability of such an organization is, therefore, highly contingent upon the economic success of the corporation. Villages in other parts of the region and country have tried to replicate the Shuping model and failed. Some failures were due to unsuccessful business ventures and the shareholding company could not distribute significant dividends to villagers; others were caused by the involuntary nature of the establishment of shareholding companies. In those villages, a very different view of the collective economy prevails. While facing appropriation of village land, villagers focus their demands on a fair distribution of the cash compensation to individuals, instead of pooling resources for collective projects. Their pessimistic outlook on the collective future makes it relatively easy for local cadres to buy out their shares in the collective enterprises at a discount price and leads to privatization of the village economy.[53]

Finally, the corporatist village model of monetary reward and localized identity limits the political imagination of villagers and village leaders. Village heads, as CEOs of the village corporation, centralize power when they consolidate the village economy. Village leaders avoid elections and face limited challenges from within. Village heads also become de facto agents of the urban government, and undertake state administrative and welfare functions in exchange for political legitimacy. While such brokering between the state and the peasantry is an integral part of village autonomy, it also allows state penetration into local social organizations, a long-standing tradition in rural governance that blurs the boundary between the state and society. In Chapter 6, I use the study of township governments to elaborate further on power brokering between the state and the peasantry, and its impact on rural land development.

Notes

1. The names of the person and village are fictionalized.
2. The name of the company is fictionalized.
3. By 2006, there were at least 5 million immigrants in Guangzhou. There were 139 villages in the city in Guangzhou, occupying 87.5 sq km, accounting for 22.7 percent of the total 386 sq km planned area of Guangzhou. See Li, Lixun, *Guangzhoushi chengzhongcun xingcheng ji gaizao jizhi yanjiu* (Study of the formation and redevelopment strategy of Village in the City in Guangzhou). Ph.D. Dissertation, Department of Geography, Zhongshan University, Guangzhou, 2002. See also, Huang, Linghua, *"Weishixian Guangzhou zhongbian zhuanjia yunji gong zhengzhongcun guanli"* (Experts discuss management of Guangzhou's

villages in the city), *Yangcheng Evening News*, June 28, 2001. Online. See <http://news.sina.com.cn/c/288764.html> accessed April 5. 2007.

4. Guangdong Provincial Gazette, Special Economic Zones, 1996, p. 70. Hu, Liping, *"Shenzhen chengshi jianshe yongdi kuozhang yu kongzhi yanjiu"* (A study on Shenzhen's expansion of construction land and its control). Master's thesis, Department of Geography, Zhongshan University, Guangzhou, 2006.

5. In 1999, less than 20 percent of the villagers had middle school or higher degrees in Shuping village. Zheng, Mengxuan, and Huang Shaowang, *Chengshihua zhongde Shipaicun* (Shipai Village in urbanization), (Beijing: Social Sciences Academic Press, 2006).

6. Interviews GZ0402 (a planning professor and consultant), Guangzhou, January 2003; SZ9701 (a high-ranking Shenzhen's Bureau of Planning and Land Management official), Shenzhen, July 1997. For policies on *liuyongdi* (reserved construction land), see "Notification on issues concerning deepening the reform of land appropriation system," Bureau of Land and Resources, Guangdong Province, Policy No. 51, 2005. Online. See <http://gddpc.gov.cn/oldver/common_file/show_file.asp?id=38328&Lanmu> accessed on February 12, 2007.

7. Originally, the government had planned to tear down and redevelop the old village. But throughout the 1990s, the government focused on *kaifaqu* in rural areas, instead of tackling the thorny issue of "village in the city" redevelopment. Villagers in the city were largely left to their devices and continued to occupy the old village homes. Jin, Cheng and Chen Shanzhe, *"Shenzhen quanmian gaizao chengzhongcun"* (Shenzhen in full gear to redevelop villages in the city), 2004.

8. In Guangzhou, very few buildings followed this code (personal observation and interview GZ980401, an urban planner Guangzhou, January 2003). In Shenzhen, the unspoken agreement was that as long as the total floor area does not exceed 480 sq m per housing site, the building would not be considered illegal. Interview SZ9701, an urban planning official in Shenzhen, July 1997 and January 2003.

9. Li, Junfu, *Chengzhongcun de gaizao* (Redevelopment of Chengzhongcun), 2004, p. 103.

10. Xie, Zhikui, *Cunluo xiang chengshi shequde zhuanxing* (Transformation from Villages to Urban Communities), 2005, p. 127.

11. Guo, Qian and Wu Haotong, *"Guangzhou chengzhongcun gaizaode wenti he gaizao kexingxing moshi yanjiu"* (A study on problems of redeveloping villages in the city in Guangzhou and redevelopment feasibility), 2007.

12. According to the China Statistical Yearbook (1991, 1996, 2001, 2006), the national average urban population density in 1990 was 279 persons per sq km. It rose to 322 in 1995, 442 in 2000, and 870 by 2005.

13. "Annual Estimates of the Population for Counties," US Census Bureau, April 1, 2000 to July 1, 2007. Online. See <http://www.census.gov/popest/counties/CO-EST2007-01.html>, accessed on December 2, 2008.

14. Site observation, July 1997 and December 2006. See also Zheng and Huang, *Chengshihua zhongde Shipaicun*, p. 8.

15. Interviews GZ0610, GZ0614 (villagers in a "Village in the City"), Guangzhou, December, 2006.

16. Interview GZ0415 (a villager in a "Village in the City"), Guangzhou, July, 2004.

17. Jin and Chen "*Shenzhen quanmian gaizao chengzhongcun*," 2004.

18. Li, Peilin, *Cunluo de zhongjie—Yangchengcun de gushi* (The End of Village: Story of Yangcheng Village), 2004.

19. Li, Junfu, *Chengzhongcun de gaizao*, 2004: 168–169.

20. Interview GZ0403 (a villager in the city), Guangzhou, July 2004. For an interesting analysis of villagers "planting houses instead of crops," see Wu, Yi, "*Nongmin zhongfang yu ruozhe de fanzhi*" (Peasants planting houses and the resistance of the weak), 2004.

21. Li, Jinkui, "*Nongcun chengshihuazhong shehui maodunde jilei*" (The accumulation of social conflicts in the process of village urbanization), 2005. The importance of housing reserve land goes beyond "villages in the city," and beyond the Pearl River Delta. A survey conducted in a rural area in northwest Fujian Province shows that, since 1987, as the government allowed villagers to purchase use rights of housing sites, massive farmland was converted legally and illegally for construction. While township and village officials took the opportunity to collect housing land use rights fees from villagers, villagers would purchase and build on the farmland to prevent urban government appropriation, or to bargain for higher compensation when appropriation appeared inevitable. Consequently, the strategy of converting farmland to assert land rights has become one of the causes of farmland loss in rural China. See Zhu, Dongliang, *Shehui bianqianzhong de cunji tudi zhidu* (Village Land System in a Changing Society) 2003, pp. 217–230.

22. Interview GZ0402 (a planning consultant). Guangzhou, December 2006.

23. See, Freedman, Maurice, Lineage *Organization in Southeastern China*, 1958; Faure, David, *The Structure of Chinese Rural Society:* 1986; Cohen, Myron, "Lineage development and the family in China," 1985; Zhang, Jing, "*Cunshe tudi de jiti zhipei wenti*" (Allocation of village collective land), 2002.

24. More than half of the construction land in the Pearl River Delta was village collective-owned land. In Shenzhen, 80 percent of its construction land was village collective land. See Yu, Li, "*Xin tudi bainge Guangdong qimu*" (A new land reform started in Guangdong), 2005. Under the state land-tenure system and the *Land Management Law*, villages are not allowed to sell collective land nor convert farmland for nonfarm uses without approval. In reality, a black and gray land market has existed in rural China since the 1980s. See Ho, Samuel, and

147

George Lin, "Emerging land markets in rural and urban China: policies and practices," 2003.

25. Jiang, Shengsan and Liu Shouying, *"Tudi zibenhua yu nongcun gongyehua— Guangdong Foshanshi* Nanhai *jingji fazhan diaocha"* (Capitalizing land and industrializing villages, 2003. The experiment in Nanhai was widely referred to as the "Nanhai model," and was promoted by central policy makers. See Jiang, Shengsan, and Liu shouying, *"Nanhai moshi"* (Nanhai Model)), 2003.

26. This is consistent with Qin Hui's observation that there has been a general shift from team-based to administrative village-based rural collective organization in the 1990s. See Qin, Hui, *Nongmin zhongguo: lishi fansi yu xianshi xuanze* (China's Peasantry: Reflections on History and Choices in Reality), 2003 p. 262; Zhe Xiaoye and Chen Yingying also noticed the power transfer from teams to administrative villages as non-farm uses of farmland increased in the 1990s. See Zhe, Xiaoye and Chen Yingying, *Shequ de shijian* (Practicing Community), 2000, p. 47.

27. Chinese villages under agricultural collectivism were organized at two levels: at the bottom was the "production team" built upon "natural villages." On the top was the "production brigade" composed of a number of teams. In the natural villages, villagers have shared history and kin and place-based identity, which became the social basis of production teams. Production teams, in turn, served as the basic economic and social unit of rural collectivism. Since the early 1980s, production teams were renamed "villagers' teams," and production brigades "administrative villages," or simply "villages."

28. PRC Constitution (1975 & 1978), Item 7, "There are three levels of collectives, the production team was the foundation of the collective system and the unit of accounting." Aided by rich local knowledge about the contracting arrangement and physical condition of the land owned by the team, leaders of villagers' teams were the ones who represented villagers to negotiate farmland transaction and sign land leases with outside investors. They also coordinated industrial estate projects on the teams' collective land. But this has been changing since the 1990s and village power has been reconcentrated at the administrative village level, as noted in the text.

29. Interview GZZS9703 (chief planner of a township under Guangzhou Municipality), Guangzhou, July 1997. As it proved to be ineffective, the authority to approve farmland conversion was further concentrated in the hands of local governments at the county and district levels. By 2003, the authority was reclaimed by municipal and provincial level governments. Other policies like the designation of super-large "central villages" above regular administrative villages was meant to further concentrate industrial and residential use of rural land. Interview GZPY0302 (chief planner of a municipal district in Guangzhou), Guangzhou, July 2003.

30. The total assets of the development company and the equity share of each shareholding team were calculated in land area rather than monetary units.

For every 6 *mu* of land contributed to the new development company, the shareholding association would be entitled to an equivalent of 4000 sq m of floor area of the company's assets. One sq m of floor area equaled one share. As a result, the village leadership held 12.11 percent of company shares; individual economic associations owned 0.06–5.94 percent of the company. The village head still represents the majority owner of the new property development venture. (Zheng and Huang, *Chengshihua zhongde Shipaicun*, p. 104).

31. Recentralization of land control from villagers' teams to the administrative villages was not without struggle and relapses. The power of the administrative village leaders has to be stabilized by keeping a satisfactory level of dividend distribution. As Secretary Deng said, his main goal as the president and party secretary of the village shareholding company was to reach the bench mark of 500 yuan dividend per share, from the current average of 350 yuan. In other villages, where collective economy was small and dividend negligible, and when the government forced the village to establish a shareholding system, villagers were reported to be reluctant to give up their land rights and join the shareholding company. The involuntary shareholding system did not lead to power consolidation or re-collectivization of the village economy; instead, it created more conflicts between villagers' teams and administrative villages. I discuss in greater detail the dialectical relationship between collective land tenure and village collectivism in Chapters 7 and 8.

32. The company had the functional offices of party branch, administrative, legal affair, real-estate management, enterprise management, personnel, security, finance, and union.

33. In the 1990s, the village expanded its water and power supply capacity, upgraded its sewer system, extended paved roads within the village, and invested in a four-lane commercial road outside the village. The village company also hired 116 security guards and 25 *hukou* registration staff, setting up 16 rental housing brokering centers, and 60 custodians for public areas. This reflected the urban government's attempt to retain a measure of control over incorporated villages like Shipai, while relying on the village to finance and coordinate local governance. See Zheng and Huang, *Chengshihua zhongde Shipaicun*, pp. 94–129.

34. Interview GZ0606 (party secretary of Shuping Village), Guangzhou, December 2006; Zhe and Chen, *Shequ de shijian—"chaoji cunzhuang" de fazhan licheng*, pp. 61–62; Lan, Yuyun, and Guo Zhenglin, "*Lun chengzhongcunde shequ baozhang ji chengshihua yiyi*" (The meaning of 'village in the city' for social security and urbanization), 2006.

35. By 2003, there were 380,000 "villagers in the city" in Guangzhou; less than 3 percent participated in the municipal social insurance program in the Tianhe District, where Shuping Village is located. Among the 80,000 villagers in Tianhe, only 2400 participated in social insurance. In Baiyun, another district in Guangzhou, only 1400 of the 140,000 villagers in the city had social insurance. See "*Guangzhou chengzhongcun jumin nanru shebao men*" (Residents of

villages in the city find it hard to get social security) Online. See <http://www.cn-insurance.cn/19_web/32153/>, accessed on November 3, 2005.

36. Mao, Dan, *Yige cunluo gongtongtide bianqian* (Transformation of a village collective), 2000; Li, Peilin, *Cunluo de zhongjie*—(End of the Village 2004), pp. 44–52.
37. Some economic associations were less endowed than others, therefore the dividends that villagers of different associations received ranged from 120 to 455 yuan per share. To help the villagers of poorer economic associations, the village-wide shareholding company set the floor share value and made up the difference for the associations whose share value was below the floor. Lan, Yuyun, *Dushi lide cunzhuang* (Village in the City), 2005, p. 142–145; Li Peilin, *Cunluo de zhongjie*, 2004, p. 47.
38. See Potter, S. H. and Potter, J. M. *China's Peasants: the anthropology of a revolution*, 1990, p. 267. Their research site was Dongguan in Guangdong. See also Faure, David, and Helen F. Siu (eds.), *Down to Earth*, 1995; Zhao, Litao, "*Jiating yu cunzhuang zhengzhi*" (Family and village politics), 1999, pp. 45–52; Sun, Qingzhong, "*Xiangcun dushihua yu dushi cunmin de zongzu shenghuo*" (Urbanization of villages and lineage organization of urbanized villagers) 2003, pp. 96–104. For an example of the relationship between political institutions and lineage in other parts of China, see Xiao, Tangbiao, "*Zhengshi tizhi yu xueyuan qinqing*" (Formal institution and blood connection), 2007.
39. Surnames are fictionalized.
40. Interviews GZ0606, Guangzhou, December 2006; GZ0403 (male villager in his fifties), Guangzhou, July 2004; GZ0604 (male villager in his thirties), Guangzhou, December 2006.
41. The leader of the first surname group served from 1964–88, followed by another from 1988 to 98 and the third served from 1998 to 2004. Then its the turn of the first surname group. Interview GZ0606, Guangzhou, December 2006.
42. Zheng and Huang, *Chengshihua zhongde Shipaicun*, pp. 35–36.
43. Interview GZ0606, Guangzhou, December 2006. For a recent analysis on armed fights in southern China, see Liu, Ping, *Bei yiwang de zhanzheng* (A Forgotten War), 2003.
44. For example, Zhang Jing suggests that it is a place-based pseudo-blood connection that is often built to reinforce the unity of the village. Zhang, Jing, "Cunshe tudi de jiti zhipei wenti" (Allocation of village collective land), 2002. p. 35.
45. Qian, Hang, *Xueyuan yu diyuan zhijian* (Between Blood and Place Connections), 2001.
46. Shuping Village Gazetteer, Guangdong remin chubanshe, 2002, p. 20.
47. Alfred Stepan's corporatism is defined as "a particular set of policies and institutional arrangements for restructuring interest representation.... In this arrangement, the state charters or even creates interests groups, attempts to regulate their number." See Stepan, Alfred, *The State and Society: Peru in Comparative Perspective*, 1978 p. 46–47. According to A. Cawson, corporatism is a model of capitalist state apparatus operation, in which major interest groups, notably those representing

capital and labor, share power with the government. See Cawson, Alan., *Corporatism and Political Theory*, 1986.

48. Oi, Jean, "Local state Corporatism in China," 1992, p. 100.
49. Gans, Herbert. J., The Urban Villagers, 1962.
50. Castells, Manuel, *The City and the Grassroots*, 1983.
51. Interview GZ0606, Guangzhou, December 2006.
52. Social stratification in prosperous villages in various regions has been discussed by Chinese sociologists. See, for example, Zhe, Xiaoye, and Chen Yingying *Shequ de shijian*, 2000; Liu, Qian, 'Cunji, diyuan yu yeyuan (Village membership, place connection, and occupation connection), 2004.
53. Interviews BJCY0701 (a former village team leader in greater Beijing), Beijing, June 2007; BJCY0702 (a villager in greater Beijing), Beijing, June 2007; BJCY0703 (a village relocation protestor in greater Beijing), Beijing, June 2007. Yang Fangquan found a similar situation in the south as well. In his research in Nanhai in the Pearl River Delta, where the shareholding system supposedly originated and was made into a model by the government, Yang reported that in the remote villages in Nanhai, where industrial and commercial activities were limited and land values low, villagers did not support the shareholding cooperative system which was imposed on them by the higher level government. This was because the involuntary shareholding scheme would have taken away their land rights in exchange for equity shares in the village's land-centered shareholding company. But land values were so low that dividends from the shareholding company were negligible. Villagers therefore resisted giving land from the team to administrative villages. Yang reported that the politics of reconcentration of land from villagers' teams to administrative village was so fierce that the shareholding system was never established. In other cases, the shareholding system led to lawsuits between villagers' teams and the administrative village. See Yang, Fangquan, *Tangcun jiufen* (Conflicts in Tang Village), 2006, pp. 104–105.

Part III

Urbanization of the Rural Fringe

Chapter 6

Township Governments as Brokers of Power and Property

In May 2006, I visited a couple of new housing projects at the rural fringe of the Beijing metropolitan region, about two hours' drive from Beijing's city center. I asked a homeowner why he bought a house built illegally by the township government in a semirural area far from central Beijing. I also asked if he worried that the municipal or district government would tear down his new home built on protected farmland. Did he worry that he did not hold the title to his apartment? The homeowner, who moved to the area after his former home was razed by a district government developer to build an office-housing complex called "Multinational Corporation Headquarters Center," said: "If it was just me alone, I would not have bought the apartment. But there were 8000 homeowners here. What government on this planet would dare tear down a new housing compound of 8000 units, even if the houses are built on protected farmland and do not have any permits?" [1]

Six years earlier, in December 2000, I met with the chief planner of a prosperous township in the Pearl River Delta. She had been transferred from the Guangdong Provincial Planning Bureau to the township in 1989, when the township planning bureau was under expansion. She recounted her experience of the first few years after she arrived in town. At that time, she said, planning was a novel idea for township leaders, and the township government had little control over villages, which were busy building factories on collective farmland. To obtain more accurate information about land-use conversion, the chief planner would bring her staff to visit every village under the township's jurisdiction and walk along rice fields to measure land parcels and record them one by one. She said, "This way the villages could not hide from us how much farmland had been converted to build commodity housing or factories." I commented that it sounded like an awful lot of work for a small planning bureau in a rapidly industrializing and urbanizing town. I then inquired about satellite imaging technologies I heard so much about during interviews with officials at Beijing's Ministry of Land and Resources. She smiled and replied: "Those satellite photos are not available for low-level offices in the townships. But these days we have a better way of conducting the land use survey ourselves to get even more accurate information. The township leaders now understand how important it is to have full control of village land. They are willing to spend money to hire photographers in low-flying helicopters to take aerial photos of villages and their land."[2]

In this chapter,[3] I examine land-development strategies employed by township governments at the rural fringe, far from metropolitan centers. Urbanism, as both physical and ideological construction of modernity, could be found not only at the urban core and urban fringe, but also in less urbanized areas. Both townships and villages were the catalysts for rural industrialization and urbanization in the 1980s and early 1990s. While their relative importance varied across different regions and subregions, the townships have a political advantage over the villages: they are a formal part of the state bureaucracy.

The township forms the lowest rung of the state hierarchy, and, as such, is endowed with formal yet limited state authority. The township is the most authoritative representative of the state in the villages. Located in this position between the state bureaucracy and the village township officials' political power has two main characteristics. One is a high level of uncertainty about their delegated power. The general principle of hierarchical supervision in China's bureaucratic system leaves the boundary of authority between levels of governments under-defined. Thus, the scale, scope, and sustainability of township governments' formal authority depend on the will of their supervisors. High-level governments can extend or withdraw authority over resource allocation and add or reduce townships' responsibilities for policy implementation. To cope with such uncertainty, township officials try to bypass scrutiny from above while increasing control over immediate resources before superiors claim them.

The second feature of township governments' power is their under-defined authority over the villages. Taking advantage of such ambiguity, township governments try to expand their influence and consolidate their control of village resources. Theoretically, villages are "autonomous organizations" and not part of the state system. In practice, however, the Chinese Communist Party (CCP) maintains a strong presence in the village. The party branch secretary of the village, appointed by the township party branch, is generally recognized as the *"yibashou"* (the number-one boss), while the elected villagers' committee chair serves as the *"erbasho"'* (the second man in charge).[4] As a result, the commanding hierarchy of the

CCP has made the villages an extension of the party state and village leaders subordinate to township governments.

At the interface between the state bureaucracy and the village, township leaders strategize to bolster their position as power brokers.[5] Land is at the center of their brokerages and, consequently, the contentious politics surrounding rural land is intertwined with township leaders' politics of power brokering. Township leaders maneuver in the gray zone of state-land tenure, and build up on the land before the superior urban government appropriates it. They also intensify the grip on subordinate villages and centralize control over villages' land conversion and construction projects.

Rural townships under urban expansionism

As shown in Chapter 4, in China's territorial hierarchy, urban governments have had the administrative legitimacy to control rural land since the 1980s. Urban dominance is buttressed by policy tools like urban development plans, farmland conversion quotas, and state monopoly over land-lease sales. Rural townships, on the other hand, have few such devices at their disposal in the quest for control over rural land.

Another constraint on township governments is their capacity limitations and administrative responsibilities. Though at the bottom of the state hierarchy, township governments bore the burden of collecting state and local taxes from peasants until 2004, and continue to carry out highly unpopular public policies such as family planning and cremation. In addition, the financial condition of the townships began to deteriorate in the latter half of the 1990s. Fiscal decentralization, which reduced provincial transfers and increased local expenditures, has left townships heavily dependent on locally generated extra-budgetary revenues, especially profits from township and village enterprises (TVEs). The TVEs began to collapse in the mid-1990s, however, due to their lack of scale economies and to the increasingly competitive markets for low-end products. Many township governments fell deep into debt and could barely pay their overheads.[6] The revenue of the townships shrank more when agricultural taxes, which were the main source of revenue of rural governments in agricultural regions, were abolished in 2004.

By the early 2000s, township leaders and officials were cast in policy discourse and media as the primary source of local corruption and excessive peasant burdens. There has also been talk about downsizing local governments, especially at the township level.[7] Already the weakest link in the state bureaucracy, the township's political legitimacy is further threatened and its power position rendered more uncertain. As noted earlier in chapter 4, this was the historical moment when urban governments launched more aggressive, mixed-use, large-scale New City projects in semirural areas.

Township government's weakened capacities, however, are not accompanied by reduced responsibilities. Quite the contrary, in the process of urban governments' appropriation of rural collective land, township officials are at the fore in negotiations with village leaders. Development projects are financed through loans, so township officials are under tremendous pressure to remove peasants and clear sites to allow construction to begin as quickly as possible. Township officials must be skillful enough to prevent conflicts. Villagers' complaints through the *shangfang* and *xinfang* system have the potential to seriously delay development, and have a negative impact on the performance evaluations of the officials involved. Further, it is not unheard of that township officials become targets of peasant antagonism and violence. From the perspective of township leaders, the rewards often don't match the trouble involved in carrying out the thankless task.

To prevent escalation and reduce political risks, township officials hold frequent mobilization meetings and do rounds of home visits to personally persuade peasants of the merits of relocation. A township cadre once complained to me that he did not sit down for dinner for a whole month during a mobilization campaign to relocate villagers.[8] By the middle of the 2000s, demolition of villages and forced relocation of peasants came to resemble low-intensity war. In addition to demolition crews, township governments hired private guards, deployed public security forces, and mobilized hundreds of township government employees, including school teachers, to be present at the site on the day of demolition, hoping to effectively intimidate and placate the peasants.[9]

One disincentive is intra-state profit sharing. The *Land Management Law* stipulates that of the total conveyance fees, 30 percent should be submitted to the central government, and 70 percent may be divided among local governments.[10] But township governments often receive little. Among local governments, provinces and prefecture-level cities get 20 percent each. The remaining 30 percent goes to county-level governments. Townships' share of the fees is usually decided on a case-by-case basis by county-level governments. Their share can be as low as 5–10 percent of the total.[11]

Throughout these hugely expensive and under-rewarding campaigns to appropriate village land on behalf of urban governments, township leaders are keenly aware that the latter profit immensely from leasing expropriated land to outside developers, usually at 10–20 times the total compensation paid to peasants.[12] Facing financial pressure and political uncertainty, under-appreciated township leaders have been moved to launch their own land-development projects. In some cases the projects are legal, such as renting out collective land zoned for construction to investors to build factories. This type of arrangement does not require the formal procedure for leasing and land rights transfer from the collective to the state prior to the rental arrangement.[13] But most of the township's projects are more complex.

Because townships are a part of the state, they can use their authority to appropriate village land in the name of "small-town construction," a loosely defined rural development program. But townships are also part of collectives.[14] According to the *Land Management Law*, rural collective land cannot be transferred to other users without first converting the ownership from the collective to the state. Conversion of ownership requires substantial fees paid to the urban government. It is not clear, however, whether townships, as a part of the collectives, need to go through the formal procedure to convert ownership of village land, and many townships choose not to do so. They build on collective land to avoid the high fees for ownership transfer and to avoid the scrutiny of the supervising urban government. Consequently, in the gray zone encompassing "small town construction" programs, townships build projects that include factories, roads, power plants, town halls, employee housing, commercial housing, and retail and wholesale markets.[15]

From the perspective of the Ministry of Land Management, most of the township development projects are illegal. In 2000, among 100,209 cases of illegal land use and transaction nationwide, 75 percent were related to unauthorized occupation of farmland.[16] According to a high-ranking official at the Ministry of Land and Resources who was on the investigation team for the nationwide land audit in 2002, township projects accounted for more than half of the cases of unauthorized occupation of farmland—and that was only the official figure.[17] In reality, the townships' "illegal land occupation" involves a series of maneuvering, including negotiation with village leaders for land, removal of peasants, financing, construction, and marketing. These extra-legal projects reflect the way township governments broker their power and land in the process of urbanization at the rural fringe.

Housing with township-granted ownership certificates

Among township-initiated, extra-legal development projects, the "housing with township-granted ownership certificates" is the most telling example

11. The wholesale market build and run by a township government, Hebei (May 2006)

of the complexity of township government brokerage of land and property rights.

The term for "housing with township-granted ownership certificates" is *"xiangchanquan"* in Chinese. *"Xiang"* means township,[18] while *"chanquan"* translates as property rights, but implicitly refers to ownership rights. The term reveals the paradoxical nature of this type of housing, since townships do not have the authority to grant ownership titles. At the rural margins of the Beijing metropolitan region, for example, township government leaders, their village collaborators, and allied developers have built commercial housing complexes in township jurisdictions. They use farmland for construction by going through neither the formal procedural for ownership transfer from the collective to the state, nor through the approval process of farmland conversion for non-farm uses. By circumventing the procedures for land-use conversion and land-ownership transfer, township governments and developers can save more than 50 percent in land costs. Cheap land helps bring down the unit price of housing, making it popular with low-budget homebuyers. In metropolitan Beijing, the average price of the township-built extra-legal housing is 40–60 percent cheaper than housing in similar locations.

To disguise housing projects built on illegally converted farmland, developers work with townships and villages to build so-called family farms to make the project qualify as agricultural use of land. These "family farms" have large greenhouses or other decorative farm activities like a recreational small animal farm in the complex, while more than 90 percent of the project area is used for commodity housing.[19] In other cases, "housing with township-granted title certificates" or *xiangchanquan* housing, is built on nonfarmland in the village. This is illegal because village housing land is not permitted for projects intended for sale to noncollective members. Buyers of such housing units receive "home ownership certificates" issued by township governments that do not, in fact, have the authority to grant ownership rights.

The *xiangchanquan* projects emerged in the late 1990s at the rural fringe of metropolitan regions like Beijing. By this time, property development, especially residential projects, had become the favorite alternative for township governments to generate local revenues. The *xiangchanquan* compounds are typically designed in grids with six-story, plain walkup buildings with minimal facilities. They are often located next to crop fields and are served by dirt roads. The growth of *xiangchanquan* housing represented a challenge to metropolitan governments' territorial control over its rural hinterlands and to the disciplinary authority of the central ministries ostensibly overseeing construction and land management.

Throughout the 2000s, official warnings and orders were issued to curb *xiangchanquan* projects. Legal professionals were mobilized to caution potential homebuyers against being duped into *xiangchanquan* housing that do not have legal titles.[20] Real-estate consultants advised people to check the "five legal certificates" of the development projects before signing the contract. The five certificates are: the certificate of use rights of construction land, the certificate of use rights of state land, the permit for development plans, the permit for project construction, and the permit of sales. If the developers do not have the five certificates, homebuyers will not be able to obtain their official home-ownership certificates. Without the certificate, homebuyers cannot get mortgages or sell the homes legally.

Despite such warnings, *xiangchanquan* units continued to be built and sold. According to a survey of metropolitan Beijing's 400-plus housing complexes in 2006, *xiangchanquan* projects accounted for 18 percent of the total floor area of residential projects for sale. In June 2007, the Ministry of Construction held a press conference to "remind consumers" not to buy *xiangchanquan* housing, and reminded people that such projects are built without construction and sales permits and are therefore illegal.[21] A week later, on June 25th, on National Land Day, the Director of Beijing's Bureau of Land and Resources announced in much tougher tones that it would take strict measures to halt the construction of *xiangchanquan* housing on illegally occupied collective land. The director threatened to launch a citywide investigation, and said he would issue warnings to halt illegal projects currently under construction.[22]

The harsh rhetoric hints at the city government's frustration with the difficulty of curbing rampant rural-land conversion that had gone beyond their control. In Beijing municipality alone, as much as 82 percent of its total 16,400 sq km of land is collectively owned. Some 13,500 sq km of collective land, comparable in size to metropolitan Paris (14,518 sq km)[23] is potentially available for projects built and sold by townships and their village collaborators. Curbing extra-legal projects scattered throughout this vast hinterland is a daunting challenge. City leaders' hands are tied because they lack legitimacy to intervene in rural-land development. In addition, skyrocketing housing prices in the city make affordable housing a pressing issue.

Although urban governments have formal and administrative authority over their rural hinterland, their authority to control rural land is a highly contentious matter. Under the discourse of "rule of law," the boundary of governmental authority has come under question by the media and scholars. Responding to the announcement of the director of Beijing's Bureau of Land and Resources that the city would adopt strict measures to halt the construction of *xiangchanquan* projects, a law professor at China People's University publicly rebutted the director. The professor, who also served as vice-general secretary of the Civil Law Committee under the China Law Society,[24] argued that the land bureau can exercise ownership rights over state-owned urban land only. Since *xiangchanquan* projects are built on collective land, they are beyond the jurisdiction of the bureau. The professor also dismissed a statement issued by the Ministry of Construction that *xiangchanquan* units are illegal because they are not granted permits for construction and sales. He pointed out that the legal support for that statement, the *Urban Real Estate Management Law*, applies only to buildings on state-owned land.[25] The *xiangchanquan* projects built on rural collective land are, again, not covered by this law, and village collectives, as the constitutionally recognized owners, retain full rights to their land. Those rights include building houses and selling them.

12. Extra-legal *xiangchanquan* housing for inner city relocatees at the fringe of Beijing (December 2007)

What is important about the professor's argument is not merely whether the argument is legalistically or logically sound. Under the dual land tenure system that separates ownership of rural and urban land, and the contentious competition for land between urban and rural governments, the argument helps create a legal space for township property projects. At a moment when the authority of rural townships has been eroded by the incorporation of rural counties and towns into the metropolitan region, and financial crisis looms, the argument in favor of rural collectives' rights effectively draws a legal boundary between rural and urban and management systems that exclude the city from interfering with the development of rural land.

The second challenge to the urban government's efforts at curbing *xiang-chanquan* projects comes from escalating housing prices since the early 2000s. In Beijing, housing prices surged 41.5 percent from 2000 to 2007, according to Beijing's statistics bureaus. The Municipal Bureau of Real Estate found a much higher increase of 226 percent from 2000 to 2006.[26] Shenzhen's average housing price increased from 5718 yuan per square meter in 2000 to 13,178 yuan per square meter in 2007, according to an international real-estate consulting firm. The official growth figure was 51.8 percent. In Shanghai, housing prices surged 280 percent from an average 3320 yuan per square meter in 2000 to 9312 yuan per square meter in 2007, with a sharp 50 percent annual increase in 2004. Again, the Shanghai Bureau of Statistics put the figure at a much lower level of 68.9 percent from 2000 to 2006.[27] Inconsistent figures for housing prices are generated by sources that use different parameters and sampling methods, and which have divergent interests. For example, data provided by the Municipal Statistics Bureaus is used to protect the municipal government from criticism over its incapacity to control real-estate speculation and housing price hikes; the much higher figures provided by real-estate boosters are cited to sustain optimism and stimulate property investment and speculation.

Regardless of the inconsistency, the prohibitive housing prices in metropolitan centers are an everyday reality for urban residents. Mortgage payments often account for more than 50 percent of average household income for middle-class families. With the abolition of welfare housing, urban home-ownership for the new generation is made possible indirectly by the one-child policy. A young couple, both the single child of their respective families, can expect help in paying for a new house from parents on both sides, who usually still have housing provided by their work units. In other words, it takes three households to pay for one housing unit.[28] For less fortunate homebuyers, an option is *xiangchanquan* housing, which costs 40–60 percent less than the average home in the same area. Immediately following the recent warnings by the Ministry of Construction and the Beijing Bureau of Land and Resources against *xiangchanquan* projects, a Beijing-based news website conducted a survey of people's attitudes towards *xiangchanquan* housing. Of the 25,000 participants in the survey, 75 percent said they would still consider buying an *xiangchanquan* unit. When asked if they were concerned about the lack of legal papers, they replied that it would be very difficult, if not impossible, for the urban government to demolish a newly built housing complex already sold and occupied by thousands of families.[29] Where would the government move them to if the new homes were to be demolished? How much can the government afford in compensation for the relocation if the *xiangchanquan* housing were demolished?

The reasoning is solid. Among *xiangchanquan* home buyers, some are recent migrants and lower-middle income urban residents, but a significant percentage of them are former inner-city residents whose houses were demolished under urban redevelopment projects, and who had been forced to relocate. Recall that such moves are an integral part of the "economics of demolition and relocation" for expansionist urban governments (see Chapter 4), as the process of demolition creates demand for new commodity housing—in New City projects for those who can afford it, and in cheaper *xiangchanquan* complexes for those who cannot. Urban redevelopment agencies and their partners purchase cheap *xiangchanquan* units to accommodate residents driven out by redevelopment projects in the inner city. Ironically, "illegal" *xiangchanquan* projects demonized by the city leaders are, in fact, an indispensable element in the city's expansion plans.

The legal ambiguity surrounding collective-owned land, coupled with the housing crisis in the city, permits the perpetuation of township governments' property projects. While the term *"chanquan"* (property rights) lends the impression of formality to *xiangchanquan* projects, the use of the term is more than being ironic. The term *xiangchanquan* should be read not in the narrow language of "property rights," but rather, as an expression of township governments' territorial strategy. Township property projects are sites through which township leaders compete with superior urban governments for land rents at the time of accelerated urban expansion and surging housing demand, and at a place on the rural fringe where urban and rural governance collide. At this temporal and locational intersection, township governments take advantage of their access to rural land and the ability to manipulate the legality of property rights. But the competition between the township and urban governments is only half the matter. The other half concerns township leaders' negotiation with the villages below them, and their strategies to consolidate control over scattered village land to launch their own development projects.

Townships' consolidation of village land

Bringing together large and contiguous land lots under a simple ownership structure is the first step toward success in real estate. To achieve this aim, the township government needs to consolidate its territorial control over villages. The logic also works in reverse: to consolidate the territorial control over the villages, the township needs to consolidate land control. Economies of scale in real estate and territorial consolidation reinforce each other and are key to township governments' financial and political maneuvers since the 1990s.

To initiate property projects, township governments are confronted by fragmented land usage in rural areas, thanks to the household contracting system implemented in the 1980s. Based on the principle of equity, village land lots were divided into small sections in different locations with different growing conditions. Each household received several small pieces of land of varying quality and in different locations. After the initial redistribution, village farmland was subject to regular readjustment, according to the changing demography of the village and the life cycle of households. Organizationally, villagers are entangled in a web of land swaps, leases, and rental arrangements with other villagers or relatives and acquaintances in neighboring villages. These practices have contributed to an increasingly fragmented pattern of land rights distribution. For township leaders who aspire to consolidate their control over land, the fragmented land-rights structure is a major impediment to their ambitions.

Taking advantage of their under-defined authority over villages, township government leaders strategize to assemble fragmented land holdings for large development projects. They have adopted regulatory, spatial, and organizational strategies as follows.

Regulatory strategies: town planning

Land-use planning is one of the most important tools of territorial governance. It provides an opportunity to restructure resource distribution and legitimize power arrangements. In the name of modernization, rationality, and efficiency, capitalistic urban planning modes are widely adopted not only in large cities, as discussed in Chapters 2 and 4, but also in small towns. Expansionist urban governments use urban planning to delegitimize socialist land masters (Chapter 2) and to legitimize annexation of large areas of village land (Chapter 4). Resourceful and ambitious townships attempt something similar with villages below them.

Township leaders draw up development plans for the entire township, including both the town center and the subordinate villages in the jurisdiction. These plans are drawn independently from metropolitan government's general plans. Most township development plans focus on zoning for the upcoming five to ten years, based on projections of population and GDP growth. But the plans are not meant to be followed. The actual function of town development plans and maps is to define the reach of township authority over village land. It gives the township legitimacy to punish or fine villages that violate the plan by building housing and factories without approval. Development plans therefore provide the township leverage over villages.

The trend for townships to make development plans can be found in many different regions, including Dongguan, in the fast-growing Pearl

River Delta. Villages in Dongguan are known to be active and aggressive, often more so than the townships, in land development initiatives.[30] In Dongguan, village-based collective economies began with export processing for Hong Kong and Taiwanese manufacturers in the 1980s. To accommodate the growing demand for factory and dormitory space, village collectives built industrial parks and housing complexes. Successful village enterprises contributed significantly to both township and village revenues in Dongguan in the 1980s, and many villages were financially stronger than townships above them. By the mid-1990s, however, most village collective enterprises were privatized, and their contribution to village and township revenues dwindled. While villages continue to receive rental income from property projects like industrial parks to compensate for the loss in collective enterprises, townships without property projects felt the financial impact of the privatization of village enterprises even more strongly. Although townships can still collect land-conversion fees from villages and industrial and commercial taxes from enterprises, they have to share revenues with higher-level governments. Moreover, scattered industrial parks located in different villages make it costly for townships to collect fees and taxes. Townships faced a growing financial crunch.

In response, township governments sought to assert administrative authority over villages and to centralize control over village land. Townships in Dongguan began to be more assertive in the mid-1990s. According to Liu Shiding's case study (2000) of a town in Dongguan, the township government announced a new local policy called "one-pen approval" (*yizhibi shenpi*) in 1994 to centralize the process of farmland conversion approval and development planning in the villages. This process of centralization and that "one pen" of approval was in the hands of the township party secretary. The township began with a thorough survey of the entire township jurisdiction, verified the boundaries of the villages, and counted the acreage of village land to be used for construction. Following the ground survey, the township government drew a development plan for the entire township of 4000 ha. In the development plan, the township reserved large areas of farmland for future property development, and began to expropriate village construction land for projects planned by the township development company. Through propaganda advocating "integrated town planning" and "regularized development," the township government also drew up a "unified land use plan" for all the villages in its jurisdiction. The plan set an annual quota of farmland conversion in each village, standardized categories of village land, and unified rates for land-lease sales.

In an interview with Liu, the township mayor emphasized the positive impact of the integrated development plan and the effective allocation of resources scattered in individual villages. He claimed that, prior to the "one-pen approval" scheme, all 13 villages under the township had tried to establish or expand their own industrial development zones. Yet, none of the villages was able to raise enough funds for infrastructure projects like connecting roads between the development zones and the main roads to ports and large cities like Guangzhou. The township government intervened to solve these problems. Township leaders first put the village development zones under township management and built 120 km of roads connecting the development zones to major transportation routes. Half of the funds for infrastructure investment came from the sale of land leases managed by the township. The township also used its connections with state banks to obtain loans for the projects. The rest of the project was funded by loans provided by contractors in the form of delayed and reduced construction payments, as well as from rents and management fees collected from enterprises located in the development zones.

Unsurprisingly, the centralized one-pen approval system created conflicts between the township and the villages. In one case, a village had planned a development zone of 4 sq km without the approval of township leaders. The township party secretary intervened and halted the project after construction had broken ground. In a separate case, a village sold a 12 sq km parcel to an outside developer at a price below the rates set by the township government. The township party secretary met with the developer and returned the deposit, with interest, and retrieved the land. In the interview, the township head insisted that the villages, no matter how unwilling in the beginning, eventually supported the one-pen approval system because the township government was able to provide public infrastructure on a scale that the villages could not match.[31]

It is unclear from Liu's report how consent to the township's dominance was eventually achieved and what the villages' counterstrategies were under the township's consolidation project. What is clear is the strong tendency of townships trying to override villages' control of land in prosperous areas like the Yangtze and Pearl River Deltas. During my visits to a township in Zhongshan City in the Pearl River Delta in 2000, and to two townships near Shanghai in the late 1990s, planners and leaders boasted about the comprehensiveness of their development plans for villages under their jurisdiction.[32] In Suzhou, in the lower Yangtze Delta, Yang et al. (2004) also reported that villages were forced to submit village land to township development zones included in township development plans. In return, villages received land compensation payments from the township in installments distributed over many years.[33]

Spatial strategies: concentration of development

Concentration of power is often expressed through spatial concentration of major construction projects. Township leaders try to concentrate resources and investment under their nose at the township seat, where the township government has immediate access and control. By concentrating major onstruction and commercial activities in places owned by the township government, the government directly manages the finance, construction, and marketing, and controls the profits. These projects include commodity housing as well as retail and wholesale markets.

In the late 1980s, rural towns encouraged the peasants in villages to move to the town seat to help build a more urbane town center. Township development companies built rows of residential-retail projects in the expanded town centers, and pre-sold the units to villagers to raise funds for construction. In exchange, the township government offered nonagricultural *hukou* to the peasants. The township hoped the scheme would accelerate the pace of urbanization, create commercial opportunities, and boost property values in the town center from which the township government could profit directly. It was also hoped the projects would boost the image of the township as an urbanized, modern place. Just as in large metropolitan centers, highly visible projects in township centers symbolize economic achievement and legitimize township leadership. For many township leaders, this image could be converted into political capital and used for career advancement.

Townships with modern buildings, high-density, commercial activity in the town center, and high GDP growth rates, which also depend significantly on property development projects, have a better chance to be upgraded in the administrative hierarchy from *xiang* (township) to *zhen* (town), or from *zhen* to *zhongxin zhen* (central town). The higher up the administrative ladder, the more resources the township can command. The administrative promotion of the township, or sometimes just the rumor of promotion, can boost the property value in the town center, because of the widely believed connection between administrative status, special transfers from the supervising government, and commercial opportunities.[34]

But the maxim that things rarely go according to plan applies here. Despite many townships' success in building up their town centers, many ended up with rows of empty or half-finished residential and mixed-use projects. Some peasants purchased housing units in town centers in exchange for township residency, but many chose to remain in the villages since there were few jobs or business opportunities in the empty town centers. This is particularly so in townships located far from major urban commercial or transportation nodes. Failed town-center projects led township governments deeper into debt crises in the late 1990s.

Some townships learned from early mistakes. Townships distant from large cities set out to create their own commercial projects. They used administrative means to channel commercial activity to locations controlled by the township government. Large wholesale and retail markets have proved to be more effective than residential and mixed-use projects as a way to attract residents, boost commercial activity, and raise property values in township seats.

In the town center and the market projects, township leaders are not only the regulators but also active developers. In addition to land rents, building markets also serve additional administrative purposes. By rounding up scattered shops in township-built markets, it is logistically easier for the township to monitor enterprises and collect taxes and fees.

The governance function of market projects can be illustrated by the case of a well-known wholesale market of handbags, backpacks, and suitcases in Beiyu Township, Hebei Province.[35] Beiyu is the hub of a handbag and suitcase production network in northern China. The area's bag industry began in the mid-1980s with small workshops scattered in villages within Beiyu Township. Workshops also clustered in the streets in the town center, with stores in the front and production in the back of the row houses. As the handbag business grew in the 1990s, neighboring towns and villages around Beiyu Township formed an extensive network for bag production, while the workshops in the town center shifted to retail and wholesale trade. The township, headed by an ambitious party secretary in the late 1990s, decided to build a large indoor wholesale market specializing in bags and backpacks, and ordered all the bag shops in town to move into the market. Initially, shop owners were reluctant to move. To press them, the township began to install underground pipelines in the areas where the shops had congregated. The ground around the shops was turned over and access to the shops was cut off. After several weeks, shop owners left their old shops and moved into the township-built market, paying rents and management fees to the township government.

But the stone was thrown to kill more than one bird. After the shops moved into the market, the township party secretary announced that he would streamline tax collection by collecting state and local (including township) taxes together. The state tax office in town protested and complained to the provincial government about the township party secretary's aggressive invasion of their turf. But the township party secretary cited the national policy to improve administrative efficiency, and he did, in fact, deliver more effective collection of both state and local taxes. His argument was persuasive because village and private enterprises regularly evade taxes, and it is prohibitively expensive for tax collectors to go after scattered small enterprises. The enterprise tax, one of the most important types of tax, is targetted by both state and local tax collectors. When an enterprise evades the state portion of the enterprise tax, it also evades the local portion of the tax. If the township is able to collect the enterprise tax by putting all the shops in one market, it helps the task of state tax collection. The provincial government responsible for collecting state taxes ultimately decided not to intervene and left Beiyu township's party secretary to his devices. To placate the state tax office and to win their cooperation after the incident, the township party secretary offered to pay the salaries of the staff in the Beiyu state tax office.[36]

In the summer of 2006, when I revisited Beiyu town after visits in 2002 and 2004, the township boasted of four more wholesale markets, now called international trading centers. Two were completed. They were much bigger than the market built in the early 2000s, each with upwards of 1000 small shops displaying backpacks, clothing, household items, and toys. Vendors rented space as small as 1.5 m by 3 m and covered the walls with merchandise. Because the shop space is so small, sales clerks sit on rows of stools in the corridor outside their shops. The scene of hundreds of sales clerks lined up outside their shops in the 2-m wide, poorly lit corridors was a vivid exhibition of the technique to discipline the small village entrepreneurs through spatial concentration. Indeed, the entire town of Beiyu has been turned into a highly regulated commercial space. Along the newly expanded six-lane streets near the grandiose gates of the international trading centers, shop fronts are adorned with colorful signs of uniform sizes and styles; licensed vendors are allowed only in certain side streets away from the town's showpiece, the trading centers, the main plaza, and the main streets. On the gate between the trading center and the plaza was a couplet that read: "*Beiyu Township is marching towards the world; let the world know about Beiyu Township.*"

But the political relationship between the township and subordinate villages is more complex than simply domination and compliance. As mentioned earlier, the township's one-pen approval scheme in Dongguan provoked conflict between township leaders and villages when a village

13. Small shop owners of the wholesale market. One shop was shared by three owners. Hebei (May 2006)

tried to sell the land lease without the township's approval. It is unclear from Liu's report how the township leader managed to solicit cooperation from villages in land projects. While the stories here tell us about the township leaders' relentless attempts to control village land and to develop their own property projects, a question remains with regard to the conditions of township leaders' exercise of power and the consent of the villages.

Organizational strategies: control and alliance with village leaders

The township's control of village resources is supported by the organizational control of village finance. Since the late 1990s, as township finance has tightened, many township governments have begun to send accountants to subordinate villages to handle bookkeeping. Major village expenditures are then approved by the township comptroller.[37] Townships also tried to exercise greater control over village personnel. Because villages are "autonomous organizations" that do not belong to the formal state apparatus, village cadres are not part of the state bureaucracy, nor are they on the state payroll. But, in practice, village administrations function as extensions of the state bureaucracy through annexation by township governments. Under the "one level down" cadre management regime implemented in the mid-1980s, village party secretaries are directly appointed by the township party branches. Village leader cadres are assigned quantitative targets for tax collection and sterilization under the family-planning policy, similar to the cadre responsibility system at the higher level of the bureaucracy.[38] Townships also interfere with the process and with the results of village elections to ensure the villages' continuous cooperation with the townships.[39]

To reinforce the alliance between townships and village cadres, cross appointments at different administrative levels are common. Party secretaries of village party branches, especially those from prosperous villages, are often appointed to party committees or government positions at the township level. Key village cadres are also put on the township payroll and pension plans. Evidence shows that the cross appointment of village and township cadres and the incorporation of the village in the township cadre management and benefit system have enhanced the control of key villages cadres.[40]

In addition to institutionalized connections between the township and villages, township governments use kinship and other social networks with villagers and village cadres to carry out policy tasks. In negotiation with villagers over relocation compensation, for example, individual township cadres are assigned to villages with which they have social connections. When visiting less cooperative villagers' homes, they are accompanied by village cadres. While lending extra legitimacy to village cadres, they also use social pressure on the villagers and plead for their cooperation. If the villagers still do not relent, the township cadre can push further by threatening the villagers with forced eviction or legal punishment. This is similar to Sun Liping and Guo Yuhua's findings (2000)[41] from their study of local officials' tactics to carry out agricultural tax collection in a northern township. They call this "mixing gentle and tough approaches" (ruanying jianshi). It takes the village and the township cadres' collaboration, along with state authority and social pressure to gain villagers' compliance.

Urbanization of rural politics and "new socialist villages"

While urban governments use administrative authority and political–legal legitimacy to attempt to control rural land, townships respond by intensifying their grip on the village and its land. Due to their weak position in the state hierarchy, township heads venture into the gray zone of extra-legality in rural property markets. Meanwhile, township governments stretch their under-defined authority downward to villages, and centralize land development, as exemplified by the one-pen approval scheme in Dongguan and the regimented wholesale markets built by Beiyu. The township government's brokering of power and property between the state and villages characterizes the urbanization of the local state at the rural township level in two ways.

One is the unprecedented advantage that townships hold over land. Compared to money minted by the central state and budgets transferred down the bureaucratic channel, land is ultimately a local resource. Localized land inevitably makes regulation of land use conversion and rights transfer more decentralized and its management more fragmented than that of money. Township leaders collaborate with village heads to gain access to rural land and pad local coffers by leasing out or developing the land for profit. Development project-based political leverage anchors the township's power position and subsequently urbanizes the elite politics of villages and townships.

Between the state and the peasantry, the townships' roles as power and property brokers reinforce one another. Their uncertain power position in the state bureaucracy raises the stakes in carving out a "fair share" of growing fortunes from land, and pushes them to develop their own projects. The projects serve as the material and political bases of township power. The township's vulnerable position in the state hierarchy could be fortified by the centrality of land rents in local accumulation.

Meanwhile, townships have waged an uphill battle. Since the late 1990s, when rural industrialism began to lose political legitimacy and economic viability, the informal and extra-legal projects confine townships to the political periphery of an emerging urban-centered territorial politics. In most of the 1990s, township construction projects were mostly ignored, as city governments busied themselves with land development at the urban fringe and in the inner city. But, as metropolitan expansion accelerated in the 2000s, township projects began to draw negative attention. Metropolitan leaders try to monitor and discipline their rural subordinates by regulating land transfer and land-use conversion with initiatives such as withdrawing township authority to approve land-use conversion and rights transfer, sending "land auditing teams" to inspect development projects in rural areas, demoting policy violators, and demolishing illegal projects. While townships enjoy direct access to, and local knowledge of rural land, they are also intensely scrutinized by the metropolitan government. Urban planners and metropolitan leaders also launched media campaigns attacking township and village projects, denouncing township government leaders' rampant construction as irresponsible and illegal. Urban planning and land management authorities regularly threaten to demolish *xiangchanquan* projects, despite the rapid increase in demand for low-cost housing.

The second feature of the urbanized rural politics at the township level, therefore, is the double movement of decentralization and reconcentration of territorial power. To be sure, at every level of the local state and in every site of authority-building, the impulse toward power decentralization is accompanied by a parallel movement of power reconcentration. The double movement in land control seems to be most contentious at the township level, because of townships' under-defined and uncertain position between the formal state bureaucracy and informal village governance, and due to the fact that the township operates in two competing land systems—those of state land tenure and collective land tenure. Townships' advantage in land access, and their in-between position amid power decentralization and reconcentration helps to explain the new national campaign of Constructing New Socialist Villages started in 2006.[41] One of the agendas of this national campaign is "to abolish villages and merge townships." Under this program, smaller and poorer villages and towns are to be abolished and their jurisdiction annexed by larger and richer "central villages" and "central towns." The stated rationale of the program was to build a leaner governance system. Yet, it could also be seen as a way to reconcile the tension between decentralization and reconcentration. The concentration of resources in fewer prosperous townships and villages will help win the cooperation of powerful rural brokers and motivate them to penetrate the rest of the rural area. Once the village or township is designated as the central village or town under the campaign of Constructing New Socialist Villages, the leaders take the term literally and start more construction projects. Rural politics is thus urbanized, as rural power brokers defend their power position through urban projects, and rural development follows urbanistic aspirations. In the next chapter, I turn to peasants at the rural edge of the metropolitan region, who are displaced and dispossessed by construction projects.

Notes

1. Interview BJ0610 (a Beijing resident and low-ranking university staff), Beijing, May 2006.
2. Interview GZXL0001, a township under Guangzhou Municipality, December 2000.
3. An earlier version of this chapter appeared in *Pacific Review*. See Hsing, You-tien, 'Brokering power and property in China's townships,' *Pacific Review*, 1/19 (2006): 103–24.
4. The CCP's dominant position in the villages is stated in the *Organic Law*, which states that the CCP party organization is the core of village organization. For the discussion of the relationship between the communist party and villagers' committee, see, Kevin O'Brien and Li Lianjiang "Selective policy implementation in rural China," 1999, pp. 167–86.
5. Important work has been done on gentry and power brokering between the state and the peasantry in Chinese history. To name a few classics: Hsiao, Kung-ch'uan, *Rural China: Imperial Control in the Nineteenth Century*, 1960; Kuhn, Philip, "Local self-government under the republic," 1975; Huang, Philip, *The Peasant Economy and Social Change in North China*, 1985; Zelin, Madeleine, *The Magistrate's Tael*, 1985; Duara, Prasenjit, *Culture, Power and the State*, 1988; Esherick, Joseph and Mary Rankin, *Chinese Local Elites and Patterns of Dominance*, 1990; Reed, Bradly, *Talons and Teeth*, 2000. But studies of contemporary power brokering is relatively scant.
6. Takeuchi, Hiroki, *Rural Tax Reform and Authoritarian Rule in China*, 2006.
7. For the debate on rural governance reform and the role of township government, see Wu, Licai, "*Zhipei, chongtu yu hezuo*" (Dominance, conflicts, and cooperation, 2002).
8. Interview CDYA0303 (a township cadre in Chengdu Municipality), Chengdu, January 2003.
9. Interviews BJMTG0701 (a village head and a villager in a rural district of Beijing), Beijing, June 2007; and BJMTG0702 (a village head and a villager in a rural district of Beijing), Beijing, June 2007.
10. Lin and Ho found that in the Yangtze River region over 98 percent of conveyance fees collected between 1989 and 1997 were retained by the municipal government and none were handed over to the central government. See Lin, George and Samuel Ho, "The state, land system, and land development processes in contemporary China," 2005: 430.
11. An official at the Kunshan Finance Bureau captured the attitude of the urban government towards collective land: "...land is owned by the state, so every level of the state is entitled to the profit from land." See Yang, Youren, Wang Hongkai, and Guo Jianlun, "*Kuaisu gongyehua xiade zhongguo dalu quyu zhili*" (Regional governance under rapid industrialization in mainland China), 2004, p. 129. However, the conveyance fee-sharing scheme varies from place to place.

In the case of Kunshan City under Suzhou Municipality of Jiangsu Province, where Yang, et al. conducted their study, township governments received 80 percent of conveyance fees after paying the provincial government compensation fees for construction land, and fees for cultivating new farmland to make up for farmland loss (p. 125). In some cases, townships are responsible for expenses incurred to cultivate new agricultural land to make up for expropriated farmland under the national policy of 'balancing between occupation (for non-farm uses) and expansion of farmland' (*zhanbu pingheng*).

12. The township gets a share of the compensation paid to villages and villagers. But the overall compensation is so low that their share pales in comparison to the large sums of conveyance fees dominated by urban governments. The *Land Law* states that compensation fees belong to village collectives and individual households. A survey shows that, in practice, individual peasant households get only 5–10 percent of total compensation, while the rest is retained by county and township governments (60–70 %) and village collectives (25–30 %). Lin, Mingyi, Lu Yuejin, and Zhou Zhenglu, *"Shiluan jinjiao chengshihua jingcheng zhongde nongmin jiti tudi chanquan zhidu jianshe"* (Establishing a peasants' collective landed property rights system in the process of urbanization in suburban areas,) 2004.

13. Townships could also build factories and workers' dormitories on the construction land and then rent the units to enterprises. See, for example, Zhang, Forrest Qian, Qingguo Ma, and Xu Xu, "Development of land rental market in rural Zhejiang," 2004.

14. The principle behind "collective ownership" of village land is that "under the three-tiered ownership system, the team (villagers' groups) is the base" (*sanji suoyou, yi dui wei jichu*). For a discussion on the ambiguity of collective ownership of land, see Ho, Peter, "Who owns China's land?" 2001.

15. Interviews ZZ0101 (director of urban planning bureau), Zhengzhou, November 2001; BJBG0305 (a township head in metropolitan Beijing), Beijing, June 2003; SHWX9601 (a town planner in greater Shanghai), Shanghai, July 1996; CDYA0303 (head of a township under Chengdu Municipality), Chengdu, January 2003. See also Zhu, Dongliang, *Shehui bianqian zhongde cunji tudi zhidu* (Village Land System in the Changing Society), 2003, p. 219.

16. Xu, Hanming, *Zhongguo nongmin tudi chiyou chanquan zhidu yanjiu* (Study on Chinese Farmers' Property Rights of Land), 2004, p. 141.

17. Interview BJC0312 (a high-ranking Ministry of Land and Resources official), Beijing, August 2003. Also, according to Xu Hanming, a vice director at the Hubei Procuratorate admitted in his investigative report that the number of unreported cases far exceeded reported ones, and most cases are resolved through fines instead of reconverting land back to farm uses. See Xu, Hanming *Zhongguo nongmin tudi chiyou chanquan zhidu yanjiu*, 2004, p. 140. According to Liu Neng's survey of villages in Shandong, since 1995 there was a visible decrease in both state expropriation and village household-initiated individual housing projects in the total farmland conversion to non-farm uses. Yet,

township-initiated and village collective-initiated projects increased from less than 20 percent to almost 80 percent of total converted area. Liu, Neng, *"Xiangzhen yunxing jizhide yici jiepo"* (An analysis of the mechanism of township operation), 2000.

18. There are two types of towns in the Chinese rural governance system: the *xiang* and the *zhen*. *Xiang* is a rural town, while *zhen* is a larger, more urbanized town usually referred to as a township. Here xiangchanquan includes both *xiang-* and *zhen-* government issued property certificates.

19. Field observation. Also see Wu, Alun, *"Jiating nongchang ganbugan zhu"* (Dare to live in a family farm?), 2000. Huang, Peijian, *"Jiti tudi liuzhuan"* Circulation of collective land, 2003.

20. Gao, Dan, "Xiangchanquan *baolu tudi guanli huise didai*" (Xiangchanquan housing exposes the gray zone of land regulation), 2005. *"Gaofangjiaxia qicheng ren jieshou xiaochanquan, gou* xiangchanquan *bieshu zhuyi shenme"* (70 percent people accepted "housing with township granted property rights" under housing price hikes: what you need to know when purchasing housing with township granted property rights), *Shichang bao* (*Market Times*), April 4, 2007. Online. See <http://paper.people.com.cn/scb/html/2007-04/04/node_175.htm>, accessed on February 10, 2009.

21. Cai, Xueqing, *"Liuyue xinpan duoshu danjia guowan, goufangzhe muguang touxiang* xiangchanquan" (Price of new housing projects in June exceeds 10,000 (per sq m), homebuyers look for xiangchanquan housing), 2007. Ma, Lin, and Wu Ying, *"Xiangchanquan fang chuyu mohu didai jianshebu tishi fengxian"* (*Xiangchanquan* housing located in a vague zone, officials in Ministry of Construction remind homebuyers of risks), 2007.

22. "Beijingshi quanmian zhankai xiangchanquan *weigui kaifa diaocha*" (Beijing launches municipality-wide investigation into illegal xiangchanquan housing), *Beijing Daily*, June 26, 2007.

23. "Ile de France," Institut National de la Statistique et des Etudes Economiques, April 2001. Online. See <http://www.insee.fr/fr/insee_regions/idf/rfc/docs/alap196.pdf>, accessed November 10, 2008.

24. See Gao, Dan, "Xiangchanquan *pulu tudi guanli huise didai.*" 2005.

25. According to the *Urban Real Estate Management Law*, Chapter 1, real-estate development is defined as activities of infrastructure and building construction on land with legally obtained state land-use rights.

26. An increase from RMB 4,557 in 2000 to RMB10,323 per sq. m by the end of 2006. For the average housing price of 2000, see *Beijingshi fangdichanye fazhan shiwu guihua* (The tenth five-year plan for Beijing real estate development). Online <http://zhengwu.beijing.gov.cn/ghxx/swjh/t888271.htm>, accessed on February 12, 2009. For the average housing price of 2006, see 2006 *Beijingshi fangwu yuexiaoshou qingkuang duibi*, December 31, 2006. Online. See <http://bj.house.sina.com.cn/scan/2006-12-31/1201168516.html>, accessed on February 10, 2009.

27. Both Shenzhen and Shanghai figures are from the website of DTZ Holdings (an international real estate consulting firm). Online. See <http://www. dtz.com/portal/site/en-cn/menuitem.1065829d8e13c873aeafe810e0108a0c/? vgnextoid=23f3c9f6b2ca4110VgnVCM1000000e01a8c0RCRD>, accessed August 27, 2007.

28. Interviews BJ0312 (a manager of a foreign firm in Beijing), Beijing, August 2004; BJ0304 (university professor in Beijing), Beijing, August 2004; BJC0312 (government official in Beijing), Beijing, August 2004; SH0401 (university professor in Shanghai), Shanghai, December 2004; GZ0402 (university professor in Guangzhou), Guangzhou, January 2003; GZ0410 (government office staff in Guangzhou), Guangzhou, January 2003.

29. 'Gaofangjiaxia *qicheng ren jieshou xiaochanquan.*' For full reference, see Note 20.

30. Dongguan was one of the main research sites (1990–2) of my first book on Taiwanese manufacturing investment in the Pearl River Delta. See You-tien Hsing (1998), *Making Capitalism in China: The Taiwan Connection* (New York: Oxford University Press).

31. Liu, Shiding, '*Xiangzhen caizheng shouru jiegou*' (Financial structure of townships), 2000, pp. 136–40.

32. Interviews GZXL0001 (a township planner in greater Guangzhou), Guangzhou, December 2000; SHSJ9701 (a township head in greater Shanghai), Shanghai, July 1997; SHXS9602 (a township head in greater Shanghai), Shanghai, May 1996.

33. Yang, Youren et al. "*Kuaisu gongyehua xiade zhongguo dalu quyu zhili.*" (Regional Governance under rapid industrialization in Mainland China), 2004.

34. Interview SH9501 (a planning professor and consultant in Shanghai), Shanghai, April 1995.

35. The name of the township is fictionalized.

36. Interview BJBG0201, (Vice mayor or the township) Beijing, June 2002. I want to thank Professor Shen Yuan of Sociology at Tsinghua University for providing additional information about this process and the township.

37. Hu, Yifan, "*Nongfu zhibian*" (Changes in agricultural taxes), 2002. Li, Linda Chilan, "Understanding institutional change," 2005.

38. Ren, Baoyu, "*nongye zhudaoxing caizheng xiade xiangzhen zhili*" (Township governance under agriculture-oriented fiscal regime), 2002. For the cadre responsibility system, see O'Brien, Kevin, and Lianjiang Li, "Selective policy implementation in rural China", 1999; and Edin, Maria, "State capacity and local agent control in China," 2003. Their discussion of the cadre responsibility system focuses primarily on township leader cadres. Townships' responsibility in tax collection and family planning, among other policy tasks, is further shared by villages below them. Tsui and Wang reported that in recent years village leaders also have had to sign responsibility contracts with the superior township government. See Tsui, Kai-yuen and Youqiang Wang "Between separate stoves and a single menu", 2004.

39. Tong, Zhihui, *"Cunmin zhijie xuanju zhongde xiangzhengfu"* (Township government in villages direct elections), 2002.
40. For a discussion on overlapping appointments at different administrative levels as an important method of cadre management, see Edin, Maria "State capacity and local agent control in China," 2003.
41. Sun, Liping and Guo Yuhua, *'Ruanying jianshi'* (Combination of soft and hard approaches), 2000.
42. Wang, Shiling, *"Siwanyi zhinong zijin de sige cengci"* (Four dimensions of the 4 trillion RMB agriculture fund), The report is an interview with Han Jun, Director of Village Department in Center for Development Research under the State Council, to interpret the policy of "Constructing new socialist village," announced in the No. 1 Document of State Council in 2006, entitled "Opinion on Constructing Socialist New Villages."

Chapter 7
Peasant Relocation and Deterritorialization

Anhui Province, 2004

In the late spring of 2004, in Ningda Village in northwest Anhui Province, tracts of village land were appropriated by the local county government to build a planned highway. Villagers were to receive compensation for appropriated land. Although households within the village held different amounts of contracted land, the land was owned by the collective. The county government therefore imposed the decision that the cash compensation would be divided evenly among all households that lost their land without considering the difference in each household's contracted land. The village leader was to distribute the cash compensation and reallocate the village's remaining land among all village households as contract land.

But the Ningda party secretary did not disclose the total amount of appropriated land, nor the total cash compensation the village received from the highway construction agency. Villagers suspected the village party secretary of embezzling the funds. They requested that the village leadership open the books on the deal before reallocating the remaining land to the villagers. But the party secretary ignored the request and began to reallocate the land. On 25 May, without the consent of the villagers, the party secretary and other village and township cadres began to reallocate village land by placing new boundary marks between land lots. That evening, the villagers erased the new marks. Two days later the party secretary and his two sons killed a villager, named Wang Yong, who had participated in erasing the boundary marks. Wang died in front of his 71-year-old father after being stabbed eleven times. The murderers were arrested that evening with several witnesses to the killing. But even after the arrest, few villagers dared to talk to Wang Yong's father. Old Wang said he felt he had become a "counter-revolutionary" in the village after he lost his son over the conflict with the powerful party secretary. Frightened villagers were reluctant to talk about the party secretary with an investigating journalist. *The party secretary was known as a local bully with significant political clout. He had been effective in collecting fees and taxes for the township government, and was rewarded as an "advanced party cadre" by the township in 2001. The villagers feared that if they talked, the party secretary would retaliate after his release from jail.*[1]

Hebei Province, 2005

June 2005, Yousheng Village, Dingzhou City, Hebei Province, about 100 miles southwest of Beijing. According to the official Xinhua news agency and the New Beijing Daily *(Xinjingbao), Yousheng villagers had been camping out in their fields from July 2004 to June 2005 to resist a compulsory and under-compensated appropriation of 380 mu (about 63 acres) of fertile farmland for a power-plant project. The resisters dug earthen fortifications under more than ten large tents on the field and dug deep trenches around their tents for defense. At 4am on June 11, 2005, the day of the Dragon Festival, more than 300 men in helmets and camouflage attacked the camps. The men came in five buses, one truck, and three cars. Some had shotguns. Others came with sharpened steel tubes with blades attached to the end. Villagers were armed with bricks and sickles. In the ensuing battle, six villagers were killed and another forty-eight were injured. The attack was captured on a three-minute video by a protester and was circulated widely on the Internet.*

The attack was not the first on the village. About two months earlier, thirty men attacked the camps at night. But that attack resulted in one of the assailants being taken prisoner by Yousheng villagers. Earlier to that, more than fifty construction trucks, eighty police cars, and hundreds of public-security officers and construction workers made more than ten attempts to force the start of construction work by first destroying the field to demoralize the peasants. But none of these attacks successfully "cleared the site," to use the official term for forced eviction. These unsuccessful attempts eventually led to the final all-out attack and the deaths.

Two days after the incident on June 11, the party secretary and the mayor of Dingzhou City was sacked. A month later, thirty-one people involved in the crime were arrested and another 131 hired hit men were detained. The provincial government ordered a halt to the appropriation of the village land. The incident was mostly presented as a criminal case in media coverage, with blame placed primarily on the construction contractors, who were said to have initiated the attack and hired the thugs.[2]

As a result of urban expansion, between 1980 and 2003, somewhere between 50 and 66 million Chinese peasants lost all or part of their farmland and houses. The total amount of collective land appropriated by the local and central state agencies totaled 100 million *mu*, about 6.6 million hectare, or 13 percent of China's total cultivable land.[3] Land grabs by local governments and their development arms in rural areas, especially in the rural fringe of metropolitan regions, have been the source of enormous grievances and the cause of considerable social unrest. Sociologist Yu Jian-rong at the Chinese Academy of Social Sciences suggests that, while protests against excessive tax burdens and compulsory birth control measures were among the main causes of peasant protests in the 1990s, land grabs and forced evictions have become the primary cause of peasants' protests since 2000. Compared to the tax protests of the 1990s, land-related protests tend to be larger and feature more frequent clashes between peasants and police forces. Violence, severe injury, and death are now more common than in the 1990s.

Yu Jianrong conducted a survey of peasants' protests from 2003 to 2004, and reported that in the first half of 2004, among the 62,466 viewers who responded to a national call-in program on CCTV focusing on social issues, 36 percent of calls concerned the "three agricultural problems" and 25 percent called with complaints about land issues. Among another 4300 complaint letters sent to CCTV, 31 percent were land-related; among the 632 effective questionnaires of a survey of peasants who went to Beijing to lodge complaints with central government agencies, 73 percent were related to land grabs. Yu's research team, which has been featured in the media, also received 172 letters from peasants, 109 of which were complaints about land grabs. He combined the letters to his research team complaining about land grabs with those sent to CCTV on the same issue, for a total of 1434 letters, and from these he randomly selected 837. Of these, 33 percent were about illegal land grabs, 23 percent concerned inadequate and undelivered land compensation, and another 22 percent complained of forced occupation and secretive selling of collective land by local cadres. Between January and June 2004, of the 87 recorded clashes between peasants and the police triggered by land appropriation in China, several hundred peasants were injured, three died, and 160 were detained. Riot police were dispatched to 12 of the 87 clashes, and armed police were called in to seven others. In the larger clashes, hundreds of police officers were mobilized to pacify the peasants.[4]

The number of aggrieved peasants is large and their grievances run deep. Displaced peasants are known as "peasants who have lost their land," or *shidi nongmin*. Like their urban counterparts, displaced peasants engage in protests against forced eviction and demand fair compensation drastically. But peasants who lose their land have even fewer options and resources at their disposal for survival and self-protection. Although, rural incomes rose sixfold between 1978 and 2000, the income gap between rural and urban residents also expanded drastically. By the late 1990s, peasant incomes began to stagnate while rural unemployment rose to nearly 20 percent.[5] To many peasants, land is the resource of last resort and a safety net, especially since health care and pensions have been largely dismantled as a result of decollectivization.

Despite the prevalence of peasant protests, peasant mobilization remains fragmented and localized. Although Yu is optimistic about peasant mobilization and argues for the emergence of organized, cross-regional peasant mobilization,[6] Li Changjin, a former township head known for sparking the public discussion of "three agricultural problems" in 2000 (see Chapter 4), has a different view. Li argues that most peasant protests were small-scale and spontaneous, and that protest organizations often dissolved after the incidents were over. Li also disagrees with Yu's labeling of rural protest representatives as "spokesmen for peasants" or "vanguards of the peasantry." Instead, he characterizes the atmosphere in the countryside as "indifference" and "alienation," and in some cases these moods evolved into "tension, incorporation, and opposition" within the village.[7] Other researchers have reached similar conclusions to Li.[8] While O'Brien and Li (2006) celebrated peasants' "rightful resistance," they did not suggest the emergence of a peasant movement.[9]

Why, then, is peasant mobilization widespread, yet fragmented and localized? A common answer points the finger at the strong party state. In other words, the Chinese Communist Party's effective and deep penetration at the grassroots level, combined with China's corporatist state and relatively weak civil society combine to make large-scale, cross-regional mobilization difficult.[10] Another explanation is that the post-Mao legal order, which provides both a platform and rhetoric for social activism, confines social mobilization to the logic of the state under the emergent discourse of "rule of law." Ching Kwan Lee (2007) argues that the "decentralized legal authoritarianism" has in fact deradicalized migrant workers in China's sunbelt.[11]

In this chapter, I focus on the territorial dimension of peasants' protests. I argue that the peasants' land loss is compounded by relocation, which triggers physical, social, and discursive processes of deterritorialization, and significantly damages the social base of solidarity necessary for effective mobilization. Deterritorialization is often seen as a natural process of modernization in China's policy circles, framed by the rhetoric of "the inevitable historical trend" of increasing agricultural productivity that leads to peasants leaving the land to become industrial labor. In other contexts, deterritorialization is considered an unintended result of relocation and could be patched up by measures like job retraining programs and social insurance schemes for peasants who lose their livelihoods.[12] In practice, however, deterritorialization is neither natural nor accidental. Local authorities actively cultivate it as a tool of territorial governance carried out through land appropriation and wholesale displacement and dispossession.

Further, territoriality—defined as the struggle to occupy and control a place—is not just a matter of state-power expansion and consolidation, but also an integral part of society's strategies of self-protection and autonomy. While state territoriality is the process by which state actors strategize to consolidate power and exercise sovereignty, civic territoriality is the process in which social actors organize to protect themselves from state extraction and market invasion, and assert territorial autonomy through negotiation with the state and market. Territoriality, therefore, is highly contested, and leads to varied results. While some villages, such as the corporatist villages in the Pearl River Delta (see Chapter 5) are successful in asserting their territoriality, other peasants are deterritorialized: they lose land, livelihood, networks of social support, and collective identities. The physical removal of peasants from the village initiates this process of deterritorialization.

As proposed in Chapter 1, territoriality includes physical, social, and discursive dimensions of space, and the connection among them. In this chapter, I begin with the decisive significance of the physical dimension of territoriality in a discussion of peasants who lose their land and are removed from their home village. I illustrate how peasants' physical detachment from the village site triggers the loss of social and discursive control over their territory.

Before proceeding, I first outline the importance of physical location by comparing the location of the corporatist village at the urban fringe depicted in Chapter 5 and that of villages at the rural edge in this chapter.

Location, location, location

Location is not just a concern for real-estate speculators. Location has a significant impact on the scope and scale of resources that a village may command at the time of appropriation of village land. The connection between physical location and territorial process is clear in the case of the corporatist village presented in Chapter 5. Since the early 1980s, the corporatist village at the urban fringe benefited from proximity to an existing urban center. Villagers achieved individual and collective accumulation, reorganized and strengthened the village collective, and learned negotiation skills with local officials prior to massive land appropriation in the mid-1990s. At the other end of the spectrum are those at the rural fringe of a metropolitan region. These villages were mainly engaged in agriculture or cottage industry when mass land appropriation occurred in the early 2000s. They were crippled by excessive tax and fee burdens in the 1980s and 1990s, saddled with debt, and had accumulated little capital. Agriculture-based village collectives were ineffective in dealing with the encroaching urban economy. As a result, villages in the rural fringe had far fewer economic and social resources at hand to deal with land appropriation.

Corporatist villages are physically adjacent to and economically connected with the existing metropolitan center, and benefit directly from the growing urban economy. In the 1980s, Shuping's villagers, the focus of my case study in chapter 5, were engaged in profitable vegetable farming to supply Guangzhou. Average incomes in Shuping were 50 percent higher than in Guangzhou City.[13] Villages in the urban fringe of coastal regions such as the Pearl River Delta were also among the first to industrialize. Individual village households started to pool their contract lands together to build industrial estates. In the early stage of industrialization, farmland was converted for the TVEs, and later was leased to outside investors. The proximity of the Pearl River Delta to Hong Kong and Taiwan helped attract overseas Chinese investment beginning in the early 1980s and generated a property boom. Revenues for villagers and village collectives from property projects soon began to outstrip those from manufacturing and agriculture.

In order to provide fair distribution of income among villagers from collective property projects, and to encourage villagers to give their contract land to the collective for such projects, villagers set about reorganizing collective asset-management systems and profit-sharing schemes in the form of shareholding companies. As more interregional migrant workers poured in, villagers also profited from renting out rooms to migrants. As a result, on the eve of land appropriations in the mid 1990s, individual villagers and village collectives at the urban fringe in the Pearl River Delta had accumulated a substantial amount of capital and had transformed village collectives into an urban-oriented economy. Among the first to experience industrialization and urbanization, these villages accumulated capital and experience in the market. They also experienced small-scale land appropriations by state units and the urban government throughout the 1970s and 1980s, and even earlier.[14] Experience in interacting with the state over land issues proved useful in negotiations with the urban government during the era of large-scale land appropriation.

Locational advantage provided corporatist villagers the opportunity for capital accumulation. The restructuring of village collectives and affirmation of village boundaries, in turn, facilitated their efforts at territorial control. The village's continued occupation in its original location and expansion of property projects were essential to sustaining village's territorial claims. Hence, in Shuping, when the redevelopment and relocation issue was reopened in 2007, the village was in a strong position to bargain with the urban government.

Compared to corporatist villages, villages at the rural fringe have experienced a very different territorial process. To begin, many villagers in the rural fringe were still engaged primarily in agriculture at the outset of massland appropriation. While some managed to accumulate some capital through cash crop farming or cottage industry, very few profited from real-estate operations, which offer much higher returns. In these villages, as in the corporatist villages, collective agriculture was weakened by the household contracting system since the late 1980s. But, unlike corporatist villages that had an incentive to reorganize the village collective and pool contract land for property projects, villagers in the less industrialized rural fringe, where demand for land conversion was much weaker, were less inclined to pool their land and capital for collective industrial or property projects.

Also, unlike corporatist villages that can bargain for high compensation for premium land tracts in the metropolitan center, villages in the rural fringe have less leverage and receive lower compensation. Urban planners and developers earmark the land in the rural fringe for catalyst projects, such as industrial parks, university cities, or public projects like highways and airports. Compared with commercial projects in the existing growth centers, the future of these pioneer projects is uncertain; it takes a long time for peri-rural areas to develop into commercial centers that command high rents. For villagers, such uncertainty can weaken their incentive to initiate collective-based property projects. The villagers' distrust of the collective asset managers in many of the poor villages further dampens the possibilities of pooling the resources together.

Corporatist villages in the Pearl River Delta strengthened their collective identity through village shareholding corporations with the prospect of continuous increase of revenues from collective real-estate operation. Conversely, the fragmented farming households on the rural fringe fought to dissolve the village collective and divide whatever collective assets were left in the village. Even in the South, Yang Fangquan (2006) found that in the remote villages at the edge of Guangzhou metropolitan region, where industrial and commercial activities were limited and land values low, villagers did not support the shareholding cooperative system, because the land values were so low that dividends from the shareholding company were negligible.[15] Villagers in the rural fringe demanded a complete division of the cash compensation for the appropriated land and collective properties. They showed little faith in collective organization and the village leadership, and sought individual shares of collective assets, following the model of farmland division under the household contracting system of the 1980s.

Relocation and deterritorialization

Location is a key element affecting the scope and scale of resources upon which villagers may draw for self-protection and establishing territorial autonomy. Yet, locational advantage does not guarantee success. Conversely, relocation almost always brings loss of control over land, disintegration of village organization, and rupture of peasants' collective identity. Location matters, but relocation matters more.

Not all cases of village land loss lead to villagers' relocation. In the case of Shuping, villagers negotiated to stay in their original homes while retaining portions of collective land for construction. In most cases, however, both farmland and housing sites are appropriated for development projects, and villagers are relocated to new housing sites.

In what follows, I use the case of Xinqing Village in the Pearl River Delta to illuminate the detrimental effect of relocation and the ways in which relocation triggers interconnected processes of physical, social, and cultural dismantlement of villages and their deterritorialization.

Relocation of Xinqing village

Xinqing is a natural village under Shuping Administrative Village since the 1950s.[16] By the early 1990s, Xinqing had about 200 households and 700 villagers. The village is distinct from other natural villages under Shuping Administrative Village in that it has been cut off from the rest of the area by a major road since the 1960s, making it physically marginal.

In 1992, the Guangzhou Municipal Government launched the Zhujiang New City project (see Chapter 4) and expropriated 900 *mu* (60 hectare) of land from Shuping. Village leaders negotiated terms that left a piece of reserved construction land for the village collective and left the village residential area intact. In order to accelerate the negotiation process and to save the cost of relocation compensation, the Guangzhou Municipal Government accepted Shuping's demands. But Xinqing was not included in the agreement. Shuping's main residential area, which housed about 10,000 villagers in more than twenty natural villages, was spared, but Xinqing was marked for demolition. Its 700-plus villagers were assigned relocation housing in the planned Zhujiang New City. Xinqing villagers initially refused to move, but without the support of the leadership at the administrative village level, their protests were in vain. After much negotiation, the municipal development agency agreed to give Xinqing village 50 *mu* (3.3 hectare) of land in the New City, where they could reconstitute the whole village. In order to persuade Xinqing villagers to move quickly and voluntarily, the municipal development agency also promised cash compensation and additional funding for the construction of the new village.

The villagers accepted the arrangement based on two expectations: that the village collective would have the right to develop the 50 *mu* of reserved land, and that the site was large enough for both village housing and commercial real-estate development. Neither expectation was realized.

Four years after the initial relocation agreement was reached, the municipal development agency contracted out the construction of the new Xinqing village to a district government-owned development company called Hualin.[17] In the contract between the municipal agency and Hualin, to which the village was not privy, the development rights of the 50 *mu* of reserved land for village reconstruction were turned over to Hualin. Hualin was to plan, design, and build high-rise relocation housing, and allocate new housing units to individual village households. In exchange, Hualin Company was granted the authority to use the rest of the 50 *mu* of land for commercial projects. The agreement between the municipal agency and Hualin stipulated that profits from the commercial development would pay for the relocation compensation to villagers, as well as the cost of demolishing the old village and costs incurred during construction of the new village housing. This arrangement relieved the municipal agency of the financial and administrative responsibility for village relocation. In other words, it was the government-sponsored development company, rather than Xinqing village, that had the control over the reserved land and the development process. Ultimately, Hualin company built high-density high-rise relocation housing for Xinqing villagers, and used the rest of the reserved land for commercial development. Profits generated from commercial development went to Hualin. In the high-rise relocation housing, relocated villagers no longer had individual sites to build rental housing as before. Neither was there space for the village collective to develop its own real-estate projects. The relocation turned out to be a deprivation and depletion of the village collective and of the villagers' sources of income. Relocated villagers, many unemployed, now live in relocation apartment units that do not generate income. Instead, their new housing depletes savings through management fees and water and power bills.

The economic degeneration resulting from relocation has been worsened by the accompanying social disintegration of the village. Upon learning about the secretive contract between the municipal development agency and Hualin in 1996, enraged Xinqing villagers took to writing letters and visiting government agencies to protest, but with few results. Early in 1998, some frustrated and disillusioned villagers chose to sign relocation agreements with Hualin. After signing the agreement, the villagers quickly moved out of their old village homes. Their houses were vandalized and then demolished. Demolition crews also damaged adjacent homes. In the summer of 1998, construction of a new road blocked the village waterway and caused a large flood. Eighty percent of the village was flooded for days, causing further damage to the remaining buildings and roads. Looming demolition and relocation discouraged any plans to repair damage. The physical deterioration of the neighborhood deepened as crime became rampant.

In 2001, in a renewed campaign to push through the Zhujiang New City project, the district government requested Shuping's Sanwan Shareholding Company to mediate the relocation negotiation with Xinqing village. With Shuping's intervention and the district government's offer of higher cash compensation, 95 percent of the villagers signed relocation agreements by 2002. Some moved into the relocation housing on the new site, living side by side with private homeowners in the commercial housing that Hualin had built.

About 100 village households, however, continued living in the old village. Lacking care and maintenance, the village had greatly deteriorated and had earned a reputation as "the largest cesspool in the world." Later in 2002, more than ten villagers were arrested over a conflict with a demolition crew. After the arrests, eighty village households signed the relocation agreement and moved out. By early 2003, only eight households were holding out on to their old sites. The last "nail households" had moved out by the year's end.

Shuping Village and Xinqing Village had similar locations, but very different development trajectories. While Shuping's story is a tale of successful defense of village autonomy and territory, Xinqing suffered dramatic loss of territorial control. While the former developed village corporatism through reinforced territorialization, the latter was deterritorialized. Their differences originated mainly in the process of relocation.

Relocation brings deterritorialization via three mechanisms. First, relocation prompts a process of economic deterioration, a downward movement that deprives those relocated of economic opportunities and income sources. Second, relocation creates and widens rifts within the village, accelerating the social and organizational disintegration of the collective; the disintegration is furthered by policies of selective conversion of villagers into urban residents. Third, relocation opens rifts among villagers, impeding their collective reterritorialization at the new relocation site.

Relocation and economic deterioration

Relocation is invariably a downward movement on the socioeconomic ladder for villagers and the village as a whole. The slide is initiated by competition between the village and urban governments over commercially valuable sites, and over control of the generation and distribution of land rents.

In this competition, the urban government uses its administrative and planning power to grab premium land from the village and forces villagers to move from the location. Xinqing village lost on many counts. The new village is located less centrally, on a site that is less commercially valuable, and is a place that offers fewer business and job opportunities. The new village site also has less complete infrastructure and services. The physical removal of the village from the city's growth epicenter marked a compulsory resource reallocation in favor of urban development powers at the expense of the village. In Xinqing, following relocation, households could no longer depend on rental incomes, and the village collective had few collective assets from which to generate dividends for villager-shareholders. The village collective's role as dispenser of dividends was thus greatly weakened. Relocation harmed the economic status of villagers and the village collective. Therefore, despite the seemingly innocent terminology, relocation is never a neutral movement between equal places.[18]

The downward movement in the process of relocation follows a spatial hierarchy within the metropolitan region. Inner-city residents are relocated to cheaper housing sites in the inner ring of the urban fringe; villagers who live along the inner ring of the urban fringe are moved to the outer ring of the urban fringe where land is even cheaper; and villagers at the outer ring are relocated to even more remote areas at the rural fringe of the metropolis.

From the perspective of the expansionist urban government and development powers, the multiple rings of urban expansion create a chain of what urban geographers call a "spatial fix."[19] As mentioned in Chapter 4, the massive demolition of inner-city housing creates a surge in housing demand. The majority of the relocated households can only afford low-cost housing in a less desirable location farther from urban services and employment opportunities. This, in turn, increases housing demand in the urban fringe. The integration of demolition and the creation of housing demand are calculated into the "economy of demolition and relocation." These are applied to every level of the spatial hierarchy, and are undertaken by different levels of the local government and their development allies. From the perspective of the urban and rural relocatees caught up in this chain of relocation, the economies of demolition and relocation entail a continuous slide down the socioeconomic scale. While the chain is a spatial fix for accumulation projects, it is a chain that creates poverty for the dispossessed.

Relocation and social disintegration

Relocation is hardly a smooth shift from site A to site B. For relocated villagers, it is a process that triggers intense conflict, drives a wedge between villagers, and reduces their ability to unite in defense of their interests. Relocation breaks up village organization much more often than it strengthens it. Some policies related to relocation help to divide villagers' interests, and officials routinely adopt divide-and-conquer tactics that feed the implosion of village solidarity.

At the outset of the relocation process, negotiation over land lease with the urban development agency usually provokes distrust among villagers. Distrust can develop within the village leadership or between the party branch and the villagers' committee, between villagers and the village heads, between villagers' teams and the administrative village, among villagers, or all of the above. For example, leaders are often offered special financial awards for securing agreements for land-use rights transfers from the rest of the village team members. Seduced by lucrative offers, some village leaders take the risk and sign agreements with development agencies without informing the villagers. In many cases, not all village leaders at the administrative and villagers' team level are informed of the secret deal, and not all agree to the deal. When villagers discover secret deals—often when bulldozers show up in their fields—the relationships between village leaders and between leaders and the villagers can erupt. Leaders involved in land-transfer deals often try to secure support from villagers by offering selected individuals a piece of the action, such as a contract to hire bulldozers to destroy fields slated for appropriation, but destroying fields provokes fierce enmity from fellow villagers.

The distribution of relocation compensation is another source of conflict within the village. One frequent sore point is discriminatory compensation offers between the administrative village, villagers' teams, and individual households. Under-the-table deals also commonly arouse suspicion, made only worse by chronically opaque village accounting systems.

The phase-by-phase physical demolition and vacating of a village also produces schisms among residents. When the first group of villagers signs the relocation agreement and leaves the village, vacant houses are immediately razed or left to deteriorate. The vacated lots, piled high with debris and garbage are blights on the landscape, and heighten villagers' anxiety. House-by-house demolition is often accompanied by intimidation. Demolition crews cut off water, telephone lines, power, and mail delivery, and even roads to make life intolerable for those who stay. Finally, after much intimidation, a second group of villagers, exhausted by living in a literal and figurative wasteland, sign the agreement and depart. At the last stage, a few households remaining in their sad shell of a village are hardly capable of collective action.[20]

In the case of Xinqing, the population dropped from 700 to 100 households in the first six years. In the second stage, eighty of the remaining households moved out after the arrests of the ten villagers. In the final stage, those who held out were the "nail households," scattered in different parts of the village "like lone ghosts." The holdouts lived in severely damaged and unsafe houses, surrounded by vacant, unsightly lots, without electricity or water. Though some "nail households" succeed in wresting better compensation packages, others are simply made to disappear. In the process of relocation, villagers are atomized and peeled off layer-by-layer from the village territory. Loss of control over territory and the disintegration of the village collectivity feed each other and accelerate the process of deterritorialization.

By the late 1990s, as local officials had accumulated more experience in negotiating with relocatees, they began to cultivate tactics for phased relocation expressly in order to create rifts among villagers. A villager in the outskirts of Beijing told me that in the first phase of his village's relocation, only a few people were willing to sign the relocation agreement with the Demolition and Relocation Office. He said those villagers were mostly "relatives and allies of the village cadre." As the first group of

14. Village housing half-destroyed for a new road at the rural fringe of Metropolitan Beijing (June 07)

villagers signed the relocation agreement, they came back from the relocation office with gifts like large bags of rice and flour, and even new bicycles
as rewards for taking the lead in the relocation program. Envious villagers
did not want to miss out on the freebees, and signed the relocation agreement. Villagers reluctant to move, meanwhile, were told that if they held
out for too long and affected the progress of the construction project, the
district government could take them to court for impeding public projects.[21] The "carrot-and-stick" approach is but one of the tactics employed
by the Demolition and Relocation Office. One official admitted that all
relocation packages are tailored to individual cases, despite the universal
formula for compensation. He said compensation negotiation is all about
manipulating relocatees by inciting jealousy among villagers who are fear-
ful of missing out on special deals, and allowing them the illusion of having
secured a better deal than their neighbors by engaging in secretive negotiations with the demolition office staff.[22] In interviews, villagers frequently
talked about their neighbors whom they believed to have provided
information to the demolition office about fellow villagers' plans for

negotiation. Informants receive cash rewards if they successfully persuaded a fellow villager to sign the relocation agreement. A former village team leader who had sided with the villagers during the negotiation told me that the discriminatory compensation packages arouse suspicion and jealousy among villagers and undermine the formation of a united front against the demolition office.[23]

Relocation and Demolition Office staff employs other divide-and-conquer tactics as well. As part of a "University City" project at the fringe of Guangzhou, for example, land from four villages was appropriated. Only half of the households in each of the four villages were relocated, however. An experienced planning consultant in Guangzhou commented that the government intentionally designed the relocation program this way in order to split the villagers, and thereby reduce the likelihood that the village would unite for negotiations or protests.[24] Relocation also greatly complicated the everyday administration of the villages. One villagers' committee chair complained to me that because the village had been split, with some households remaining in the old village and others relocated to a site 45 minutes away by motorbike, he had to travel constantly between the two sites to carry out his administrative routines. It had been impossible to call a village-wide meeting since the relocation.

When physical separation implies conflicting interests, rifts can easily arise. One of the most important factors contributing to the divergence of villagers' interests is the policy of "conversion from agricultural to urban residency," or *nongzhuanju*. This policy entails shifting villagers' *hukou* from agricultural to nonagricultural, and villagers' resident status from peasant-village members to urban residents. The change of status is paired with the change in ownership of village land from the collective to the state. It is a dual strategy of transferring villagers out of the village organization and village land out of the control of the collectives. Under *nongzhuanju*, both villagers and village collectives lose their legal claims over land.[25]

Under this policy, those who lose their land are entitled to conversion from agricultural to nonagricultural status. Some choose or are persuaded to convert their status, while others insist on retaining their agricultural residency and land rights. As a result, among those who are relocated are a mix of agricultural and urban resident households. Similarly, of those who stay in the old village, some keep the agricultural household status because they are not entitled to the conversion, while others are entitled to conversion but refuse to do so, and still others who are converted to urban residency but do not want to leave the village. While converted urban residents and village members live side by side in the village, village administration is divided between the urban residents' committee and villagers' committee.

For those who retain their agricultural residency, the main advantage is their legitimacy in making claims over village collective assets and welfare benefits covered by the village collective, including shares of the village shareholding company. For this group, the main concern is fair distribution of profits generated from village assets. Those who convert to urban resident status no longer enjoy rights over collective assets, but are covered by the social security and employment package provided by the urban government. For them, the major concern is mainly monthly wages, pension payments, and other urban welfare programs. Further, of those who choose to convert to urban resident status, there is a generational gap. Those who have reached retirement age (60 for male and 55 for female) are placed in the category of "surplus-converters" no longer eligible for job allocation, and receive minimal monthly pension payments. Those under the retirement age are assigned jobs like street sweeping, and receive wages that are often higher than the pension.[26] While older "surplus-converters" feel they

15. A peasant, who lost her land, working as a street sweeper, Beijing (June 2007)

still need the village collective for welfare provisions because the pension provided by the urban government is too low, villagers who retained their agricultural status feel pinched by the retirees who technically are no longer entitled to village welfare.

In addition to those who converted to urban-resident status, and those who maintain agricultural residency, there are also villagers wavering between the two options, weighing the pros and cons while negotiating with the urban government and relocation staff over compensation packages. While the phased relocation process creates rifts between villagers who relocate and those who stay behind, and between villagers who relocate at different phases, the policy of *nongzhuanju* triggers additional friction among villagers in both the old village and the new site. In interviews with a group of Beijing villagers who represented the village lodging complaints to the municipal government about low and undelivered relocation compensation, I found that different representatives from the same village had divergent demands. Those who had become urban residents wanted higher pension and health coverage, which were promised but not delivered; those who retained their agricultural status demanded transparency in village accounting.[27] The long process of relocation, complicated by the manipulation of villagers' emotions and divisive relocation policies, had created multiple fractions among villagers.

Relocation and identity rupture

Relocation also undercuts villagers' identities. The physical removal of villagers disconnects them from their historically formed sense of place and place-based collective memory. As villagers try to settle in a relocation site, they encounter new territorial dynamics that intensify the rupture of identities, with an immediate impact on their capacity to regain control over their lives and to reterritorialize in their new homes.

A "new" place is new only to new arrivals, and is never an empty place. In theory, if an entire village were relocated together to a new site with its social organization intact, collective control would stand a good chance of being reestablished in the new place. That, at least, was the hope held out by Xinqing villagers when they agreed to relocate to the designated new village site. But that proved overly optimistic. Relocation housing is usually built on land that belongs to other villages in a more remote area controlled by the development arms of local townships or village collectives (see Chapter 6). Moving onto other people's turf, the relocatees are no longer "locals" or "natives" with moral claims over land and place, like the corporatist villagers outlined in chapter 5. Nor do the relocatees have extensive histories or social networks to call upon to strengthen their standing. Hence, villagers are reduced to timid outsiders and illegitimate intruders in an alien environment, with few political or economic resources in hand. Relocated villagers find it difficult to rebuild a connection with the place they move to, let alone regain territorial control.

Moreover, relocation-housing compounds often house people of various backgrounds and from different parts of the country. The new housing site is, in fact, a meeting point of many histories. Very few relocated villages move to a new housing compound occupied exclusively by them. Most are mixtures of relocatees from different villages, joined by former residents of inner-city neighborhoods, homebuyers unable to afford better-located commercial housing, and immigrant tenants from other provinces, who speak various dialects. In the housing compounds, drab buildings are built in grids with few meeting points or public spaces to encourage spontaneous interaction between residents. The most common scene in the public spaces of the new compounds is uniformed security guards standing alone or in pairs smoking and looking bored (see photo on page 163 of a relocation housing compound, *xiangchanquan* housing). Most of the guards are young men from the villages hired as a part of agreements stipulating that the development company provides jobs to villagers whose land was appropriated.

The relocation compound thus creates entirely different social dynamics from the old villages. It takes time to get to know the new neighbors. The elderly complain about the many flights of stairs that prevent them from seeing and visiting friends in other buildings. Meanwhile, among villagers from the same village, interests and action plans diverge greatly. The younger generation moves to other places with more promising employment oppor-tunities. "Nail households" hold out in the old village and entrepreneurial villagers manage to move to other housing compounds in better locations. Under such circumstances, organizing collective action to gain territorial control over the new place becomes a daunting, long-term project.

Such alienation is apparent in the case of Ma Yehong, a relocatee-activist in the metropolitan fringe of Beijing.[28] In the summer of 2007, Ma led me on a tour of what remained of his old village, which was being transformed into a commercial project called "Olympics Media Village." What was to me an immense, noisy, and dusty construction site dotted with newly finished and semifinished buildings seemed very different to Ma. He led me through hidden shortcuts to visit several "nail households" scattered in different parts of the site. He recounted in detail the history of the place, telling me which villagers' teams used to own which parts. He pointed to a tract that spread from a 22-storey condominium with a billboard atop reading "Green Garden Villa," to the middle of a six-lane road adjacent to an empty lot, and told me, "that was the land of my team." His demolished house had sat in the middle of what was now a construction site behind a 10-foot fence painted with images that promised another 22-storey condominium. His prized possession, a roadside restaurant built on the village's land, is now a small triangle-shaped green space at the junction of two main roads. Ma knew the place intimately and could vividly describe it, though it was now totally changed. When asked how he felt about the changes, he replied with a heavy trace of nostalgia: "I always turn my head to look at this place each time I pass by."

After the tour of the old village site, Ma took me to see his new home in a relocation-housing compound near Beijing's sixth ring road, one of the city's concentric peripheral highways. He acted differently in his new neighborhood. Some of his fellow villagers had moved to the same housing compound, and about 80 percent of the residents in his six-storey condo and seven other condos in his compound originated from neighboring villages. But he said he did not have much to say to his old neighbors in the new housing compond, nor was he interested in getting to know other new neighbors. Upon my request, he walked with me around the compound just to be courteous. He told me that the developer of the new compound, which is illegal (see Chapter 6 on *xiangchanquan* housing), wanted to expand the compound into a neighboring village but was stopped by the village. Then he concluded, "... but that was none of my business. Situations vary in different villages. We need to resolve our own problems first." I asked if he knew about the "Grand Litigation of Ten Thousand Plaintiffs" in Beijing (see Chapter 3). He said he had heard about it, but had not contacted the organizers. He explained that they were urbanites dealing with the issue of state-owned land in the city. His was the issue of collective land in the village. "These are two entirely different matters," Ma said emphatically.

Ma and a fellow villager surnamed Li have formed a two-men protest team. The two have written petition letters to the State Council, the National People's Congress, the Political Mediation Committee, and the National Office of Laws and Regulation to lodge their complaints about the district government and its development allies over the illegal appropriation of village land and unfair compensation. Ma said he and Li shared evidence they gathered to expose illegal actions of the demolition office and other government officials. But, they said, they did not trust fellow villagers who also tried to gather evidence. They complained about the lack of solidarity among villagers, and said other villagers used collected evidence to blackmail the staff of the demolition office in order to wrest better compensation packages for themselves. Another group of relocated villagers told me about their attempt to network with relocatees in neighboring villages. More than thirty representatives from different villages in the region met several times, but no collective action was taken. The representatives were mostly self-appointed, rather than elected by fellow villagers. In a recent report by Wang Guolin (2007),[29] based on a survey of fifty-seven villages in a coastal county of Zhejiang Province, there was one case of three villages whose land was appropriated for an industrial park project. After many failed attempts at protesting separately, the three villages eventually decided to write petition letters and visited the township government jointly. However, the alliance did not last longer than six months.

In a relocation compound for villagers displaced by Guangzhou's University Town that I visited in the winter of 2006, groups of unemployed men gathered to gamble in a dark room of the community center, while women sewed beads to pieces of silk cloth as subcontracting work in the open parking lot at the ground level of their apartments. The relocated villagers had many complaints over unfair relocation arrangements and the lack of jobs and services in their new housing compound and said they had tried to organize protests. One of the villages in the compound organized a visit to Beijing to lodge complaints. Each village household contributed to the representatives' travel expenses between Guangdong and Beijing. But the visit did not bring any results, and the protest ended quickly. A villager said, "I paid money for the representatives to go to Beijing, and it did not work. So I won't pay for it again."[30]

More investigation is needed before a conclusion can be drawn about the level of organization in peasants' land-based mobilization. Given the fragmented information I have, it seems that relocation has largely tamed landless peasants. The contentious process of relocation weakens the village economy and organization, creates or worsens internal distrust, lowers villagers' morale, and ruptures their collective identity. All these contribute to village deterritorialization. For sure, relocation is not the only driving force behind village deterritorialization, nor is the village in a perpetual state of cohesion and solidarity before relocation. But relocation can widen rifts that are already present and trigger new conflicts that hasten the disintegration of the village.

"Nail households" and the body politics of holding out

The connection between relocation and deterritorialization helps explain the increasing number of holdouts during village demolition and forced eviction. When all other attempts at self-protection fail, peasants resort to using their own bodies to guard their land and homes. Given the imbalanced power relationships at play in property development and China's deficient legal institutions, the physical occupation of disputed property is one of the few options available to villagers to keep themselves in the battle. As presented in Chapters 4 and 5, both urban governments and corporatist villages make their physical presence recognized by marking boundaries, erecting structures, and intensifying land use as the first step in establishing territorial control. Their territorial strategy is to establish their physical presence through occupying the place with boundary markers and buildings.

Villagers in the rural fringe also strategize to establish claims to the place. With few resources at their disposal, and under the threat of losing land and livelihood, villagers on the defensive resort to using their own bodies to occupy and mark their turf. Their bodies become the moral leverage in the bargaining process. Their actions force officials to choose between violence, which carries certain inherent political risks, and financial compromises. Villagers use their bodies to push the issue of unfair compensation and illegal land appropriation to the fore. The term "nail households," therefore, can be interpreted in two ways. From the perspective of government officials, nail households are those that defy orders and cause trouble. From the perspective of peasants, nail households evoke a metaphor of people hammered into a tight spot. In response, they, hold on tighter to their land and gamble on the intangible legitimacy concerns of government officials involved in the ruthless project of land-centered capital accumulation. Villagers collectively and individually use their bodies to hold their grounds.

Group "nail households"

Collective occupation of the land under dispute is a common strategy of protest and is usually undertaken in the village's crop fields. Upon learning about secretive land deals and when disputes arise and trust between cadres and villagers breaks down, villagers begin to squat the land under dispute. They erect tents in the fields and organize 24-hour occupation in rotating shifts to watch for bulldozers and demolition crews. These actions can involve hundreds of villagers. Many villagers have been known to occupy fields for months, and are ready to fight tooth and nail. Sociologist Yu Jianrong reported that from January to June 2004, among the eighty-seven reported land appropriation-related clashes between protesting peasants and the police, more than half of the clashes erupted on the site of the disputed land. Other clashes happened in front of the city hall, the train station, and at highways or railway tracks, where peasants had blocked traffic and organized sit-ins.[31]

As noted in the opening episode of this chapter, one of the few publicized and officially acknowledged land-related incidents took place in Yousheng Village in Dingzhou City, Hebei Province. The villagers had set up tents to occupy the disputed land tract for a year, during which they rebuffed more than ten attempts by developers to forcibly take over the land, and survived an armed attack by a large gang of thirty or more hired thugs. The standoff came to a head in June 2005 in the widely publicized pitched battle in which six villagers were killed and forty-eight were injured. While people used their bodies to occupy the land, the deaths of villagers caused by violent battles elevated the villagers' moral claims over the land. After the incident, villagers went to the hospital to "snatch" two of the dead from the hospital and bring them back to the village. As a routine practice, patients who die in the hospital cannot be taken home before the doctor examines the body and issues the death certificate. But villagers were worried that the hospital might be pressured by the city government to quickly cremate the bodies to get rid of evidence of the killings. Facing the outraged peasants, and knowing the power of local customs which claim that death outside of one's own home will disturb the spirits of the dead and affect the lives of the living, the hospital official agreed to let the villagers take the bodies home, and sent the doctor to the village to issue the death certificates. Yousheng villagers converted the office of the villagers' committee into a memorial hall, displaying the corpses in six open coffins, and playing funeral music day and night through the outdoor audio broadcasting system, commonly used for policy announcement in the villages since the Mao era.

In other recorded cases of villagers occupying disputed land, the duration of the occupation ranged from a few days to a few months, usually accompanied by letters and visits to higher-level government officials, and occasionally by legal action. According to reports, most villagers involved in these actions experienced violence and brutality. The Yousheng incident is extreme, but is not an isolated case of death and injury of protesters. In many of these cases, a number of police, security guards, and hired thugs are also injured. While some of the protesting villagers managed to squeeze more cash compensation from the demolition office, and Yousheng villagers won their land back after the six deaths, most resisting peasants are forced to retreat after devastating and violent conflicts.[32] As most villagers retreat from disputed land, and as crops and irrigation systems are purposely destroyed by the demolition office to demoralize villagers, only a few choose to continue the physically, politically, and economically costly fights against land appropriation.

Individual "nail households"

The politics of land loss and resistance against land appropriation is not a straightforward story of peasants acting as natural guardians of the land and farms. Villagers, as political actors, do not act upon one abstract principle of farmland protection or environmental causes. Instead, they consider the multifaceted gains and losses of land appropriation. In many cases, especially in more industrialized and commercialized areas and for the younger generation, peasants are not opposed to conversion of farmland, as long as they are fairly compensated. In the rural fringe, where peasants are caught between low returns from staple agriculture and a shortage of non-farm jobs, the promise of a sizeable amount of cash for land is extremely alluring. Promised compensation can bring new hope to dead-end rural lives. The young and the entrepreneurial count on the cash compensation to start a small business, while others hope to use the cash to repay debts, or build additions to the family home. But for many villagers, the rewards of cooperation with land appropriation seem disproportionate to the gains reaped by the officials who lease out the appropriated land at the price that is often a hundred times higher than the compensation payment to the peasants. Moreover, promises made in negotiations over relocation are seldom kept by the government. To bargain for higher compensation and to ensure that officials deliver on their promises, some individual villagers place their bodies on the line. The site of their protest is usually not the open fields but their own homes slated for demolition. The purpose of their protest is not protection of land, but the economic interests tied to the land.

However, nail households who succeed in getting higher compensation are mostly inner-city residents or residents of the urban fringe, rather than those in rural or semirural areas. One of the most famous cases of individual "nail households" in recent years was in Chongqing. An entire

16. The house of a "nail household" standing alone in the empty site, Beijing (June 2007)

neighborhood of 280 households was demolished to make way for a commercial housing project, but a lone house, owned by a media-savvy business couple, refused to move from their home, which teetered atop a 10-m-deep construction pit that had been dug around the entire house. The house stood for three years in the center of the construction site before it began to receive attention nationwide. Pictures of the house circulated widely in the media, and the issue of the owners' property rights were debated heatedly on the Internet, in newspapers, and on TV programs, just as the *Property Rights Law* was to be passed at the National People's Congress in the spring of 2007.[33] A month after their story had become a fixture of national public debate, the couple reportedly signed a relocation agreement with the demolition office worth an unprecedented 1.5 million yuan in cash, and new relocation housing in the city center.[34] In another case, in a "village in the city" in Shenzhen, after more than a year of solitary resistance, a villager won a package worth 12 million yuan in October 2007 for a six-storey house that stood alone on the site of a planned new financial center.[35] More stories of holdouts can be found in other large cities where residents occupy strategic locations. After watching neighbors pay dearly for accepting compensation packages too readily, and after witnessing twenty years of urban redevelopment and expansion, some urbanites and urbanized villagers have learned to calculate their bargaining leverage and to fight for greater benefits. The steady criticism of "selfish" and "greedy" nail households who slow down and block modernization continues unabated. Yet, with the passing of the *Property Rights Law*, the policy discourse of "harmonious society," and more high-ranking officials getting sacked over connections with development interests, the moral position of the nail households has been bolstered in the battle to secure a larger share of China's growing urban fortunes.[36]

Along with persistent occupation of homes and using their bodies to stand in the way of the wrecking ball, individual nail households have also used threats of suicide as a tactic to resist eviction. In such cases, protesters bring a can of gasoline to the demolition office threatening to self-immolate as a show of determination. Some death threats succeed in winning protesters higher compensation, but some backfire. The threat could, for example, be dismissed as a hoax, thereby forcing the protester to set him or herself alight to save face. The resulting injury or death may be compensated with a better relocation package for surviving family members, or it may simply lead to the closure of the case.

A far less risky tactic is to enlist more bodies in the negotiation game. In 2006, as demolition and relocation became increasingly controversial, the Shanghai Municipal Government announced a new formula to calculate compensation for each household. One important aspect of the new formula is that relocatees can choose to use the number of registered residents in the household, instead of the size of the old homes, as the baseline for compensation. Each eligible resident can receive 150,000 yuan, in addition to a discount on the purchase of a new housing unit. Eligibility for "registered residents" includes unborn babies and relatives.

This head-counting policy triggered a wave of divorces in a village of 2000 households in the Pudong area, the fast growing urban fringe of Shanghai that has become a posh business center. Some of the villagers had been relocated to the current location from the old city center, Puxi area twenty years earlier as a result of an inner-city redevelopment project. This time, the relocation was for a new office tower in Shanghai's showcase financial district. By the summer of 2007, after a year's negotiation, there were still 150 households remaining in the village. These families took advantage of the new policy in various ways. For example, couples filed for divorce, with the husband then marrying a pregnant immigrant girl, or a single mother with children. The wife would also try to do the same with a new husband. Their adult children also quickly married. Then all the added family members would register for residency in the village. A household of two or three members could thus show itself to be eligible for a compensation package for six or more residents. After they received their compensation, the new couples would file again for a divorce, and the original couples would remarry. The family would then pool the compensation to buy a new apartment. Some even had enough compensation cash to start a small business such as a majiang house.

The entire scheme was facilitated by relocation brokers, who helped them with the divorce procedures, and with finding appropriate marriage partners, all for a fee. As a result, there were cases in which a household managed to increase the number of residents eligible for compensation from four to ten; another from one to eleven. In Pudong District, where Shanghai's demolition and construction projects were concentrated, 2100 couples filed for divorce in the first five months of 2007, a 10 percent increase over the same period the year before. Nail households in Shanghais' Pudong area were relatively successful in their self-protection. Compared to many displaced and deterritorialized at the rural fringe, politically savvy and strategically located Pudong villagers have managed to squeezed more cash from the development power. Yet, theirs was also a highly individualized and isolated defense of individual economic interests. Such individualization of resistance seems to be the ultimate manifestation of peasants' deterritorialization in the face of forced relocation.

Location, relocation, and localized resistance

In this chapter, I looked at the peasants in the rural fringe of metropolitan regions and compared their territorial struggles with those of the corporatist villagers discussed in Chapter 5. I argue that their respective locations determine the scope and scale of resources the peasants have at their disposal when facing land grabs by expansionist urban governments. While locational resources are necessary but not sufficient factors in building territorial autonomy, involuntary relocation invariably leads to the deterritorialization of the village and villagers. Deterritorialization, in turn, significantly affects the results of villagers' protests against land grabs, forced eviction, and unfair compensation.

While Ching Kwan Lee's legal authoritarianism (2007) helps explain the cellularization of workers' activism in post-Mao China, deterritorialization provides another explanation of peasants' fragmented organization despite grave grievances and widespread rural agitation. Although corporatist villages in the Pearl River Delta are successful in maintaining their territorial autonomy as compared to the deterritorialized villages at the rural fringe, the phenomenon of corporatist villages remains highly localized. In fact, it is only because of localization through reinforcement of village identities and fixation of village boundaries that the corporatist villages maintain territorial autonomy. Built on location-specific real-estate fortunes, corporatist villages choose to exclude outsiders from their good fortune. While advantageous locations provide resources to build territorial autonomy, such location-specific resources and territorial autonomy do not seem to have political implications for social activism. In short, localization is a common feature of social activism in China today, including the relatively successful case of corporatist villages.

Nail household resistance to eviction is the ultimate form of localized social activism. Deterritorialized villagers resort to using their own bodies to protect property and protest its appropriation. Some nail house holds are lucky enough to occupy land in a strategic spot, and are persistent enough to effectively slow down construction, thus wresting better compensation packages for themselves. Nonetheless, very few known cases exist in which the logic of land-centered accumulation monopolized by development powers was altered, or those evicted succeeded in reterritorializing in their original village or at a new site. The struggles of individual nail households, heroic as they may be, are the struggles of deterritorialized villagers with limited implications for the broader politics of redistribution.

Notes

1. Bao, Xiaodong (2004), '*Anhui Fuyang Funanxian cunzhishu sharen shijian diaocha*' (Investigation into a murder committed by a village party secretary in Funan County, 2004. No longer accessible on *Southern Metropolitan Daily* website. For a partial report online, see <http://news.163.com/40705/9/0QH3133D0001126G.html>, accessed on February 10, 2009.
2. '*Hebei Dingzhou xiji cunmin shijian shimo: bei kongju longzhao de cunzhuang*' (The attack on villagers in Dingzhou, Hebei: the village under the shadow of horror), *San Lian shenghuo zhoukan* (San Lian Life Weekly), posted to *Jinan Shibao*, July 1, 2005. No longer accessible on San Lian's website. Online. See <http://news.qq.com/a/20050701/001470.htm>, accessed on February 12, 2009.
3. Yu Jianrong estimates the number at 66 million. See Yu, Jianrong, "Protection of peasants" land rights and urbanization in China,' 2006. According to Wang Guolin,

about 100,000 million *mu* of farmland was lost between 1996–2003, pushing about 50 million peasants off their land). See Wang, Guolin, *Shidi nongmin diaocha* (Investigation of Peasants Who Lost Their Land), 2007.

4. Yu, Jianrong, '*Tudi wenti yichengwei nongmin weiquan kangzhengde jiaodian*' (Land has become the focus of peasants' rights protests), *Guangming guancha*, 2006.

5. Lum, Thomas, "Social Unrest in China," 2006.

6. Yu, Jianrong, "*Dangqian nongmin weiquan huodong de yige jieshi kuangjia*" (An explanatory framework for current peasant rights protests), 2006. See also Yu Jianrong, "*Dangdai zhongguo nongmin weiquan zuzhide fayu yu chengzhang*" (Development of peasant mobilizational organization in China today), 2004.

7. Li, Changjin, '*Wokan nongcun xingshi jianyu Yu Jianrong boshi shangque nongmin youzuzhi kangzheng*' (My observations of the countryside and discussion with Dr. Yu Jianrong about peasant 'organized protests'), 2004. Li outlines his disagreement with Yu as follows: 'From my long tenure working in the rural areas, the relationship between local cadres and peasants is best described as isolation, alienation, indifference; and in some places and times the relationship is about tension, opposition, non-cooperation, even resistance.... In general, letters and visits, friction, and confrontation are small-scale and isolated; there were very few large-scale, well-organized, violent incidents with casualties. Most incidents are spontaneous and poorly prepared. In larger protests, the organization and division of labor among participants is simple and is resolved quickly afterwards.... There were few that could rightly be called "peasant leaders."

8. Lum, Thomas, 'Social Unrest in China,' 2006.

9. Working in a different sector, Ching Kwan Lee's conclusion (2007) from her studies of urban labor activism in post-Mao China is that workers' protests have been "cellularized" and "localized," limited to resolving grievances within their own factories, and mostly centered on economic demands. This is similar to peasant protests.

10. Whyte, Martin, "Urban China," 1992. For debates on China's civil society and public sphere, see Huang, Philip (ed.),"Special Issue on Civil Society," 1993; Kluver, Randy and John H. Powers (eds.), *Civic Discourse, Civil Society, and Chinese Communities,* 1999; Madsen, Richard, *China's Catholics,* 1998; White, Gordon, Jude Howell, and Shang Xiaoyuan, *In Search of Civil Society,* 1996; Perry, Elizabeth J. and Mark Selden (eds.), *Chinese Society,* 2003 and Hsing, You-tien and Ching Kwan Lee (eds.), *Reclaiming Chinese Society: The New Social Activism,* 2009.

11. Lee, Ching Kwan, *Against the Law,* 2007.

12. Wu, Xiaoming, '*Dangqian jianli shidi nongmin shehui baozhang gongzuo zhong yingguanzhude liangge wenti*' (Two major issues in providing social security to peasants who lost their land), 2004. The author, who was affiliated with the research division of the Bureau of Finance of Zhejiang Province, suggested that "it is proved by world history that peasants leaving the land and becoming

urban citizens is an important road for the sustainable development of a country. In China, with a large population and little land, and with a rural population of 0.8 billion, or 64 percent of the total population, urbanization is a fundamental way of realizing a *xiao-kang* society." See also Zhang, Jihui, *"Shen-fen zhuanbian yu guannian gengxin"* Change of status and perceptions, 2006. The author says that "it is an inevitable trend that peasants are "peeled off" from land in the process of urbanization. But most peasants who lost their land, including young peasants who lost their land are not fully employed in the city. There are many reasons for this. The most fundamental reason was that young peasants who lost their land are slow to change their perception."

13. Zheng, Mengxuan and Huang Shaowang, *Chengshihua zhongde Shipaicun (Shipai Village in urbanization)*, 2006.

14. For example, Shuping experienced more than 100 instances of land appropriation of different scales by different state units and urban government agencies since the 1950s. *Shipai Village Gazetteer*, 2002, Guangzhou renmin chubanshe.

15. Yang, Fangquan, *Tangcun jiufen*, (Conflicts in Tang Village), 2006, pp. 104–105.

16. Village name is fictionalized. "Natural village" was the "production brigade" under agricultural collectivism, and became "villagers' team" under the reforms, and an "economic association" under the shareholding system. An administrative village consists of several natural villages. The information of Xinqing's relocation is taken from Lan, Yuyun, *Dushi lide cunzhuang* (Village in the City). 2005, pp. 403–423.

17. Company name is fictionalized.

18. Li, Jinkui, *"Chengshi shuaixian xiandaihua zhiyi"* (Questioning the urban priority in modernization), 2005. The author cites a national survey conducted by the National Bureau of Statistics in 2003 of more than 2900 peasant households whose land was expropriated. Forty-three percent of the surveyed households had lost all their land, and 46 percent experienced decreased income after land appropriation.

19. Harvey, David, *The Urbanization of Capital*, 1985.

20. The tactic of intimidating the nail households in order to speed up redevelopment can be found in different parts of the world. For the case of New York's renewal in the 1950s–1960s and the strategies that the city used to demoralize residents, see Caro, Robert, *The Power Broker*, 1974.

21. Interview BJCY0702 (a villager in greater Beijing), Beijing, June 2007.

22. Interview BJ0306 (manager of a semi-official relocation company), Beijing, August 2003; see also Chai, Huiqun, *"Chaiqian douzhiji"* (Demolition games), 2007.

23. Interview BJCY0701 (a former village team leader in greater Beijing), Beijing, June 2007.

24. Interview GZ0402, (a planing professor and consultant) Guangzhou, Dec 2006.

25. The most extreme case of this strategy is found in Shenzhen. The Shenzhen Municipal Government announced a complete abolition of "villages" in Shenzhen. All Shenzhen villagers were converted into urban residents overnight in October 2003.

By doing so, the Shenzhen government incorporated the villages and took over collective land. See "Opinion on accelerating urbanization in Baoan and Longgang Districts," Shenzhen Communist Party Committee and People's Government Document No. 15, October 29, 2003. Online. See <http://www.sz.gov.cn/zfgb/2003/gb365/200810/t20081019_95667.html>, accessed on November 12, 2008.

26. In a village in greater Beijing, the difference is 290 yuan per month for the former, and 1000 yuan for the latter. Interview BJCY0701, Beijing, June 2007.

27. Interview BJCY0709, Beijing, June 2007.

28. Fictionalized name, interview BJCY0703, Beijing, June 2007 .

29. Wang, Guolin, *Shidi nongmin diaocha* (Investigation of Peasants Who Lost Their Land), 2007.

30. Interview GZ0606 (a villager in a relocation village in greater Guangzhou), Guangzhou, December 2006.

31. Yu, jianrong, "*Tudi wenti yichengwei nongmin weiquan kangzhengde jiaodian.*" 2006.

32. Wang, Guolin, *Shidi nongmin diaocha,* 2007; see also '*Chengdu wenjiang sanbaiduo nongmin jiti xingdong duohui bei qiangzheng tudi*' (More than 300 peasants in Wenjiang, Chengdu took collective action and forcefully took back their appropriated land), Radio Free Asia, November 7, 2007. Online. See <http://www.rfa.org/cantonese/xinwen/2007/11/07/china_rights_land/>, accessed on November 12, 2007.

33. "*Lishishang zuiniude dingzihu*" (The toughest nail household ever), *Zhongguo fazhi baodao (Law and Governance in China)*, March 21, 2007. Online. See <http://news.sina.com.cn/c/2007-03-21/143412575843.shtml>, accessed on March 2, 2008.

34. Zhang, Qin and Zhang Guilin, "*Chongqing dingzihu huo chaiqian anzhi fang ji 90 wanyuan yingye sunshi*" (Chongqing nail household received relocation housing and 900,000 yuan compensation for business loss), 2007.

35. Fu, Jianfeng, "*Zhongguo zuigui dingzihu*" (The most expensive nail household in China), 2007.

36. Chai, Huiqun, "*Chaiqian douzhiji,*" (Game of demolition and relocation), 2007. Chai reported that in October 2007, the vice-chief of the Pudong District was detained for allegedly accepting bribes of 24-apartment units. This official was also a high-level manager of the Lujiazui Finance and Trade Zone Development Company in Pudong. The development company was directly responsible for village demolition. In the month when the governor was detained, none of the villagers signed relocation agreements with the demolition office. Villagers claimed that they have seen the weakening of the semi-governmental demolition office since 2007. Street Committee and Residents' Committee staff stopped accompanying demolition office staff to visit residents to try to get residents to move. Residents believed this was due to the scandals involving high-level officials, and because of the passage of the *Property Rights Law*, which made demolition office staff more reticent to use violence in forcing residents to move. Therefore, despite repeated court orders telling them to move, nail households were optimistic about the results of their resistance.

Chapter 8

A New Territorial Order

To conclude, I'd like to broaden the scope of this book and make programmatic connections both between the *urbanized local state* and China's emerging territorial order, and between *civic territoriality* and the prospects of grassroots mobilization in Chinese cities and the countryside.

The territorial order of the land-centered regime of accumulation manifests itself in the double movement of power decentralization and reconcentration at different levels of local states as they compete for territorial control and land rents. In this process, major metropolitan centers, such as Beijing, Shanghai, Chengdu, and Nanjing emerge as the predominant force in China's new territorial order, and become new sites of central–local contention. This new territorial ordering helps to analyze the politics behind the management of the 2008 real-estate crisis.

On the distribution front, housing protests in large Chinese cities help to revisit the classic dichotomy between class- and community-based grassroots mobilization; while the disempowering consequences of peasants' deterritorialization contribute to disentangle the recent controversy over rural land rights reform in the fall of 2008. China's new territorial order, featuring regional leading cities' dominant position in accumulation, and spatially-framed social activisms of varied distributional consequences, concludes this study of the great urban transformation in China.

Urbanized local states and leading cities of metropolitan regions

In Chapters 2, 4, and 6, I presented three sets of state actors competing to control land in three types of places. In the urban core, the leading players are municipal governments and socialist land masters; at the urban fringe, urban governments battle subordinate rural governments; and in the rural fringe of the metropolis, township leaders' broker power and property between the state bureaucracy and peasants. These three sets of state actors represent the three main axes of state power in China today, and all are shaped by land development. But competition over land has done more than shape intra-state power dynamics. I argue that, as intra-state power is realigned along land interests, local states themselves are urbanized. Driven by the expectation of a continuous property boom, urban expansionism has overtaken industrialism as the ultimate goal of development and become the definition of modernity. The fiscal effects of this change are significant—land-lease sales provide 50–60 percent of the local government revenue. As a consequence, local development is invariably wrapped up in urban agendas, mega urban projects become testaments to territorial authority, and urban spectacles and property-value increases are held up as evidence of the governing capacity of local leaders. In short, the city and the local state are mutually constitutive. While local states build the city, the city builds the local state.

The territorial implications of the urbanized local state and its connection with the politics of accumulation are twofold. The first is decentralization and reconcentration in the restructuring of the territorial order for real-estate development. The second is the emergence of leading cities of metropolitan regions operating as leading sites of land-based accumulation, and key players of central–local contention.

Decentralization and reconcentration of territorial power

Land is an inherently local resource, so a land-centered regime of accumulation leads to a decentralized territorial order. Authority can be built and unbuilt by urban projects, and successful urban builders emerge as dominant territorial powers who challenge the jurisdictional hierarchy of the state. In some cases, rapidly growing minor towns outpace their supervisory cities and push for the upgrading of their administrative status to obtain greater power. Jurisdictional ranks and boundaries between territorial units were therefore readjusted multiple times throughout the 1980s and 1990s, resulting in thousands of rural towns and counties officially becoming cities.[1]

In the meantime, the impulse of local leaders to push for decentralization creates a countermovement toward power reconcentration. Counties and cities swallow up prosperous towns and villages around them, while large cities incorporate rapidly growing counties at their fringe and claim their resources. The struggle over jurisdictional annexation, merger, and detachment is bitterly fought. Ultimately, large municipalities have emerged as the victors. Supported by a central policy of administrative streamlining and coordinated urban development, counties at the fringes were formally dissolved, and their jurisdictional status converted to municipal districts. In Shanghai, for example, there were nine rural counties and twelve urban districts within the municipal jurisdiction prior to 1991. By 2005, only one rural county remained, while the others were either incorporated into existing municipal districts or became a new district under the municipal jurisdiction. In Beijing, there were eight rural counties and ten urban districts in 1996. By 2005, they had turned into two rural counties and twelve enlarged urban districts. In the 2000s, most provincial capitals made similar moves, especially targeting prosperous counties in efforts to grab land and power over personnel and finance.

Jurisdictional consolidation was also supported by an emergent policy discourse of land-focused macroeconomic contraction. Beginning in the early 2000s, land issues had gained political momentum amid a new phase of macroeconomic growth fueled primarily by expansion in the real-estate sector. The real-estate markets, especially the commodity housing sector, grew at 30 percent a year. In 2003, as GDP growth reached 10 percent, a land-centered macroeconomic adjustment policy package was set in motion.[2] For the first time since the 1980s, land was employed as a primary policy tool for macroeconomic contraction. Along with other tools of monetary and fiscal control, such as tightening credit for property development projects and mortgages for second homebuyers,[3] control over land supply was considered a fundamental cure for excessive investments that were overheating the economy. Thus, scattered land-development projects in rural areas were politically delegitimized, and the appeal of rural industrialism diminished. Further, rural governments were stripped of the authority to approve land-use conversion and rights transfers.

This land-focused macroeconomic adjustment maneuver was followed up by a series of government actions. As presented in Chapter 4, central leaders and ministries issued policies to reclaim unused land and tighten control over land-use conversion and rights transfers. Special work teams were dispatched to conduct land audits. The campaign resulted in the abolition of 70 percent of the 6866 development zones nationwide. That amounted to 24,900 sq km, or about 65 percent of the total area earmarked for development zones.[4] Under the new territorial order, land had also become a disciplinary tool of the state. Between 2000 and 2007, about 14,000 cadres were issued warnings by the Communist Party or under criminal investigation for land-related charges.[5]

Under the new ethos of "more rational, concentrated, and efficient land use," powerful and resourceful municipal governments firmed up their control over rural land and launched mega projects, such as "new towns" and "university towns." These run from ten to a few hundred square kilometers each, making them much larger than the industrial estates of the 1980s and 1990s. As outlined in Chapter 4, such new towns are both territorial and accumulation projects. Real-estate profits are maximized through multiphase, large-scale projects requiring considerable land reserves acquired through jurisdictional merger and territorial consolidation. While these projects contributed little to the central government's efforts at macroeconomic contraction, they were exploited to boost the leading city's control over the rural hinterland.

Banking reforms in the 2000s further fueled the political economy of scale evident in such moves. As national commercial banks were restructured into shareholding systems, and as risk management became more important for lenders, large borrowers ready to offer land as collateral were much preferred over small firms. This trend has encouraged local governments to take up two expansionist strategies. One is to assemble many small firms and turn them into a few star firms with impressive asset portfolios, and hence have greater creditworthiness. In some cases in the Lower Yangtze Delta, local governments have handpicked small firms, including private ones, and helped them expand by granting them land and tax subsidies.[6] The second mechanism is land expropriation. While a small portion of the expropriated land is used for immediate development, the remainder serves as collateral to finance development. A similar logic of scale also works in accessing central government grants: the larger the proposed infrastructure project, the bigger the match-up funds local governments can expect from the central government.[7] In brief, in the 2000s, massive scale, as the result of recentralized resource control, has displaced the former belief that "small boats turn faster"—held on to in the 1980s and early 1990s.

Political economy of scale and metropolitan centers

As a result of a rescaled political economy, major cities like Beijing, Shanghai, Guangzhou, Nanjing, Hangzhou, Chongqing, and some provincial capitals like Xi'an, Chengdu, Shenyang, Zhengzhou, and Jinan have emerged as leading cities of metropolitan regions, amassing large areas of land and hosting the most ambitious infrastructure and commercial projects.

Metropolitan centers have also become primary sites of central–local contention and targets for the central government efforts at macroeconomic contraction. Land-related scandals, which brought down rural cadres in townships and villages in the 1990s, began to bring down leader cadres of large cities like Zhengzhou, Shaoxing, Beijing, Shanghai and Shenzhen in the 2000s.[8] After several failed attempts to curtail rampant land development in the 1990s and early 2000s, the Ministry of Land and Resources in 2004 initiated a reorganization of the land management bureaucracy and imposed a "vertical system of land management" which gave the ministry direct control over local land-management bureaus, bypassing local governments. By 2006, a national system of urban land supervision was established.[9] Under the new system, the minister assumed the role of national land superintendent overseeing regional offices in nine cities: Beijing, Shanghai, Shenyang, Nanjing, Jinan, Guangzhou, Wuhan, Chengdu, and Xi'an. It is no coincidence that these nine cities are also where mega development projects are most concentrated. Barry Naughton (2007) has insightfully pointed out that "although all these cities are provincial capitals, by setting up the offices in individual cities, rather than in provinces per se, the objective was to create a national supervisory system separate from the governmental hierarchy."[10] Along with direct central–state monitoring of the primary sites of land-centered local regimes of accumulation, the system also indicates the emergence of a new territorial order. In this new order, the focus of central–local interaction has shifted from the provinces to major centers of real-estate development in leading cities of metropolitan regions.

But the real-estate-based territorial ordering was only possible in boom times. In 2008, the first significant downturn in China's real-estate market, compounded by the global financial meltdown, started to threaten the viability of debt-financed urban mega projects. Housing values plunged by 10–50 percent in seven months. Consequently, open land auctions in large cities, which used to provoke fierce bidding wars, failed to make sales. Lessees breached land leases with governments' land reserve centers and returned land parcels.[11] Land revenue was reduced to less than half of the previous year in cities like Guangzhou, Hangzhou, and Shanghai.[12]

The central leadership responded to the crisis with an announcement that emphasized the importance of providing affordable housing.[13] Metropolitan governments interpreted this announcement as a signal to prioritize market rescue, for which they promptly came up with bold plans. By November 2008, eighteen cities, including major real-estate markets like Shanghai, Hangzhou, Nanjing, Chengdu, and Xi'an introduced measures to prop up the market. These included cuts in transaction taxes and even subsidies for homebuyers. The minimum down payment on first homes was reduced to 20 percent from 30 percent, the stamp tax was eliminated, and mortgage rates cut. Hangzhou's municipal government, well-known for its bold measures to promote real estate, had gone so far as to offer homebuyers urban-residence certificates.[14] But the main targets of the rescue plans were developers: development surcharges and land value appreciation taxes were significantly reduced, payment schedules for land leases were extended, and time limits on developing held land were relaxed. As a boom city builds the local state, the real-estate downturn threatened to shatter the local state. Declining property prices were as strong a signal of official incompetence as rising prices were of official competence. To save themselves, urban leaders rushed to prop up the property market in order to secure land revenues and their careers. In Shenyang, for example, the municipal government reportedly organized a monopolistic coalition among developers to prop up property values in the city, and threatened to punish those who slashed housing prices.[15]

Metropolitan governments' rescue packages in 2008 have presented a challenge to the central government contraction policies. Only a few years earlier, in 2004, when the property market was at its peak, policy reports were loaded with cautionary language calling for the constriction of land supply and capital to prevent overheating in the real-estate sector and the economy as a whole. As the contraction measures started to show signs of effectiveness in 2006 and 2007, the crisis in 2008 immediately set them back. Cities' rescue packages were almost a point-by-point eradication of central government policies on constraining capital and land supplies. For example, in January 2008, the State Council announced that leases would be invalidated without compensation if developers did not break ground on a site within two years of lease signing.[16] But with the surge of failed land auctions and growing numbers of land-lease defaults since, urban governments were too desperate for land revenues to impose such a rule. One commentator predicted that the crisis might bring back the pre-2004 practice of illegal land-lease sales by local governments.[17] Amid the new round of accumulation crisis, the leading cities of metropolitan regions stood at the center of the politics of crisis management between the central and the local states.

Social activism and civic territoriality

In an uncertain policy environment, different social groups find space for mobilization within policy gaps and devise strategies in accordance with their interpretation and anticipation of state actions.[18] The great transformation, therefore, is also marked by society's creative experiments with ways of seizing opportunities when dealing with the state and market.

In Chapters 3, 5, and 7, I reported the ways that land grabs and development projects have triggered different types of social activism in various locales. In the urban cores of large cities, redevelopment projects have provoked protests by displaced inner-city residents. Inner-city protesters have launched litigation and petitions using the legal and administrative order of the state. They then stretched beyond the realm of the state in two directions. They expanded from "lawful resistance" to "rightful resistance," similar to what O'Brien and Li (2006) have found in their studies of peasant protests, by using the law as a rhetorical weapon of the weak to take the state at its word. But urban protesters did not merely employ legal texts discursively. They took legal action as a platform for social mobilization that moved beyond the logic of state-delineated legality. Moreover, while protesters engaged in property rights debates and framed their demands as "property rights protection," they moved beyond the concept of property rights to embrace a moral call for entitlement to a livelihood in the city, which I have termed residents' rights. Both homeowners and tenants in the inner city, regardless of their ownership status, make claims on social rights as city dwellers.

At the rural fringe of metropolitan regions, peasants who lose their land to urban expansion have launched protests against unfair compensation and forced relocation. Like urban protesters identified as *chaiqianhu*, or "households that are relocated and whose homes are demolished," rural peasants are known as *shidi nongmin*, or "peasants who have lost their land." Despite widespread protests in different parts of China, especially at the peripheries of industrialized areas, peasant mobilization has largely remained fragmented and localized. I have used the concept of deterritorialization of villagers to explain this puzzle. Deterritorialization, understood in this context as the process of losing physical, socioeconomic, and discursive control over homes and villages, is brought about through involuntary relocation. Relocation leads to economic deterioration, social disintegration, and a rupture of identity, which deterritorialize villagers. Deterritorialization tames dispossessed villagers and fragments their mobilization.

The relationship between the local state and society in the process of urban expansion is not confined by the sequential dynamic of land grabs, displacement, and resistance. At the urban edge of metropolitan regions in southern China, I have found another mode of state–society interaction in the process of urban expansion, as shown in Chapter 5. These "corporatist villagers" do not directly confront the state-sponsored development powers through protest or litigation. Instead, they skillfully negotiate with the state, and find opportunities for self-protection in the cracks between the state and the market. Instead of being deterritorialized like peasants at the rural fringe, corporatist villages manage to reterritorialize. They represent an important variant of social activism in the violent process of urban expansion, in which society finds its bargaining leverage and space for autonomy in the gap between the state's expansionist ambition and its regulatory capacity.

The variety of social action in different territorial contexts means that territorial power relationships are not an exclusive domain of the power elite. The lens of civic territoriality reveals the critical role that social actors play in shaping territorial politics. Civic territoriality finds different expressions in different local contexts, and presents possibilities and constraints for localized social mobilization. In the urban core, activists mobilize territorial strategies to protect their entitlement to property, place, and a livelihood in the city. Their grievances are framed spatially as losses of home, job, and social networks built to particular inner-city neighborhoods. They employ territorial rhetoric and the logic of location and relocation in the legal mobilization for property rights and residents' rights. At the urban fringe of metropolises, corporatist villagers achieve relative territorial autonomy for the village by reinforcing the village's collective economy, organization, and identity, which, in turn, fortifies successful territorialization. At the rural fringe, in contrast, displaced and dispossessed peasants are weakened economically and organizationally, and their collective identity dissipates. Displaced and dispossessed peasants are deterritorialized, undermining their political capacity to organize sustainable collective action. In other words, civic territoriality brings uneven results in civil autonomy.

The interconnection between the politics of distribution and civic territoriality can be pursued further along the lines of two theoretical debates: one concerns the debate on the relative importance of community and class in urban mobilization; the other concerns the relationship between land ownership and collectivism.

Community and class in urban mobilization

The discussion of the community and class arises from the tendency for localization that dominates the territorial logic of social mobilization. Social mobilization in the three different locales presented in this book demonstrate both the possibilities and limitations of localized social mobilization. When inner-city protesters localize their identity through long-term residence in specific neighborhoods, localization is a discursive and legal strategy against unfair compensation and forced relocation. For corporatist villagers at the urban fringe who try to reinforce collective identities and organization in the original site of the village, localization functions as leverage for relative territorial autonomy. To displaced and dispossessed peasants at the rural fringe, however, the loss of localized economic and organizational resources through forced relocation deterritorializes villagers and weakens their mobilization capacity, as demonstrated by "nail households" and their individualized protest actions.

The question of localization prompts the classic question of the strength and weakness of community-based mobilization compared with class-based mobilization. In the literature on urban mobilization in the United States, the strength of urban mobilization seems to lie in its inclusiveness, which stretches across different economic sectors or classes, and the immediacy of urban collective consumption, which appeals to a wide spectrum of urban residents. On the other hand, unlike workers facing off with capitalists in class struggles, urban residents seem to have less leverage in protests against the elite. Further, the inclusiveness of urban mobilization can also be a source of division within the community along class, race, or gender lines. Observers of American cities have found an uneasy relationship between labor unions and community organizations with different social bases and agendas.[19] In these studies, class and community occupy two distinctive physical, sociopolitical and discursive spaces. These differences tend to provoke division more often than unity, while racial and gender politics only add more challenges to their solidarity.

Recent work on Chinese urban workers suggests a different type of urban mobilization in which class and community overlap. In her research on labor protests in China's rustbelt, Ching Kwan Lee (2007) found two types of linkages between labor and urban community. One concerns the Chinese socialist *danwei* system that housed workers of the same factory in shared housing compounds. The long-term physical proximity of workspaces and residential quarters is important in building solidarity and encouraging participation in collective actions at the moment of contention. The focus of contention, according to Lee, is also reinforced, involving workers' concerns over both lost wages and unemployment, and collective consumption issues, such as heating subsidies in the long winter in China's northeast. In other words, the social and spatial overlap of class and community in Chinese state-owned factories facilitates urban mobilization. In a separate problematique, Lee also suggests that while Chinese state factory workers protest against nonpayment or unemployment, what prevents these desperate workers from further radicalization is the *danwei* housing, which provides a basic safety net for middle-aged and retired state factory workers and their families, which often include several unemployed or underemployed family members who do not have access to either *danwei* or commercial housing. In Lee's formulation, integration of the urban community and industrial workers is the basis of the socialist state's legitimacy, and such space of integration also dialectically facilitates socialist workers' protests under market reform. What remains to be seen, however, is what workers will do, and whether their protests will turn more radical, when encroaching urban redevelopment projects destroy this last resort of security, the welfare housing. The case of Tiexi District in Shenyang is exemplary. Tiexi is Lee's primary fieldwork site in the northeast. It is also one of China's largest compounds of traditional industry and the oldest working-class neighborhood in Shenyang, the provincial capital of Liaoning. Since the early 2000s, worker-residents of Tiexi have gone through massive demolition and relocation to make way for urban redevelopment projects planned by the municipal government aimed at thoroughly revamping the old and unfashionable, industrial area. Lee reported that workers protested against unfair relocation compensation, but more research is needed to see whether desperate workers, who have now lost their resource of last resort, will turn to more radical actions.

What is also unclear is the possibility for cross-class coalitions in urban mobilization, as Manuel Castells (1983) suggested in his studies of urban social movements in Europe, the United States, and Latin America. In addition to the three types of mobilization I have outlined in this book, there is another significant type of urban social activism arising among middle-class homeowners in the commodity-housing complex. Since the early 2000s, in large cities like Beijing, Shanghai, and Guangzhou, a growing number of homeowners have organized homeowner associations in individual housing compounds.[20] These owners, mostly white-collar professionals, are relatively young, well-educated and Internet-connected. They began to mobilize around the basic right to organize homeowner associations, as permitted by law, which was often obstructed by developer-affiliated property management firms and local officials. They subsequently launched litigation against developers over property-rights infringements, such as secretively leasing out public spaces within housing compounds to businesses. These disputes involve other issues as well, like false advertising, breach of contract, violation of housing density regulations, and insufficient public facilities in the compounds. Some homeowners have taken municipal governments and urban planning bureaus to court for issuing development permits that violate zoning regulations; and opposing urban development plan revisions that allow, for example, construction of residential towers on the community green.[21] These better-endowed homeowners frame their demands in a rich repertoire that includes community self-governance, grassroots democracy, citizenship rights, and property rights. In Beijing, in addition to homeowner associations organized in individual housing compounds, activists try to network among more than a hundred homeowner associations across the city.[22] While there have been signs of coalition across different districts and neighborhoods, one wonders whether cellularized and localized urban mobilization is the only structural opportunity with which social actors are able to engage in the struggle for civic territorialization.

Collective land ownership and rural collectivism

In the countryside, the link between distribution politics and civic territoriality can help clarify the policy debates on the reform of collective ownership of rural land. Peasant land rights, hardly a new point of contention in China, moved again to the fore in October 2008, during the Third Plenary Session of the 17th Central Committee of the Chinese Communist Party. Prior to the meeting, which was to focus on rural development, there had been high expectations for a revolutionary decision to allow peasants to buy, sell or lease the use rights to their fields—changes that would bring China's land tenure closer to a de facto private ownership system. But the meeting ended with a communiqué that reaffirmed the collective ownership of rural land and the reaffirmation of a ban on farmers mortgaging their land and houses.

The decision to maintain collective land ownership attracted criticism by Western media about the Chinese Communist Party's infringement of peasants' property rights and denial of peasants' access to capital. It was interpreted as a triumph of communist hardliners who dogmatically associate private property with class exploitation and a sign of the Chinese Communist Party's weakening grip on society.[23] The critics suggested that the CCP was stubbornly clinging to collectivism out of power lust and ideology. China-based intellectuals and policy thinkers were more split on the issue. For market-minded reformers disappointed by the conclusion of the meeting, privatizing rural land is the best way to protect peasants' interests against land grabs. For the socially concerned who endorsed the communiqué, land serves as a form of social security for peasants, and collective land tenure is the best way to sustain this safety net. While both camps have peasants' best interests in mind, they favor opposite solutions.

To respond to this recent round of debate on collective land ownership, two points of clarification can be made. First, we must decouple the paired concept of market and private property, and disrupt the dichotomy of public and private ownership. The post-Mao reforms have proved that it is not necessary to have "genuinely private" firms to energize a market. Nevertheless, this dogma has persisted. In media commentaries, collective land ownership is considered a barrier to land trades in rural China. In reality, land lease sales have been carried out in the Chinese countryside for at least two decades. A mixed set of actors, private, public and mixtures of both, have participated in this market. Individual households have been trading and renting their own housing sites and homes, village organizations have leased out construction land and farmland, and sold housing units they developed on village land. Local officials have exercised state authority to convert collective land to state land to allow for its sale, and have changed the use of land from agricultural to construction. While many of these transactions and conversions were found to be illegal in the eyes of state land managers in the 1980s and 1990s, the central policy toward land lease sales started to liberalize in the 2000s. Farmers are now permitted to lease out contracted land in accord with the *Rural Land Contracting Law* of 2002.[24] There have been local experiments, approved by the State Council, on rural land lease sales in Tianjin, Jiangsu, Zhejiang, Anhui, Guangdong, Shanghai, Shandong, Sichuan, and other provinces even in the 1990s,[25] long before the Third Plenary Session and the establishment of the first land-use rights exchange center in Chengdu in October 2008, which was widely celebrated as a breakthrough allowing farmers to sell or rent out land-use rights.[26]

In other words, despite the image of a stagnant land market controlled by unflinching communist ideologues, land lease sales in both legal and extralegal markets have been extremely active in rural China in the past two decades, and these changes have been far more complex than the bipolar model of private and public ownership can convey. What matters, therefore, is not the legalistic or ideological divide between private and collective land ownership. Qin Hui, a Beijing-based historian of agrarian questions, maintains that peasant land rights are a matter of political rights. For him, the fundamental contradiction lies not between private and public ownership, but emerges as a result of competing interests between the peasants and the state (and its agents) in a highly unbalanced power relationship. Even if land rights are completely privatized in legal terms, he argues, privately owned land is still subject to government expropriation for the "public interest," a condition similar to the practice of eminent domain in the United States. The critical question from this standpoint is what constitutes the "public interest," and who determines the "public interest" and how?[27] Li Changping, the former township head who initiated the public debate on the "three agricultural questions" in 2000 (see Chapter 4), has suggested that land rights are a matter of redistribution of land rents and profits, regardless of the form of ownership.[28]

A second point of clarification is to separate out three concepts that are often mixed together in the discussion of collectivism. These are: collective land ownership, village collective organization, and villagers' collective identity. While the central government's land policy seems to buttress collective ownership, other rural policies have contributed to the dissolution of village collective organizations and identity. I argue that such contradictions between collective land ownership and collective organization may be necessary for the state to sustain a land-centered regime of accumulation.

As discussed in Chapter 7, the policy of "agricultural to urban resident conversion," or *nongzhuanju*, is one of the major tools used to restructure village organization, with an explicit purpose to separate peasants from their land. This policy entails shifting villagers' *hukou* from agricultural to nonagricultural, and peasants' status from village members to urban residents. As a result, villagers are transferred out of the village, and collective land out of the control of village collectives. The dual shifts have decisively weakened the material base of village collective organization. *Nongzhuanju* usually operates jointly with another widely implemented policy of the 2000s, which turns village collective units into shareholding companies, capitalizing village land assets and turning villagers into shareholders.

Most important, this twin policy has been imposed on villages at the moment of land expropriation and village relocation. As villagers are removed from village sites and village land turned into New Towns, and as villagers are moved into different relocation housing compounds, their interests diverge and their sense of control over collective assets diminishes. Most consequently choose to cash out from shareholding companies, often at a discount rate, and village shareholding companies become private for all practical purposes. In my analysis of deterritorialized peasants in Chapter 7, I have connected the villages' physical relocation with their economic degradation and organizational disintegration, which, I argue, led to the rupture of collective identity and subsequently to the deterritorialization of peasants. Deterritorialization, in turn, helps to explain the difficulty of peasant collective mobilization. Out of the ruins of village organization and solidarity, the state's control over collective land emerges as powerful as ever, and the latter is paradoxically dependent on the former. In short, while much of the recent debates focused on the collective ownership of land, what has slipped out of the public attention is the equally detrimental impact of the government policies that have systematically and effectively dismantled peasants' collective organization and identity. Without the collective organization and identity, the villagers' control over the village territory is easily liquidized, regardless of the legalistic stipulation of their land ownership rights. Indeed, the case of corporatist villages in southern Chinese cities (see Chapter 5) proved to be a relative success. With the combination of strategic location, bargaining skills, and village corporatism, the southern villagers managed to strengthen their territorial autonomy. Yet, it remains to be seen whether these urban enclaves of corporatist villages, a welcome alternative to the wholesale destruction of the peasantry, will survive the long-term modernist impulse toward the territorial integration of urban economy, polity, and society.

Notes

1. Wang, Yuqin, "1997 *nian yilai woguo chengshi xingzheng quhua tiaozheng de bian hua jiqi yingxiang fenxi*" (An analysis of the impact of jurisdictional readjustment since 1997), 2008.
2. Wu, Jinglian, *Dangdai zhongguo jingji gaige* (*China's Contemporary Economic Reform*), 2003, pp. 349–61.
3. People's Bank of China Document No. 121, "*Guanyu jinyibu jiaoqiang fangdichan xindai yewu guanli de tongzhi*" (Notification of reinforcing credit control of real-estate development), 5 June 2003. Online. see <http://www.law-lib.com/law/law_view.asp?id=77576>. Accessed on February 1, 2009.
4. Dai, Shichao, "*Cuntu cunjin kaifaqu*" (Precious land and *kaifaqu*), 2004.
5. Ministry of Land and Resources, State Council, press conference report, "Report on 100-Day Action of *National Land Law* reinforcement," November 21, 2008. Online. See <http://www.mlr.gov.cn/zt/qt/jbszn/dsj/200811/t20081121_112390.htm>, accessed October 4, 2008. More than a third of cases occurred in 2007.
6. Shen, Minggao, "*Cuiruo de kuozhang*" (The fragile expansion), 2008. Yang, Binbin, "*Chonghui 'xiaozhengfu,*" ' (Return to "small government"), 2008.
7. Jiang, Haiyan, "*Difang tuzi weihe dayuejin?*" (Why is there a "Great Leap Forward" in local investment?), 2008.
8. Song, Wei, "*Gaoguan yidi shenpan zhidu chulu duanni*" (First experiments of the system of judging high-ranking officials in different jurisdictions), 2006. "*Zhejiang Shaoxing fushizhang shouhui baiwan beixingju huoqi tudi*" (Shaoxing vice

mayor arrested for taking millions in land bribes), Xinhua, September 9, 2008. Online. See <http://big5.xinhuanet.com/gate/big5/news.xinhuanet.com/legal/ 2008-09/09/content_9875641.htm>, accessed on December 3, 2008; "*Beijingshi renda changwei jueding mianqu Liu Zhihua fushizhang zhiwu*" (The standing Committee of People's Assembly of Beijing removes Vice Mayor Liu Zhihua), Xinhua, June 11, 2006. Online. See <http://big5.xinhuanet.com/gate/big5/ news.xinhuanet.com/newscenter/2006-06/11/content_4679450.htm>, accessed on November 12, 2008; "*Zhonggong zhongyang jueding geiyu Chen Liangyu kaichu dongji, kaichu gongzhi chufen*" (CCP Politburo abolishes Cheng Liangyu's party membership and removes him from Party Secretary post), Central People' Government of the People's Republic of China, July 26, 2007. Online. See <http://big5. gov.cn/gate/big5/www.gov.cn/jrzg/2007-07/26/content_698318.htm>, accessed on October 4, 2008. Jiang, Xun, *Shenzhen shizhang Xu Zongheng luoma muhou* (Behind the demotion of Shenzhen mayor Xu Zongheng), 2009.

9. Office of State Council, Document No. 50, "Notification on establishing national land superintendent system," July 24, 2006.

10. Naughton, Barry, "The assertive center" (2007b). Naughton also suggests that the land superintendent system is a parallel to structures established in other key areas of intensive central control, including the People's Bank of China (in 1998) and the Bureau of Statistics.

11. Zhang, Yingguang, "*Tudi kuangbiao zhihou*" (After land price hikes), 2008. Zhao, Hejuan and Fu Yanyan, "*Shanghai Shenzhen fangdichan jiangjiasheng siqi*" (Real-estate price drops in Shanghai and Shenzhen), 2008. Gong, Jing, "*Hengda dichan dafu tiaojia Nanjing loupan doujiang 35%*" (Hengda development company's big price cuts, property prices in Nanjing drop 35 percent), 2008. Jing, Baojie and Wang Li, "*Jiangjiachao manyan Beijing loushi*" (Waves of price cuts spread in Beijing), 2008. These are figures from journalists. Official figures of price drops were much smaller. According to Xinhua News Agency, the largest decline in housing prices in 70 cities was Shenzhen's at 10.8 percent in September 2008, compared with the same month the previous year. See "*Jiuyue70 chengshi fangjia Shenzhen jiangfu zuida—xinfang tongbi jiang10.8%*" (Shenzhen sees largest drop in housing prices in September of 70 cities—new home prices drop 10.8 percent from last year), Xinhua, October 22, 2008, <http://news.xinhuanet.com/fortune/ 2008-10/22/content_10233310.htm>, accessed January 9, 2009.

12. Ge, Hui, "*2008 Hangzhou tudi churangjin suoshui yuban*" (Land revenue is more than halved in 2008), 2008. Chen, Baifan, "*Zhengfu maidi jinnian shaoshou guo baiyi*" (Reduction of land sales revenues exceeds 10 billion yuan this year), 2008. In Beijing, while some news sources claimed that the revenues from land sales did not decline in Beijing, unlike in other cities, but housing prices nevertheless were stagnated or declined, with the implication of declined land sales revenues. Zhou, Hong, "*Beijing tudi churangjin shouru bujian fan ceng*" (Beijing land sale revenues don't drop, they rise), 2008. Li, Yinghui, *Beijing fangjia zi 2004 nian yilai shouci tongbi xiajiang*" (First drop of housing price in Beijing since 2004), 2009.

13. Jia, Haifeng, *"Zhongyang loushi xinzheng dingdiao baotouzi bu tuoshi"* (New central policy on real estate, protecting investment but not upholding market), 2008. This new policy refers to the "Ten measures of stabilizing and stimulating economic development" announced by the State Council Standing Committee Working Meeting on October 17th, which emphasized the increase in affordable housing, lowering taxes on housing transaction, and supporting homebuyers. Online. See <http://news.xinhuanet.com/newscenter/2008-10/19/content_10218973_1.htm>, accessed on October 30, 2008. This was followed by the Office of the State Council Document No. 131, "Opinions on facilitating the healthy development of real estate markets," December 21, 2008. Online. See <http://www.gov.cn/zwgk/2008-12/21/content_1184227.htm>, accessed on January 3, 2009.

14. Chenzhong, Xiaolu, *"Shanghai fabu fangdichan jiushi shisi tiao"* (Shanghai government announces 14 measures for market rescue), 2008. Zhang Yingguang, *"Hangzhou 24 tiao jiushi"* (Hangzhou government announces 24 measures for market rescue), 2008. Gong, Jing, *"Nanjing banbu 20 tiao jiushi xinzheng"* (Nanjing government announces 20 measures in new policy of market rescue), 2008. "What goes up," *The Economist*, p. 7, October 23, 2008. Note that the Nanjing and Hangzhou governments announced their market rescue measures prior to the State Council's "Ten measures." The municipal governments were too desperate to wait any longer, and were said to have detected the green light from central leaders' prior to the State's Council's formal announcement.

15. Zhang, Yingguang, *"Jinfang difang jiushi yuejie"* (Caution needed to prevent local governments' market rescue measures from going too far), 2008.

16. State Council, Document No. 3, "Notification on land conservation and concentration of land use," January 7, 2008. Online. See <http://www.gov.cn/zwgk/2008-01/07/content_851750.htm>, accessed on October 1, 2008.

17. Zhang, Yingguang, *"Ganga de dichan tiaokong zhengce"* (Macroeconomic adjustment policies of land caught in an embarrassing situation), 2008.

18. Lee, Ching Kwan Lee, *Against the Law*, 2007.

19. For a classic treatment of urban mobilization in the United States, see Katznelson, I., *City Trenches*, 1981. For a recent review of urban mobilization in United States' cities, see Sites, William, "Contesting the Neoliberal city?" 2007.

20. This is generated mainly by the abolition of *danwei* housing and the new home mortgage schemes in the early 2000s. For a study of homeowner associations, see Read, Benjamin, "Democratizing the neighborhood?" 2003.

21. Interviews BJ0403 (a homeowner association activist), Beijing, July 2004; and BJ0301 (a real-estate development consultant), Beijing, August 2004.

22. Conversation with a Beijing-based social researcher, July 2007.

23. "Still Not to the Tiller," *The Economist*, p. 54, October 23, 2008; Magnier, Mark, "China land reform disappears from radar," 2008.

24. According to the *Law of the People's Republic of China on Land Contract in Rural Areas*, Article 32: The right to land contractual management obtained through

household contract may, according to law, be circulated by subcontracting, leasing, exchanging, transferring or other means. Adopted August 29, 2002.

25. Zhao, Xiaofeng and Li Kuan, *"Nongcun tudi liuzhuan yuanhe chule wenti?"* (Why are there problems in rural land circulation?), 2008. Wu, Hongying, *"Chongqing nongdi liuzhaun qianye sheilai xiangshou tudi zengzhi shouyi dangao?"* (Who benefits from land profits on the eve of rural land circulation in Chongqing?), 2008. Jia, Haifeng, *"Guotubu nichu nongdi liuzhuan guanli banfa"* (The Ministry of Land and Resources announces guidelines for rural land circulation), 2008.

26. Anderlini, Jamil, "China lets farmers trade land use rights," 2008.

27. Qin, Hui, *"Qiangdiao nongmin diquan xianzhi quandi yundong"* (Prioritize peasants' land rights, hold back "land enclosure movement"), 2008; the director of the China Academy of Social Sciences Research Center for Rural Development, Zhang Xiaoshan, made similar comments. See Zhou, Zhenghua, *"Tudi chanquan yaokao minzhu quanli lai baozhang"* (Protection of land rights depends on democratic rights), 2008. This article is an interview of Zhang Xiaoshan.

28. Yuan, Ying, *"Tudi zhidu dehexin shi sheizhanyou dizu he tudizibenhua shouyi"* (Who monopolizes land rents and profits from land capitalization are the core issues of the land system), 2008.

Bibliography

Abram, Philip, Notes on the difficulty of studying the state (1977), *Journal of Historical Sociology* 1/1 (1988): 58–89.

Agnew, John, *Place and Politics* (Boston, MA: Allen and Unwin, 1987).

Anderlini, Jamil, China lets farmers trade land use rights, *Financial Times*, October 16, 2008.

Alonso, William, *Location and Land Use* (Cambridge, MA: Harvard University Press, 1964).

Altshuler, Alan, The ideologies of urban land use politics, *Land Lines* 6/8 (1996): 1–5.

Bao, Xiaodong, *Anhui Fuyang Funanxian cunzhishu sharen shijian diaocha* (Investigation into a murder committed by a village party secretary in Funan County, Fuyang Municipality, Anhui Province), *Southern Metropolitan Daily*, July 5, 2004.

Baum, Richard and Alexei Shevchenko, The state of the state, in Merle Goldman and Roderick Macfarquhar (eds.), *The Paradox of China's Post-Mao Reforms*, 333–60 (Cambridge, MA: Harvard University Press, 1999).

Beijing Municipal Bureau of Statistics, *Beijing Statistical Reports*, 2003, 2004, 2005.

Bendix, Reinhard, *Nation Building and Citizenship: Studies of Our Changing Social Order*, new enlarged edn. (Berkeley, CA: University of California Press, 1977).

Bi, Xiangyang, *Cong caomin dao gongmin: dangdai Beijing dushi yundong* (*From the Masses to Citizens: Contemporary Urban Social Movement in Beijing*), unpublished Ph.D. dissertation (Beijing: Sociology Department, Tsinghua University, 2006).

Bjorklund, E. M., The Danwei: Social-spatial characteristics of work units in China's urban society, *Economic Geography* 1/62 (1986): 19–29.

Brenner, Neil, Beyond state centrism? Space, territory, and geographical scale in globalization studies, *Theory and Society* 28 (1999): 39–78.

Broudehoux, Anne-Marie, "Spectacular Beijing: The Conspicuous Construction of an Olympic Metropolis." *Journal of Urban Affairs*, 4/29 (2007): 383–399.

Burawoy, Michael, The state and economic involution: Russia through a China lens, *World Development*, 6/24 (1996): 1105–17.

Cai, Xueqing, *Liuyue xinpan duoshu danjia guowan, goufangzhe muguang touxiang xiangchanquan* (Price of new housing projects in June exceeds 10,000 (per sq. m), homebuyers look for *xiangchanquan* housing), *Beijing yule xinbao*, June 21, 2007. Available at: http://news.soufun.com/2007-06-21/1104998.htm (accessed on December 14, 2008).

Cai, Yongshun, Collective Ownership or Cadre's Ownership? The Non-agricultural Use of Farmland in China, *The China Quarterly* 175 (2003): 662–80.

Caldeira, Teresa, *City of Walls: Crime, Segregation, and Citizenship in São Paulo.* (Berkeley: University of California Press, 2000).

Cao, Jianhai, *Zhongguo Tudi Gaoxiao Liyung Yenjiu* (*Studies of Efficient Use of Urban Land in China*) (Beijing: *Jingji guanli chubanshe*, 2002).

Cao, Shengjie and Lu Shangchun, *Hepingli beijie erhao: nanyi kaizhang de tudi chaoshi?* (Hepingli North Street No. 2: a "land supermarket" that could not have a grand opening), *Economic Observer News*, September 12, 2004.

Caro, Robert, *The Power Broker: Robert Moses and the Fall of New York* (New York: Alfred A. Knopf, 1974).

Castells, Manuel, The Urban Question: A Marxist Approach. (Cambridge, Mass: MIT Press, 1979).

—— *The City and the Grassroots* (Berkeley: University of California Press, 1983).

—— The Rise of the Network Society. (Oxford UK: Blackwell Publishing 1996).

Cartier, Carolyn, *Globalizing South China* (Oxford: Blackwell, 2001).

—— "Zone Fever", the arable land debate, and real estate speculation: China's evolving land use regime and its geographical contradictions, *Journal of Contemporary China* 10(28) (2001): 445–69.

Cawson, Alan, *Corporatism and Political Theory* (Oxford: Blackwell, 1986).

Chai, Huiqun, *Chaiqian douzhiji* (Game of demolition and relocation), *Nanfang zhoumo* (*Southern Weekend*), November 29, 2007.

Chan, Kam Wing, Misconceptions and complexities in the studies of China's cities: Definitions, statistics, and implications, *Eurasian Geography and Economics* 4/48 (2007): 383–412.

—— *Cities with Invisible Walls: Reinterpreting Urbanization in post-1949 China* (Hong Kong: Oxford University Press, 1994).

Chan, Roger and Xiaobing Zhao, The relationship between administrative hierarchy position and city size development in China, *GeoJournal* 56 (2002): 97–112.

Chen, Baifan, *Zhengfu maidi jinnian shaoshou guo baiyi* (Reduction of land sales revenues exceeds 10 billion yuan this year), *Guangzhou Daily*, December 12, 2008. Available at: http://gzdaily.dayoo.com/html/2008-12/12/content_406329.html (accessed on December 29, 2008).

Chen, J., *Liushi de Zhongguo: guoyou zichan luishi xianxiang toushi* (Lost China: inspection of the loss of state assets) (Beijing: zhongguo chengshi chubanshe, 1998).

Chen, J. J. and D. Wills (eds.), *The Impact of China's Economic Reforms upon Land, Property and Construction* (Aldershot: Ashgate, 1999).

Chenzhong, Xiaolu, *Shanghai fabu fangdichan jiushi shisi tiao* (Shanghai government announces 14 measures for market rescue), *Caijing*, October 23, 2008. Available at: http://www.caijing.com.cn/2008-10-23/110022393.html (accessed on November 5, 2008).

China National Bureau of Statistics, China Statistical Yearbooks (1991, 1996, 2001, 2006).

Bibliography

Chung, Jae Ho and Tao-chiu Lam, "City system" in flux: explaining post-Mao administrative changes, *The China Quarterly* 180 (2004): 949–50.

Cohen, Myron, Lineage development and the family in China, in Hsieh Jih-chang and Chuang Ying-chang (eds.), *The Chinese Family and Its Ritual Behavior* (Institute of Ethnography, Academia Sinica, Taipei, Taiwan, 1985).

Cooper, Mary Comerford, New thinking in financial market regulation: Dismantling the "split share structure" of Chinese listed companies, *Journal of Chinese Political Sciences* 1/13 (2008): 53–78.

Corinna-Barbara, Francis, Quasi-public, quasi-private trends in emerging market economies: The case of China, *Comparative Politics* 3/33 (2001): 275–94.

Corrigan, Philip and Derek Sayer, *The Great Arch: English State Formation as Cultural Revolution* (New York: Basil Blackwell, 1985).

Cresswell, Tim, *In Place/Out of Place: Geography, Ideology and Transgression* (Minneapolis, MN: University of Minnesota Press, 1996).

—— *Place: A Short Introduction* (Oxford: Blackwell, 2004).

Dai, Shichao, *Cuntu cunjin kaifaqu* (Precious land and *kaifaqu*), *China Real Estate News*, September 8, 2004.

Debord, Guy, *The Society of the Spectacle* (New York: Zone Books, 1995).

Defilippis, James, Alternatives to the new urban politics: Finding locality and autonomy in local economic development, *Political Geography* 18 (1999): 973–90.

Delaney, David, *Race, Place and the Law, 1836–1948* (Austin, TX: University of Texas Press, 1998).

Delaney, David, *Territory: A Short Introduction* (Oxford: Blackwell, 2005).

Deleuze, Gilles and Felix Guattari, *A Thousand Plateaus: Capitalism and Schizophrenia*, translated by Brian Massumi (Minneapolis, MN: University of Minnesota Press, 1987).

Dreyfus, Hubert and Paul Rabinow, *Michel Foucault, Beyond Structuralism and Hermeneutics*, 2nd edn. (Chicago, IL: University of Chicago Press, 1982).

Du, Z., *Bienhu qimin* (*Organizing Households and Governing People*) (Taipei: Lianjing Publisher, 1990).

Duara, Prasenjit, *Culture, Power and the State: Rural North China, 1900–1942* (Palo Alto, CA: Stanford University Press, 1988).

Edin, Maria, State capacity and local agent control in China: CCP cadre management from a township perspective, *The China Quarterly* 173 (2003): 35–52.

Esherick, Joseph and Mary Rankin, *Chinese Local Elites and Patterns of Dominance* (Berkeley: University of California Press, 1990).

Evans, Peter, ed., Livable Cities? Urban Struggles for Livelihood and Sustainability. (Berkeley: University of California Press, 2002).

Ewing, Kent, China goes back to the land, *Asian Times* (online), May 6, 2006. Available at: www.atimes.com/atimes/China/HC09Ad03.html (accessed on January 9, 2009).

Fan, Cindy, The vertical and horizontal expansions of China's city system, *Urban Geography* 6/20 (1999): 493–515.

Fang, Ke, *Dangdai Beijing jiucheng gengxin: diaocha, yanjiu, tansuo* (*Contemporary Conservation in the Inner City of Beijing: Survey, Analysis, and Investigation*) (Beijing: Zhongguo jianzhu gongye chubanshe, 2000).

Fan, Lixiang, *Nanjing: zhengfu caopan xincheng tiaokong dichan baoli* (Nanjing: municipal government controls *xincheng* and regulates huge profits), *21st Century Business Herald*, May 3, 2004.

Faure, David, *The Structure of Chinese Rural Society: Lineage and Village in the Eastern New Territories, Hong Kong* (Hong Kong: Oxford University Press, 1986).

—— and Helen F. Siu (eds.), *Down to Earth: The Territorial Bond in South China* (Palo Alto, CA: Stanford University Press, 1995).

Foucault, Michel, The subject and power, in Hubert Dreyfus and Paul Rabinow, *Michel Foucault, Beyond Structuralism and Hermeneutics*, 2nd edn. (Chicago, IL: University of Chicago Press, 1982).

Freedman, Maurice, *Lineage Organization in Southeastern China*, London School of Economics Monographs on Social Anthropology, Vol. 18 (London: Athlone Press, 1958).

Fu, Jianfeng, *Zhongguo zuigui dingzihu: zaofang huabaiwan buchang yuqianwan* (The most expensive nail household in China: more than 10 million yuan cash compensation for a house that costs 1 million to build), *Southern Weekend*, October 24, 2007. Available at: http://news.sina.com.cn/s/2007-10-25/101314161204.shtml (accessed on February 2, 2008).

Fung, Kai-yu, "Urban sprawl in China: some causative factors," in Ma, Laurence and Edward Hanten (eds.), *Urban Development in Modern China*, 194–200 (Boulder, CO: Westview Press, 1981).

Gans, Herbert J., *The Urban Villagers: Group and Class in the Life of Italian Americans* (New York: Free Press of Glencoe, 1962).

Gao, Dan, *Xiangchanquan baolu tudi guanli huise didai* (*Xiangchanquan* housing exposes the gray zone of land regulation), *Beijing Youth Daily*, July 7, 2005. Available at: http://bjyouth.ynet.com/article.jsp?oid=21811180 (accessed on February 10, 2009).

Gao, Xu, *Beijing chaiqian fenqi, xietiao, yu gongping* (*Housing Demolition in Beijing: Disagreement, Negotiation and Justice*), unpublished master's thesis (Beijing: Department of Sociology, Beijing University, 2002).

Ge, Hui, 2008 *Hangzhou tudi churangjin suoshui yuban* (Land revenue is more than halved in 2008), *Jinri caobao*, December 25, 2008. Available at: http://house.china.com.cn/land/view/27620.htm (accessed on December 29, 2008).

Gong, Jing, *Hengda dichan dafu tiaojia Nanjing loupan doujiang* 35% (Hengda development company's big price cuts, property prices in Nanjing drop 35 percent), *Caijing*, September 8, 2008. Available at: http://www.caijing.com.cn/2008-09-08/110011054.html (accessed on October 11, 2008).

Gong, Jing, *Nanjing banbu* 20 *tiao jiushi xinzheng* (Nanjing government announces 20 measures in new policy of market rescue), *Caijing*, September 28, 2008.

Available at: http://www.caijing.com.cn/2008-09-28/110016898.html (accessed on November 5, 2008).

Grzymala-Busse, Anna and Pauline Jones Luong, Reconceptualizing the state: lessons from post-Communism, *Politics and Society* 4/30 (2002): 529–54.

Guan, Shuang, *Aoyun shi fangdichan shengyan zuigao ke zengzhang* 30% (The Olympic Games: A banquet for real estate, estimated growth to be 30 percent), *Xinjing bao* (*New Beijing Daily*), November 28, 2005.

Guo, Qian and Wu Haotong, *Guangzhou chengzhongcun gaizaode wenti he gaizao kexingxing moshi yanjiu* (A study on problems of redeveloping villages in the city in Guangzhou and redevelopment feasibility), *Sichuan Architecture Research* 3/33 (2007): 183–5.

Guo, Qiang, *Zeyang yifa chaiqian jiucheng gaizhao de dingzihu fangwu?* (How to legally demolish the houses of *chaiqian* nail households?), *Shidai Business News*, June 25, 2004.

Guo, Sujian, The ownership reform in China: What direction and how far? *Journal of Contemporary China* 36/12 (2003): 553–73.

Guo, Xiaolin, Land expropriation and rural conflicts in China, *The China Quarterly*, 166 (2001): 422–39.

Guo, Yan, '*Jiejue 20 nian yiliu wenti, yiwanduo hu banchu biaozhunzu sifang*' (A 20-year historical problem resolved; more than 10,000 tenants moved out of *biaozhunzu* housing), *Beijing Youth Daily*, January 13, 2005.

Hanlon, Bernadette, Thomas Vicino, and John Rennie Short, The new metropolitan reality in the US: Rethinking the traditional model, *Urban Studies* 12/43 (2006): 2129–43.

Harvey, David, *The Urbanization of Capital* (Oxford: Blackwell, 1985).

—— From space to place and back again, in Jon Bird et al. (eds.), *Mapping the Futures: Local cultures, Global Change* (London: Routledge, 1993) pp. 3–29.

He, Qinglian, *Cunchaiqian xingwei kan zhongguo zhengfu xingweide heishehuihua* (Mafia behavior of Chinese government from the perspective of demolition and relocation), December 14, 2005. Available at: http://www.danke4china.net/shgc/9.htm (accessed on December 1, 2008).

He, Zhongping, *Chengdu mofang: jingying chengshi yu shouyeren benwei* (Chengdu complex: Urban entrepreneurialism and urban guardian), *21st Century Business Herald*, December 22, 2003.

Hinsley, Francis H., *Sovereignty* (Cambridge: Cambridge University Press, 1986).

Ho, Peter, Who owns China's land? Policies, property rights and deliberate institutional ambiguity, *The China Quarterly* 166 (2001): 394–421.

Ho, Samuel and George C. S. Lin, Emerging land markets in rural and urban China: Policies and practices, *The China Quarterly* 175 (2003): 681–707.

—— —— Non-agricultural land use in post-reform China, *The China Quarterly*, 179 (2004): 758–81.

Ho, Samuel and George Lin, The state, land system and land development processes in contemporary China, *Annals of the Association of American Geographers* 2/95 (2005): 411–36.

Holston, James, Insurgent Citizenship: Disjunctions of Democracy and Modernity in Brazil (Princeton, NJ: Princeton University Press, 2008).

Hong, Yanjie and Yang Baochuan, 212 *hu biaozhunzu sihu jinqian xinju* (212 *biaozhunzu* private homeowners moved into new homes today), *Beijing Evening*, November 18, 2004.

Hong, Yu-hung, Myths and Realities of Public Land Leasing: Canberra and Hong Kong, *Land Lines* 2/11 (1999).

—— and Steven. C. Bourassa, *Leasing Public Land: Policy Debates and International Experiences* (Lincoln Institute of Land Policy, 2003).

Hsiao, Kung-ch'uan, *Rural China: Imperial Control in the Nineteenth Century* (Seattle: University of Washington Press, 1960).

Hsing, You-tien, *Making Capitalism in China: The Taiwan Connection* (New York: Oxford University Press, 1998).

—— Land and territorial politics in urban China, *The China Quarterly* No. 187 (2006): 575–91.

Hsing, You-tien, Foreign capital and local real estate development in China, in Wu Fulong (ed.), *Globalization and Chinese Cities*, 167–89 (New York: Routledge, 2006).

—— Brokering power and property in China's townships, *Pacific Review* 1/19 (2006): 103–24.

—— and Ching Kwan Lee (eds.), *Reclaiming Chinese Society: The New Social Activism* (New York: Routledge, 2009).

Hu, Liping, *Shenzhen chengshi jianshe yongdi kuozhang yu kongzhi yanjiu* (*A Study on Shenzhen's Expansion of Construction Land and Its Control*), master's thesis (Department of Geography, Zhongshan University, Guangzhou, 2006).

Hu, Yifan, *Nongfu zhibian* (Changes in agricultural taxes), *Caijing*, August 5, 2002. Available at: http://magazine.caijing.com.cn/20020805/2356.shtml.

Huang, Chiling, *Gaige kaifang zhong Shanghai dushi duti fazhan yu dushi kongjian zaijiegou* (*Urban Land Development and Urban Space Restructuring in Shanghai During Economic Reforms*), unpublished master's thesis (Shanghai: Department of Urban Planning, Tongji University, 1997).

Huang, Peijian, *Jiti tudi liuzhuan: zouxiang bianfa* (Circulation of collective land: moving towards a policy change), *The Economic Observer*, August 11, 2003. Available at: http://www.fsa.gov.cn/web_db/sdzg2004/internet/person/BGOV/gzgdbtt/g2003080010.htm (accessed on February 10, 2009).

Huang, Philip, *The Peasant Economy and Social Change in North China* (Palo Alto, CA: Stanford University Press, 1985).

Huang, Philip (ed.), Special issue on civil society, *Modern China* 2/19 (1993).

Jia, Haifeng, *Zhongyang loushi xinzheng dingdiao baotouzi bu tuoshi* (New central policy on real estate, protecting investment but not upholding market), *21st Century Business Herald*, October 21, 2008. Available at: http://www.21cbh.com/HTML/2008/10/21/HTML_4F5HR2XDJNIV.html (accessed on October 30, 2008).

—— *Guotubu nichu nongdi liuzhuan guanli banfa* (The minsitry of land and resources announces guidelines for rural land circulation), *21st Century Business Herald*, October 30, 2008. Available at: http://www.21cbh.com/Content.asp/?NewsId=85734 (accessed on November 5, 2008).

Jiang, Yun, *Chanquan jieding de quanli shijian: yi jingzusifangzhu de weiquan huodong wei gean (Rights Practice in Property Rights Confirmation: A Case Study of Rights Protection of jingzufang Private Home Owners)*, unpublished master's thesis (Beijing: Department of Sociology, Tsinghua University, 2006).

Jian, Xia, *Chaiqian, haishi jiaofei?* (Is it demolition or attacking bandits?), *China Economic Times*, May 27, 2004.

Jiang, Haiyan, *Difang tuzi weihe dayuejin?* (Why is there a "Great Leap Forward" in local investment?), *Caijing*, November 25, 2008. Available at: http://www.caijing.com.cn/2008-11-25/110031694.html (accessed on November 30, 2008).

Jiang, Shengsan and Liu Shouying, *Tudi zibenhua yu nongcun gongyehua—Guangdong Foshanshi Nanhai jingji fazhan diaocha* (Capitalizing land and industrializing villages—a survey of economic development in Nanhai in Foshan City, Guangdong Province),*Guanli shijie (Management World)* 11 (2003): 87–97.

—— —— *Nanhai moshi: rang nongmin yitudi quanli canyu gongyehua* (Nanhai Model: allows peasants to participate in industrialization with their land rights—an interview with Jiang Shengsan and Liu Shouying), *China Economics Times*, May 15, 2003.

Jiang, Xun, *Shenzhen shi zhang Xu Zongheng luoma muhou* (Behind the demotion of shenzhen Mayor Xu Zongheng), Yazhou Zhoukan (The International Chinese Newsweekly), June, 21, 2009. pp. 38–39.

Jin, Cheng and Chen Shanzhe, Shenzhen quanmian gaizao chengzhongcun (Shenzhen in full gear to redevelop "villages in the City"), *21st Century Business Herald*, August 16, 2004.

Jing, Baojie and Wang Li, *Jiangjiachao manyan Beijing loushi* (Waves of price cuts spread in Beijing), *21st Century Business Herald*, October 17, 2008. Available at: http://www.21cbh.com/HTML/2008/10/17/HTML_FN4QMK26R3T5.html (accessed on November 13, 2008).

Jing, Hua, *chengxiang jumin shouruchaju jinwanyuan* (Rural-urban income gap almost reaches 10,000 yuan mark), *Nanfang Daily*, August 30, 2008. Available at: http://www.nanfangdaily.com.cn/epaper/nfrb/content/20080830/Article-1A01004FM.htm (accessed on October 15, 2008).

Katznelson, I., *City Trenches: Urban Politics and the Pattern of Class in the United States* (New York: Pantheon, 1981).

Kim, A., A market without the "right" property rights: Ho Chi Minh City, Vietnam's newly emerged private real estate market, *Economics of Transition* 2/12 (2004): 275–305.

Kirkby, Richard, *Urbanization in China; Town and Country in a Developing Economy 1949–2000 AD* (New York: Columbia University Press, 1985).

Kluver, Randy and John H. Powers (eds.), *Civic Discourse, Civil Society, and Chinese Communitie*s (Stamford, CT: Ablex Publishing Corporation, 1999).

Kuhn, Philip, Local self-government under the republic, in Wakeman, Frederic and Carolyn Grant (eds.), *Conflict and Control in Late Imperial China* (Berkeley: University of California Press, 1975).

Lake, Robert, Negotiating local autonomy, *Political Geography* 13 (1994): 423–42.

Lan, Yuyun, *Dushi lide cunzhuang:yige xincunshe gongtongti de shidi yanjiu* (*Village in the city: Case study of a "New Village Collective"*) (Beijing: *sanliang shudian*, 2005).

—— and Guo Zhenglin, *Lun chengzhongcunde shequ baozhang ji chengshihua yiyi: yi Guangzhou yi chengzhongcun weili de yanjiu* (The meaning of "village in the city" for social security and urbanization: the case of a "village in the city" in Guangzhou), *Shehui kexue zhanxian* (Battle Fields in Social Sciences), 2 (2006): 188–93.

Lee, Ching Kwan, *Against the Law: Labor Protests in China's Rustbelt and Sunbelt* (Berkeley: University of California Press, 2007).

Lefebvre, Henri, *The Production of Space* (Oxford: Blackwell, 1991).

—— *The Urban Revolution* (Minneapolis, MN: University of Minnesota Press, 2003).

Li, Changjin, *Wokan nongcun xingshi jianyu Yu Jianrong boshi shangque nongmin youzuzhi kangzheng* (My observations of the countryside and discussion with Dr. Yu Jianrong about peasant "organized protests"), *Sannong zhongguo*, Spring 2004. Available at: http://www.snzg.cn/member1/member.php/username=%C0%EE%B2%FD%C6%BD (accessed on November 11, 2006).

Li, Jinkui, "*Nongcun chengshi huazhong shehui maodunde jilei*" (The accumulation of social conflicts in the process of village urbanization), Beijing: kexue shibao (Science Times), December 15, 2005. Online. See <http://tech.memail.net/051215/132,33,2209510,00.shtml>. accessed on October 9, 2008.

—— *Chengshi shuaixian xiandaihua zhiyi—zhongguo hexie chengshihuade guanjian suozai* (Questioning the urban priority in modernization: the key to harmonious urbanization in China), Beijing: *Kexue shibao* (*Science Times*), December 16, 2005. Online. See <http://www.cas.cn/html/Dir/2005/12/16/13/65/76.htm> accessed on October 9, 2008.

Li, Junfu, *Chengzhongcun de gaizao* (*Redevelopment of Chengzhongcun*) (Beijing: *Kexue chubanshe*, 2004).

Li, Ling Hin, *Urban Land Reform in China* (London: McMillan Press, 1999).

Li, Linda Chilan, Understanding institutional change: fiscal management in local China, *Journal of Contemporary Asia* 1 (2005): 87–108.

Li, Lixun, *Guangzhoushi chengzhongcun xingcheng ji gaizao jizhi yanjiu* (*Study of the Formation and Redevelopment Strategy of Village in the City in Guangzhou*), Ph.D. dissertation (Department of Geography, Zhongshan University, Guangzhou, 2002).

Li, Peilin, *Cunluo de zhongjie—Yangchengcun de gushi* (*The End of Village: Story of Yangcheng Village*) (Beijing: *Shangxu chubanshe*, 2004).

Li, Peng, *Zhongguo difang zhengfu zhaiwu fengxian cheng touhao weixie, chuyu shikong bianyuan* (Chinese local governments' debts are the No. 1 threat, at the edge of losing control), *China News*, February 23, 2004. Available at: http://finance.sina.com.cn/nz/dept/index.shtml (accessed on September 7, 2008).

Li, Shufeng and Po Ren, *Shanghai tudi chubeizhi zhuanxing* (Transformation of Shanghai's land reserve system), *Caijing*, 76 (2003).

Li, Yinghui, *Beijing fangjia zi 2004 nian yilai shouci tongbi xiajiang* ("First drop of housing price in Beijing since 2004"), *Xinhua News*, February 13, 2009. Available at: http://big5.xinhuanet.com/gate/big5/news.xinhuanet.com/house/2009-02/13/content_10810665.htm (accessed on February 16, 2009).

Lichtenberg, Erik and Chengri Ding, Assessing farmland protection policy in China, *Land Use Policy* 1/25 (2008): 59–68.

Lin, Chun, Against privatization in China: A historical and empirical argument, *Journal of Chinese Political Science* 1/13 (2008): 1–27.

Lin, George C. S., The growth and structural change of Chinese cities: A contextual and geographic analysis, *Cities* 5/19 (2002): 299–316.

—— Towards a post-socialist city? Economic tertiarization and urban reformation in the Guangzhou metropolis, China, *Eurasia Geography and Economics* 1/45 (2004): 18–44.

—— Peri-urbanism in globalizing China: A study of new urbanism in Dongguan, *Eurasian Geography and Economics* 1/47 (2006): 28–53.

—— Reproducing spaces of Chinese urbanization: New city-based and land-centered urban transformation, *Urban Studies* 9/44 (2007): 1827–55.

—— and Samuel Ho, The state, land system, and land development processes in contemporary China, *Annals of the Association of American Geographers* 2/95 (2005): 411–36.

Lin, Ke, *Dalu pinfu chongtu yichujifa* (Conflicts between the poor and the rich in mainland is a time bomb), *Shangye Zhoukan* (*Business Weekly*), Taipei, 88 (September 29, 2003).

Lin, Mingyi, Lu Yuejin, and Zhou Zhenglu, *Shiluan jinjiao chengshihua jingcheng zhongde nongmin jiti tudi chanquan zhidu jianshe* (Establishing a peasants' collective landed property rights system in the process of urbanization in suburban areas), *Turang* (*Soil*) 3/26 (2004): 25–7.

Liu, Junde, Zhongguo zhuanxingqi tuxian de 'xingzhengqu jingji' xianxiang fenxi (An analysis of "jurisdictional economy"), *Lilun qianyan* (*Theoretical Frontiers*) 10 (2004): 20–2.

Liu, Neng, *Xiangzhen yunxing jizhide yici jiepo* (An analysis of the mechanism of township operation), in Rong Ma, Liu Shiding, and Qiu Zeqi (eds.), *Zhongguo xiangzhen zuzhi bianqian yanjiu* (*Transformation of Chinese Township Organization*) (Beijing: *Huaxia chubanshe*, 2000).

Liu, Ping, *Bei yiwang de zhanzheng—Xianfeng, Tongzhi nianjian Guangdong tuke daxiedou yanjiu* (*A forgotten War: A Study of Armed Fights during the Reigns of Xianfeng and Tongzhi*) (Beijing: *Shangwu chubanshe*, 2003).

Liu, Qian, *Cunji, diyuan yu yeyuan—yige zhongguo zhongbu cunzhuang de shehui fencing* (Village membership, place connection, and occupation connection: social stratification of a village in central China), Chinese Academy of Social Sciences, May 8, 2004. Available at: http://www.sociology.cass.cn (accessed on December 6, 2008).

Liu, Shiding, '*Xiangzhen caizheng shouru jiegou*' (Financial structure of townships), in Ma, Rong, Liu Shiding and Qiu Zeqi (eds.) *zhongguo xiangzhen zu zhi bianqian yanjiu* (Transformation of Chinese Township Organization), (Beijing: Huaxia chubanshe, 2000).

Liu, Zhiming, *Chaiqian chai de rangren xinhan* (Demolition chills people's hearts), *China News Weekly* (*Zhongguo xinwen zhoukan*), September 29, 2003.

—— *Sushi fufu: shei chaile wode fangzi?* (Mr. and Mrs. Su: who tore down my house?), *China News Weekly* (*Zhongguo xinwen zhoukan*), September 29, 2003.

Logan, John and Harvey Molotch, *Urban Fortunes: The Political Economy of Growth* (Berkeley: University of California Press, 1987).

Lu, Dadao et al., *Zhongguo quyu fazhan baogao—chengshihua jincheng ji kongjian kuozhang* (*Report on China's regional development: Progress in urbanization and spatial expansion*) (Beijing: Shangwu Yinshuguan, 2006).

Lu, Duanfang, *Rebuilding Chinese Urban Form.* (London: Routledge, 2006).

Lu, Xiaobo and Elizabeth Perry (eds.), *Danwei: The Changing Chinese Workplace in Historical and Comparative Perspective* (Armonk, NY: M.E. Sharpe, 1997).

Lubman, Stanley, *Bird in a Cage: Legal Reform in China After Mao* (Stanford, CA: Stanford University Press, 1999).

Lum, Thomas, "Social Unrest in China," Congressional Research Service (CRS) Reports and Issue Briefs, 2006, Cornell University. Online see <http://digitalcommons.ilr.cornell.edu/cgi/viewcontent.cgi?article=1018&context=crs>, accessed on November 1, 2008.

Luo, Xiaojun, *Zhejiang chuangzhi: guifan difang zhengfu juzhai* (Zhejiang's policy innovation: regulating local governments' borrowing), *21st Century Business Herald*, February 5, 2005.

Ma, Hongshou, Zhou Renjie, Xiong Manling, and Su Yan, *Zhongguo xuyao duoshao CBD?* ("How many CBDs does China need?"), *China Central TV-News*, April 15, 2003.

Ma, Laurence, Urban transformation in China, 1949–2000: A review and research agenda, *Environment and Planning A* 34 (2002): 1545–69.

—— Urban administrative restructuring, changing scale relations and local economic development in China, *Political Geography* 24 (2005): 477–97.

—— The state of the field of urban China: A critical multidisciplinary overview of the literature, *China Information* 20 (2006): 363–89.

—— and Gonghao Cui, Administrative changes and urban population in China, *Annals of the Association of American Geographers*, 3/77 (1987): 373–95.

Ma, Lin and Wu Ying, *Xiangchanquan fang chuyu mohu didai jianshebu tishi fengxian* (*Xiangchanquan* housing located in a vague zone, officials in Ministry of Construction remind homebuyers of risks), *China Real Estate News*, June 25, 2007. Available at: http://house.focus.cn/news/2007-06-25/328121.html.

Madsen, Richard, *China's Catholics: Tragedy and Hope in an Emerging Civil Society* (Berkeley: University of California Press, 1998).

Magnier, Mark, China land reform disappears from radar, *The Los Angeles Times*, October 15, 2008.

Makielski, S. J. Jr., *The Politics of Zoning: The New York Experience* (New York: Columbia University Press, 1966).

Mao, Dan, *Yige cunluo gongtongtide bianqian* (*Transformation of a Village Collective*) (Beijing: Xuelin chubanshe, 2000).

Mao, Shoulong, *Cun zhidushang fansi Taole de jue zhaiwu* ("Reflections on the massive debt of Taole"), *Xinjing Bao* (*New Beijing News*), October 5, 2004.

Marcuse, Peter, Privatization and its discontents: Property rights in land and housing in the transition in Eastern Europe, in Andrusz, G., M. Harloe, and I. Szelenyi (eds.), *Cities after Socialism: Urban and Regional Change and Conflict in Post-Socialist Societies*, 119–91 (Oxford: Blackwell, 1996).

Marshall, T. Humphrey, *Citizenship and Social Class*. London: Pluto Press, 1992.

Massey, Doreen, *Space, Place and Gender* (Minneapolis: University of Minnesota Press, 1994).

Mitchell, Don, *The Right to the City: Social Justice and the Fight for Public Space* (New York: Guilford, 2003).

Mo, Chengshun, *Hainan fangdichan: paomo yichan zhongju sijin huanyuan* (property bubbles in Hainan: whether the end is near is unclear), *Caijing* 76, January 20, 2003. Online. See <http://magazine.caijing.com.cn/20030120/3341.shtml> (accessed on January 13, 2009).

Murray, Martin, *Taming the Disorderly City: The Spatial Landscape of Johannesburg after Apartheid* (Ithaca: Cornell University Press, 2008).

Nan, Xianghong and Ma Jieting, *Chule Qianmen daona anjia?* (Where to after moving out from Qianmen?), *Nanfang zhoumo* (*Southern Weekend*), October 12, 2006.

Naughton, Barry, *Growing Out of the Plan: Chinese Economic Reform 1978–93* (New York: Cambridge University Press, 1996).

—— *The Chinese Economy: Transitions and Growth* (Cambridge, MA: MIT Press, 2007a).

—— The assertive center: Beijing moves against local government control of land, *China Leadership Monitor*, 20 (2007b).

Nolan, Peter and Wang Xiaoqiang, Beyond privatization: Institutional innovation and growth in China's large state-owned enterprises, *World Development* 1/27 (1999): 169–200.

O'Brien, Kevin and Lianjiang Li, Selective policy implementation in rural China, *Comparative Politics* 1/99 (1999): 167–86.

—— —— *Rightful Resistance in Rural China* (Cambridge: Cambridge University Press, 2006).

Oi, Jean, Fiscal reform and the economic foundations of local state corporatism in China, *World Politics* 1/45 (1992): 99–126.

Oi, Jean, and A. Walder (eds.), *Property Rights and Economic Reform in China* (Stanford, CA: Stanford University Press, 1999).

Pannell, Clifton, China's continuing urban transition, *Environment and Planning A* 34 (2002): 1571–89.

Perry, Elizabeth and Mark, Selden (eds.), *Chinese Society: Chang, Conflict and Resistance*, 2nd edn. (NY: Routledge Curzon, 2003).

Phan, Pamela, Enriching the land or the political elite? Lessons from China on the democratization of the urban renewal process, *Pacific Rim Law and Policy Journal* 14 (2005): 607–52.

Po, Lan-chih, *Strategies of Urban Development in China's Reforms: Nanjing, 1984–2000*, Ph.D. dissertation (Department of City and Regional Planning, University of California at Berkeley, 2001).

Potter, Sulamith H. and Jack M. Potter, *China's Peasants: The Anthropology of a Revolution* (Cambridge: Cambridge University Press, 1990).

Pratt, Geraldine, Geographies of identity and difference: making boundaries, in Doreen Massey et al. (eds.), *Human Geography Today*, 151–68 (Cambridge: Polity, 1999).

Pred, Allan, Place as historically contingent process: Structuration and the time-geography of becoming places, *Annals of the Association of American Geographers* 2/74 (1984): 279–97.

Prosterman, Roy, Tim Hanstad, Brian Schwarzwalder, and Ping Li, *Rural Land Reform in China and the 1998 Land Management Law* (Seattle, WA: Rural Development Institute Reports on Foreign Aid and Development #98, 1998).

Qian, Hang, *Xueyuan yu diyuan zhijian: Zhongguo lishishang liangzong yu liangzong-zuzhi* (*Between Blood and Place Connections: Lineage Alliance and Its Organization in Chinese History*) (Shanghai: Shanghai *shehui kexue chubanshe*, 2001).

Qin, Hui, *Nongmin zhongguo: lishi fansi yu xianshi xuanze* (*China's Peasantry: Reflections on History and Choices in Reality*) (Zhengzhou: Henan renmin chubanshe, 2003).

—— *Qiangdiao nongmin diquan xianzhi quandi yundong* (Prioritize peasants' land rights, hold back "land enclosure movement"), *Luye*, No. 11, December 5, 2008. Available at: http://www.snzg.cn/article/show.php/itemid-12750/page-1.html (accessed on December 5, 2008).

Qin, Wen, *Beijing weifanggaizao jinru weixunhuan shidai* (Redevelopment in Beijing enters a new period of "microcirculation"), *New Beijing Daily* (*Xinjingbao*), January 4, 2005.

Read, Benjamin, Democratizing the neighborhood? New private housing and home-owner self organization in urban China, *The China Journal* 49 (2003): 31–59.

Reed, Bradly, *Talons and Teeth: County Clerks and Runners in the Qing Dynasty* (Palo Alto, CA: Stanford University Press, 2000).

Ren, Baoyu, *nongye zhudaoxing caizheng xiade xiangzhen zhili* (Township governance under agriculture-oriented fiscal regime), in *Shandong keji daxue xuebao shehui kexueban* 2/4 (2002): 57–62.

Ren, Po, *chengshi tudi zhimi* (Secret of Urban Land), *Caijing* 76, January 20, 2003. Available at: http://magazine.caijing.com.cn/20030120/2101.shtml (accessed on February 12, 2009).

—— *Beijing yuhui zhilu* (The winding path that Beijing took), *Caijing* 76, January 20, 2003. Available at: http://magazine.caijing.com.cn/20030120/2135.shtml (accessed on February 12, 2009).

—— *chaiqian zhisu* (Law suites over demolition), *Caijing* 87, July 5, 2003. Available at: http://magazine.caijing.com.cn/20030705/3379.shtml (accessed on February 12, 2009).

—— *xinquandi yundong molu* (The end of "New Land Enclosure") *Caijing* 90, August 20, 2003. Available at: http://magazine.caijing.com.cn/20030820/3380.shtml (accessed on February 12, 2009).

Ren, Zhiqiang, *Ruhe nadi?* (How to obtain land?), Beijing: *Jingji guanchabao (The Economic Observer News)*, September 24, 2003.

Ren, Zhiqiang, *Renren pingshuo (Ren's Commentaries on Real Estate)* (Beijing: *Zhonghua gongzhang lianhe chubanshe*, 2003).

Sargeson, Sally, Subduing "the Rural House-Building Craze": Attitudes towards housing construction and land use control in four Zhejiang villages, *The China Quarterly* 172 (2002): 927–55.

—— Full circle? Rural land reforms in globalizing China, *Critical Asian Studies* 4/36 (2004): 637–56.

Scott, James, *Seeing Like a State: How Certain Schemes to Improve the Human Condition Have Failed* (New Haven, CT.: Yale University Press, 1998).

Shanghai chengshi guihua (Shanghai's City Planning) (Shanghai: Shanghai Municipal Bureau of Urban Planning, 1998).

Shen, Lang, *Shanghai tudi xianzhi zhimi* (The mystery of vacant land in Shanghai), Beijing: *The 21st Century Business Herald*, September 15, 2004.

Shen, Minggao, *Cuiruo de kuozhang* (The fragile expansion), *Caijing*, November 11, 2008. Available at: http://www.caijing.com.cn/2008-11-11/ (accessed on November 12, 2008).

Shen, Yuan, *Shichang, jieji, yushehui: zhuanxing shehuixue de guan jian wenti*, (Market, class and society: critical issues in the sociology of transformation) (Beijing: Social Science Documentation Publishing House, 2008).

Shi, Fayong and Cai, Yongshun, Disaggregating the state: networks and collective resistance in Shanghai, *The China Quarterly* 186 (2006): 314–32.

Shi, Mi, The evolving law of disputed relocation: Constructing inner city renewal practices in Shanghai, 1990–2005, *International Journal of Urban and Regional Research* Fourthcoming 1/34 (2010).

Shi, Yi and Zhao Xiaojian, *Sunan yuyan* (The tale of southern Jiangsu), *Caijing*, May 5, 2001. Available at: http://magazine.caijing.com.cn/20010505/2288.shtml (accessed on May 5, 2006).

Shue, Vivienne, Legitimacy crisis in China? in Peter Hays Gries and Stanley Rosen (eds.), *State and Society in 21st-Century China: Crisis, Contention, and Legitimation*, 24–49 (New York: RoutledgeCurzon, 2004).

Simmons, James and Larry Bourne, Defining urban places: Differing concepts of the urban systems, in James Simmons and Larry Bourne (eds.), *Systems of Cities: Readings on Structure Growth and Policy*, 28–41 (New York: Oxford University Press, 1978).

Singer, Joseph, *Entitlement: The Paradox of Property* (New Haven, CT: Yale University Press, 2000).

Sites, William, Contesting the neoliberal city? Theories of neoliberalism and urban strategies of contention, in Helga Leitner, Jamie Peck, and Eric Sheppard (eds.), *Contesting Neoliberalism: Urban Frontiers*, 116–38 (New York: Guilford Press, 2007).

Smith, Neil, *The New Urban Frontier: Gentrification and the Revanchist City* (New York: Routledge, 1996).

—— and Cindi Katz, Grounding metaphor: Towards a spatialized politics, in Michael Keith and Steve Pile (eds.), *Place and the Politics of Identity*, 66–81 (New York: Routledge, 1993).

Song, Wei, *Gaoguan yidi shenpan zhidu chulu duanni* (First experiments of the system of judging high-ranking officials in different jurisdictions), *News of the Communist Party of China*, December 25, 2006. Available at: http://cpc.people.com.cn/BIG5/64093/64371/5209949.html (accessed on December 12, 2008).

Song, Yan and Chengri Ding eds., *Smart Urban Growth for China*, (Cambridge, Mass.: Lincoln Institute of Land Policy, 2009).

Stepan, Alfred, *The State and Society: Peru in Comparative Perspective* (Princeton: Princeton University Press, 1978).

Su, Si, *Zijin queshi houde zhujiang xincheng xiezilo kaifa lujing* (Capital shortage and development strategies of office space in Zhujiang New City), *21st Century Business Herald*, September 22, 2004.

Sun, Liping and Guo Yuhua, *Ruanying jianshi: zhengshi quanli feizhengshi yunzuode guocheng fenxi* (Combination of soft and hard approaches: a process analysis of informal exercise of formal power), *Tsinghua Sociological Review*, May 2000: 21–46.

Sun, Qingzhong, *Xiangcun dushihua yu dushi cunmin de zongzu shenghuo: Guangzhou chengzhong sancun yanjiu* (Urbanization of villages and lineage organization of urbanized villagers: Three "villages in the city" in Guangzhou), *Dangdai zhongguoshi yanjiu* (*Research of Contemporary Chinese History*) 3/10 (2003): 96–104.

Takeuchi, Hiroki, *Rural Tax Reform and Authoritarian Rule in China*. Ph.D. Dissertation, Department of Political Science, University of California at Los Angeles, 2006.

Tang, Zheng, *8–31 da-xien* (The 31 August deadline), *Caijing* 110 (2004): 96–99.

Teaford, Jon, *City and Suburb: The Political Fragmentation of Metropolitan America, 1850–1970* (Baltimore: Johns Hopkins University Press, 1979).

—— *The Twentieth-Century American City* (Baltimore, MD: The Johns Hopkins University Press, 1986).

Bibliography

The Economist, What goes up, p.7, October 23, 2008.

—— Still Not to the Tiller, p.54, October 23, 2008.

Tian, Qilin, *Weigai zhimi* (Secrets of "Dangerous" housing renovation), *Caijing*, 24, December 20, 2003.

Tian, Xinjie, *Shibohui jinru shizhi yunzuo Shanghai chengjian kuaipao* (The World Expo preparation proceeds, Shanghai urban construction runs fast), *21st Century Business Herald*, December 7, 2005.

Tong, Zhihui, *Cunmin zhijie xuanju zhongde xiangzhengfu* (Township government in villages direct elections) in Xu, Yong (ed.), *Zhongguo nongcun yanjiu* (*China Rural Studies*), (Beijing: China Social Science *chubanshe*, 2002) pp. 46–63.

Tsui, Kai-yuen and Youqiang Wang, Between separate stoves and a single menu: Fiscal decentralization in China, *The China Quarterly* 177 (2004): 71–90.

Verdery, Katherine, The elasticity of land: Problems of property restitution in Transylvania, *Slavic Review* 4/53 (1994): 1071–109.

Walker, Richard, *The Country in the City: The Greening of the San Francisco Bay Area* (Seattle: University of Washington Press, 2008).

Wang, Fengjun, *Guotu ziyuanbu de gaige luxiantu* (Map of reform of the Ministry of Land and Resources), *21st Century Business Herald*, February 18, 2004.

Wang, Guolin, *Shidi Nongmin diaocha* (*Investigation of Peasants Who Lost Their Land*) (Beijing: Xinhua Publisher, 2007).

Wang, Hao, *Zhujian xincheng* CBD *zhilu zaoyu hongdeng* (Red lights on the road to Zhujiang New City CBD), *Nanfang Daily*, June 3, 2005.

Wang, Shiling, *Siwanyi zhinong zijin de sige cengci* (Four dimensions of the 4 trillion RMB agriculture fund), *21st Century Business Herald*, February 24, 2006. Available at: http://www.zzz-hnagri.gov.cn/news/1533.html.

Wang, Wei, *43 jian pingfang lingchen zao yeman tuiping* (43 housing units were razed to the ground after midnight), *Jinghua Times*, August 8, 2005.

Wang, Xiaoxia, *Shehei chaiqian: Beijing yi jumin shenye zaobang bei yiweipingdi* (Gangster-involved chaiqian: A civilian home was razed to the ground at the deep night), *China Economic Times* (*Zhongguo jingji shibao*), September 24, 2003.

Wang, Yuesheng, *Ruhe zouchuchaiqiande liangnan jingdi* (How to resolve the dilemma of *chaiqian*), February 18, 2005. Available at: http://pr15.sdsc.edu (accessed on November 7 2006).

Wang, Yuqin, *1997 nian yilai woguo chengshi xingzheng quhua tiaozheng de bian hua jiqi yingxiang fenxi* (An analysis of the impact of jurisdictional readjustment since 1997), Center for Policy Research, Ministry of Civic Affairs, January 4, 2008. Available at: http://www.mca.gov.cn/article/mxht/llyj/200801/20080100009424.shtml (accessed on January 4, 2008).

Wang, Zongli et al. (eds) *Beijing fangdichan* (Beijing Real Estate) Beijing: *Hangkong gongye chubanshe*, 1996.

Weimer, David (ed.), *The Political Economy of Property Rights: Institutional Change and Credibility in the Reform of Centrally Planned Economies* (New York: Cambridge University Press, 1997).

White, Gordon, Jude Howell, and Shang Xiaoyuan, *In Search of Civil Society: Market Reform and Social Change in Contemporary China* (Oxford: Clarendon Press, 1996).

Whyte, Martin, Urban China: A civil society in the making?, in Arthur Rosebaum (ed.), *State and Society in China: The Consequence of Reform*, 77–102 (Boulder, CO: Westview, 1992).

Wong, Zongli et al (ed.), *Beijing fangdi chan* (*Beijing Real Estate*) (Beijing: *Hangkong gongye chubanshe*, 1996).

Wu, Alun, *Jiating nongchang ganbugan zhu* (Dare to live in a family farm?), *Caijing*, August 5, 2000. Available at: http://magazine.caijing.com.cn/20000805/6249.shtml (accessed on February 10, 2009).

Wu, Chenguang, *Beijing biaozhunzu sifang de jiejue zhidao* (Ways to resolve the problem of *biaozhunzu* private homes), *Nanfang zhoumo* (*Southern Weekend*), July 31, 2003.

Wu, Hongying, *Chongqing nongdi liuzhaun qianye sheilai xiangshou tudi zengzhi shouyi dangao?* (Who benefits from land profits on the eve of rural land circulation in Chongqing?), *21st Century Business Herald*, October 27, 2008. Available at: http://www.21cbh.com/Content.asp/NewsId=86951 (accessed on November 5, 2008).

Wu, Fulong, The new structure of building provision and the transformation of the urban landscape in metropolitan Guangzhou, China, *Urban Studies* 2/35 (1998): 259–72.

—— The game of landed property production and capital circulation in China's transitional economy, with reference to Shanghai, *Environment and Planning A* 33 (1999): 1757–71.

—— China's changing urban governance in the transition towards a more market-oriented economy, *Urban Studies* 7/39 (2002): 1071–93.

Wu, Jich-min, Launching satellites: Predatory land policy and forged industrialization in interior China, in Si-ming Li and Wing-shing Tang (eds.), *China's Regions, Polity, and Economy: A Study of Spatial Transformation in the Post-Reform Era*, 309–50 (Hong Kong: The Chinese University Press, 2000).

Wu, Jinglian, *Dangdai Zhongguo jingji gaige* (*China's Contemporary Economic Reform*) (Shanghai: Yuandong Books, 2003).

Wu, Licai, *Zhipei, chongtu yu hezuo: shilun xiangcun guanxi* (Dominance, conflicts, and cooperation: An analysis of township village relationships), in Xu, Yong (ed.), *Zhongguo nongcun yanjiu* (*China Rural Studies*), 64–86 (Beijing: China Social Science chubanshe, 2002).

Wu, Weiping, *Pioneering Economic Reform in China's Special Economic Zones: The Promotion of Foreign Investment and Technology Transfer in Shenzhen* (Aldershot, UK: Ashgate, 1999).

Wu, Xiaoming, *Dangqian jianli shidi nongmin shehui baozhang gongzuo zhong yingguanzhude liangge wenti* (Two major issues in providing social security to peasants who lost their land), *Jingji yanjiu cankao* (*Review of Economic Research*) 25 (2004): 26–30.

Wu, Yi, *Nongmin zhongfang yu ruozhe de fanzhi* (Peasants planting houses and the resistance of the weak), *Shucheng* 5 (2004). Available at: http://www.xschina.org/show.php/id=5559 (accessed on February 12, 2009).

Xiao, He, *Zhou Zhengyi an baofa shimo* (The scandal of Zhou Zhengyi), Hong Kong: *Kaifong Magazine*, July 2003: 23–7.

Xiao, Hua, *kaifashang nangao? jiogao gueihuaju!* ("Too difficult to sue developers? Sue the Planning Department!"), *Nanfang zhoumo* (*Southern Weekend*), November 27, 2003.

Xiao, Tangbiao, *Zhengshi tizhi yu xueyuan qinqing—difang ganbu duinongcun zongzude lichang yu taidu fenxi* (Formal institution and blood connection: an analysis of local cadres' attitude towards village lineage), *Jingji shehui tizhi bijiao* (*Comparative Studies of Economic and Social Systems*) 2 (2007): 111–15.

Xie, Ju, *Shouchuang sanwen* (Three questions about capital land), *Xincaijing* 41 (2003): 34–7.

Xie, Wei, Liao Ailing, and Xie Yanjun, *Beijing tupo tudi guanlifa xianzhi jiansheyundi shidian liuzhuan* (Beijing breaks away from *Land Management Law*, experiments with circulation of (rural) construction land), *Xinjing Bao* (*New Beijing Daily*), October 21, 2004.

Xie, Zhikui, *Cunluo xiang chengshi shequde zhuanxing* (*Transformation from Villages to Urban Communities*) (Beijing: *Zhongguo shehui kexue chubanshe*, 2005).

Xu, Hanming, *Zhjongguo nongmin tudi chiyou chanquan zhidu yanjiu* (*Study on Chinese Farmers' Property Rights of Land*) (Beijing: Social Sciences Documentation Publishing House, 2004).

Xu,Wei, Yan Gun, Gu Guo-cai, and Shan Yi-hu, *Nanjing hexi xinchengqu fangdichan fazhan qushi fenxi* (Analysis of the prospect of real estate development in Nanjing Hexi New City), *Xiandai chengshi yanjiu* (*Studies of Modern City*), June 2002: 57–60.

Xu, Xueqiang., F. Xue, and X. Yen (eds.), *Zhongguo xiangcun chengshi zhuanxing yu xietiao fazhan* (*China's Rural-Urban Transformation and Coordination*) (Guangzhou: Zhongshen University Press, 1998).

Xuan, Zegang, *ludi biancheku, gueihua shigemi* (Mystery of planning: Greens turned into Parkade), *Nanfang zhoumo* (*Southern Weekend*), January 29, 2003.

Yang, Binbin, *Chonghui "xiaozhengfu"* (Return to "small government"), *Caijing*, November 12, 2008. Available at: http://www.caijing.com.cn/2008-11-12/110027818.html (accessed on November 15, 2008).

Yang, Dali, *Remaking the Chinese Leviathan: Market Transition and the Politics of Governance in China* (Palo Alto, CA: Stanford University Press, 2004).

Yang, Fangquan, *Tangcun jiufen: yige nanfang cunlode tudi, zongzu yu shehui* (*Conflicts in Tang Village: Land, Lineage and Society in a Southern Village*) (Beijing: China Social Science *chubanshe*, 2006).

Yang, Liping, *Ni Pengfei: chengshi pinpai diyixiang* (Analysis of competitive edge: The first report on branding the city: An interview with Ni Pengfei), *21st Century Business Herald*, September 29, 2004.

Yang, Liping, *Wang Zhigang: chengshi jingying shi raobukaide* (Wang Zhigang: We cannot avoid entrepreneurial management of cities), *21st Century Business Herald*, September 29, 2004.

—— *Tudi xinzheng: hongguan tiaokong shashoujian* (New land policies: The teeth of macroeconomic adjustment and control), *21st Century Business Herald*, November 22, 2004.

Yang, Liping, *Tudi: hongguan tiaokong disanzhong liliang?* (Land: The third force in macro adjustment and regulation?), *21st Century Business Herald*, January 5, 2005.

Yang, Lei, *Huanbao fengbao beihou* (Behind the storm of environmental protection), *21st Century Business Herald*, January 19, 2005.

Yang, Youren, Wang Hongkai, and Guo Jianlun, *Kuaisu gongyehua xiade zhongguo dalu quyu zhili: Yi Suzhou diqu tudi chanquan tizhi zhuanhua weili* (Regional governance under rapid industrialization in mainland China: a case of land rights transformation in Suzhou region), *Zhongguo dalu yanjiu (Main-land China Studies)* 3/47 (2004): 111–41.

Yeh, Anthony Gar–an and Fulong Wu, The new land development process and urban development in Chinese cities, *International Journal of Urban and Regional Research* 20 (1996): 330–53.

Ying, Xue, *Fangdichan hongguan tiaokong: chengbai xiyu fangjia?* (Real estate macro-economic adjustment and control: its success depends on housing price?), *21st Century Business Herald*, January 5, 2005.

Yu, Chengyao, 2008 *nian sanjidu jingji pingshu: suoxiao chengxiang shouru chaju yingdui guoji jinrong weiji* (Economic commentary of the third quarter of 2008: Reduce rural-urban income gap, deal with international financial crisis). Online. See <http://finance.sina.com.cn/roll/20081110/08382506232.shtml> accessed on December 19, 2008.

Yu, Jianrong, *Dangdai zhongguo nongmin weiquan zuzhide fayu yu chengzhang* (Development of peasant mobilizational organization in China today), Collection of essays from the International Seminar on Chinese Peasant Organization, December 7, 2004. Online. See <http://www.snzg.cn/article/show.php/itemid-1399/page-1.html> accessed on October 23, 2007.

—— *Dangqian nongmin weiquan huodong de yige jieshi kuangjia* (An explanatory framework for current peasant rights protests), *Sannong zhongguo*, January 2, 2006.

—— Protection of peasants' land rights and urbanization in China, speech at the Forum on China's urbanization, Beijing, *Sannong zhongguo*, March 15, 2006. Online. See <http://www.snzg.cn/member1/member.php/username=%D3%DA%BD%A8%E1%C9> accessed on August 12, 2007.

—— *Tudi wenti yichengwei nongmin weiquan kangzhengde jiaodian* (Land has become the focus of peasants' rights protests), *Guangming guancha*, November 9, 2006. Online. See <http://www.snzg.cn/article/show.php/itemid-1429/page-1.html> accessed on November 9, 2006.

Yu, Li, *Xin tudi biange Guangdong qimu* (A new land reform started in Guangdong), *Nanfang zhoumo (Southern Weekend)*, September 29, 2005.

Yuan, Mei and Xiang Zhang, *Shanghai tudi tunji zhimi* ("Secrets of land hoarding in Shanghai"), *Caijing* 127 (2005): 28–34.

Yuan, Ying, *Tudi zhidu dehexin shi sheizhanyou dizu he tudizibenhua shouyi: fang Hebei daxue zhongguo xiangcun jianshe yanjiu zhongxin yanjiuyuan Li Changping* (Who monopolizes land rents and profits from land capitalization are the core issues of the land system: an interview with Li Changping, researcher at the Center for Village Construction, Hebei University), *Shangwu zhoukan (Business Weekly)*, November 19, 2008.

Zelin, Madeleine, *The Magistrate's Tael: Rationalizing Fiscal Administration in Nineteenth Century Ch'ing China* (Berkeley: University of California Press, 1985).

Zhang, Forrest Qian, Qingguo Ma, and Xu Xu, Development of land rental market in rural Zhejiang: Growth of off-farm jobs and institution building, *The China Quarterly* 180 (2004): 1050–72.

Zhang, Jianjun, *Zhengfu quanli, jingying guanxi he xiangzhen qiye gaizhi—bijiao Sunan he Wenzhou de butong shijian* (Government power, elite relationships, and TVE reform: A comparison between southern Jiangsu and Wenzhou), *Sociological Research* 5 (2005): 92–124.

Zhang, Jihui, *Shenfen zhuanbian yu guannian gengxin—duishidi qingnian nongmin jiuye zhangaide zaisikao* (Change of status and perceptions: Reflections on employment issues of young peasants who lost their land), *Research Journal of Zhejiang Youth Party Academy* No.1 (2006): 1–4.

Zhang, Jing, *Cunshe tudi de jiti zhipei wenti* (Allocation of village collective land), *Zhejiang Xuekan (Zhejiang University Research Journal)* 2 (2002): 32–9.

Zhang, Li, *Stranger in the City: Reconfigurations of Space, Power, and Social, networks within China's Floating Population* (Stanford: Stanford University Press, 2001).

Zhang, Li and Aihwa Ong eds., *Privatizing China: Socialism from Afar.* (Ithaca: Cornell University Press, 2008).

Zhang, Li and Simon X. B. Zhao, Re-examining China's "urban" concept and the level of urbanization, *The China Quarterly* 154 (1998): 330–81.

Zhang, Qin and Zhang Guilin, *Chongqing dingzihu huo chaiqian anzhi fang ji 90 wanyuan yingye sunshi* (Chongqing nail household received relocation housing and 900,000 yuan compensation for business loss), *Xinhua News*, April 3, 2007. Online. See <http://news.xinhuanet.com/legal/2007-04/03/content_5929258.htm> accessed on February 2, 2008.

Zhang, Wenhao, *Beijing tudiye chushi* (Land masters in Beijing), *Caijing*, 61 (2002): 38–43.

Zhang, Yingguang, *Tudi kuangbiao zhihou* (After land price hikes), *Caijing*, No. 209, April 14, 2008. Online. See <http://magazine.caijing.com.cn/20080413/56486.shtml> accessed on September 5, 2008.

—— *Hangzhou 24 tiao jiushi, dichan hongtiao poju* (Hangzhou government announces 24 measures for market rescue, breaking macroeconomic adjustment policies), *Caijing*, October 14, 2008. Online. See <http://www.caijing.com.cn/2008-10-14/110020214.html> accessed on November 5, 2008.

—— *Ganga de dichan tiaokong zhengce* (Macroeconomic adjustment policies of land caught in an embarrassing situation), *Caijing*, October 25, 2008. Online. See <http://www.caijing.com.cn/2008-10-25/110023192.html> accessed on November 5, 2008.

Zhang, Yingguang, *Jinfang difang jiushi yuejie* (Caution needed to prevent local governments' market rescue measures from going too far), *Caijing*, December 11, 2008. Online. See <http://www.caijing.com.cn/2008-12-11/110037592.html> accessed on December 15, 2008.

Zhang, Zhihui, *Shanghai Xintiandi juqu gaizao jihua gean yanjiu* (*A Case Study of "New World" Urban Renewal Project in Shanghai*), unpublished master's thesis (Taipei: Institute of Urban Design and Town Planning, National Taiwan University, 2002).

Zhao, Hejuan and Fu Yanyan, *Shanghai Shenzhen fangdichan jiangjiasheng siqi* (Real estate price drops in Shanghai and Shenzhen), *Caijing*, September 10, 2008. Online. See <http://www.caijing.com.cn/2008-09-10/110011469.html> accessed on October 19, 2008.

Zhao, Ling, *chaiqian shinien beixiju* (Ten years of relocation drama), *Nanfang zhoumo* (*Southern Weekend*), September 4, 2003.

Zhao, Litao, *Jiating yu cunzhuang zhengzhi, 1950–70* (Family and village politics: 1950–70), *Twenty-first Century* (Hong Kong), 55 (1999): 45–52.

Zhao, Xiaofeng and Li Kuan, *Nongcun tudi liuzhuan yuanhe chule wenti?* (Why are there problems in rural land circulation?), *Sannong zhongguo*, November 25, 2008. Online. See <http://www.snzg.cn/article/show.php=itemid-12613/page-1.html> accessed on December 13, 2008.

Zhe, Xiaoye and Chen Yingying, *Shequ de shijian—chaoji cunzhuang de fazhan licheng* (*Practicing Community: Development of a "Super Village"*) (Hangzhou: *Zhejiang renmin chubanshe*, 2000).

Zheng, Dingquan, *Jin 20 nian woguo difang xingzheng quhua de bianhua* (Changes in local jurisdictions in China in the past 20 years), *Zhongguo Jingji gaige yanjiuhui* (China Research Association of Economic Reform), July 9, 2007. Available at: http://www.Chinareform.net (accessed on March 2, 2008).

Zheng, Mengxuan and Huang Shaowang, *Chengshihua zhongde Shipaicun* (*Shipai Village in Urbanization*) (Beijing: Social Sciences Academic Press, 2006).

Zhongguo Jingji yanjiu zhongxin (Research Center of Chinese Economy) *Tudizhidu, chengshihua yu hongguan tiaokong* (Land system, urbanization, and macroeconomic adjustment and control), Beijing University, June 14, 2004.

Zhou, Hong, *Beijing tudi churangjin shouru bujian fan ceng—zhuzhai lei dikuai gongxian da* (Beijing land sale revenues don't drop, they rise—housing tracts are large contributors), *Beijing Youth Daily*, December 18, 2008. Online. See <http://www.soufun.com/news/2008-12-18/2292911.htm> accessed on January 9, 2009.

247

Zhou, Le, *Dui Beijing dongqian da guimo weijiufang gaizaode sikao* (Thoughts on massive urban redevelopment in Beijing), *Beijing City Planning and Construction Review* 4 (2002): 43–7.

Zhou, Min and John Logan, Market transition and commodification of housing in urban China, in Logan, J. (ed.), *The New Chinese City: Globalization and Market Reform*, 135–52 (Oxford: Blackwell, 2002).

Zhou, Yingying, Han Hua, and Stevan Harrell, From labour to capital: Intra-village inequality in rural China, 1988–2006, *The China Quarterly* 195 (2008): 515–34.

Zhou, Yixing and Laurence Ma, Economic restructuring and suburbanization in China, *Urban Geography* 3/21 (2000): 205–36.

Zhou, Yixing and Laurence Ma, China's urbanization levels: Reconstructing a baseline from the fifth population census, *The China Quarterly* 173 (2003): 176–96.

—— —— China's urban population statistics: A critical evaluation, *Eurasian Geography and Economics* 4/46 (2005): 272–89.

Zhou, Yixing and Yanchun Meng, *Beijing de jiaoquhua jiqi duece* (*Suburbanization and Policies in Beijing*) (Beijing: *kexue chubanshe*, 2000).

Zhou, Zhenghua, *Tudi chanquan yaokao minzhu quanli lai baozhang* (Protection of land rights depends on democratic rights), *China News Weekly*, November 26, 2008. Online. See <http://www.snzg.cn/article/show.php?itemid-12622/page-1.html> accessed on November 30, 2008.

Zhu, Dongliang, *Shehui bianqianzhong de cunji tudi zhidu* (*Village Land System in a Changing Society*) (Xiamen: Xiamen University Press, 2003).

Zweig, David, The externalities of development: Can new political institutions manage rural conflicts?, in Perry, E. and M. Selden (eds.), *Chinese Society: Chang, Conflict and Resistance*, 2nd edn., 120–42 (NY: Routledge Curzon, 2003).

Index

Note: page numbers in *italic* refer to illustrations and the table.